THE PHILOSOPHICAL
ASSESSMENT OF
THEOLOGY

THE
PHILOSOPHICAL
ASSESSMENT OF
THEOLOGY

Essays in honour of
Frederick C. Copleston

EDITED BY GERARD J. HUGHES, SJ

SEARCH PRESS

GEORGETOWN UNIVERSITY PRESS

First published in Great Britain and U.S.A. 1987

by Search Press Ltd
Wellwood, North Farm Road
Tunbridge Wells
Kent, TN2 3DR

in association with

Georgetown University Press
Intercultural Center 111
Washington, D.C. 20057

ISBN (UK) 0 85532 599 2

ISBN (USA) 0-87840-449-X

Library of Congress Cataloging-in-Publication Data
The Philosophical assessment of theology.

   Bibliography.
   1. Religion—Philosophy.   2. Philosophical theology.
3. Catholic Church and philosophy   4. Catholic Church—
Doctrines.   5. Copleston, Frederick Charles.
I. Copleston, Frederick Charles. II. Hughes, Gerard J.
BL51.P525 1987   200'.1   87–94

Set by Pentacor Ltd, High Wycombe, Bucks
Printed and bound in Great Britain by
Robert Hartnoll (1985) Ltd., Bodmin, Cornwall

CONTENTS

THE CONTRIBUTORS

Dr P.J. FitzPatrick is Reader in Philosophy at the University of Durham, and chaplain to the Little Sisters of the Poor at Sunderland.

Garth Hallett, SJ is Dean of the College of Philosophy and Letters at St Louis University.

D.W. Hamlyn is Professor of Philosophy and Vice-Master of Birkbeck College, University of London. He was also the first Chairman of Governors of Heythrop College.

Gerard J. Hughes, SJ who has edited this volume, is Vice-Principal and Head of the Department of Philosophy at Heythrop College, University of London.

A.H.T. Levi is Buchanan Professor of French Language and Literature in the University of St Andrews.

Hugo Meynell is Professor of Philosophy at the University of Calgary.

Basil Mitchell is Professor Emeritus of the Philosophy of the Christian Religion, University of Oxford.

Stewart Sutherland is Professor of the History and Philosophy of Religion, and Principal of King's College, University of London.

Richard Swinburne is Nolloth Professor of the Philosophy of the Christian Religion, University of Oxford.

Janice Thomas is a Lecturer in Philosophy at Heythrop College, University of London.

EDITOR'S INTRODUCTION

by GERARD J. HUGHES, SJ

Professor F.C. Copleston, SJ, celebrates his eightieth birthday early in 1987. Some of his many friends and colleagues, wishing to take advantage of that occasion to express their appreciation for his contribution to philosophical scholarship over so many years, have collaborated to produce this volume of essays in his honour.

Fr Copleston — Freddie, as his friends like to think of him — became a Catholic in 1925, and, after taking his degree at St John's College in Oxford, a Jesuit in 1930. After his Jesuit studies in theology, he began his teaching career in 1939 at Heythrop College in Oxfordshire, lecturing to young Jesuit students. To this task he devoted the next thirty years of his life, until he became the first Principal of the newly founded Heythrop College in the University of London in 1970. By that time, he had lectured in the Gregorian University in Rome, had broadcast on radio and on television, was well on the way to completing his major philosophical work, and had been elected a Fellow of the British Academy. Since then, and even after his retirement in 1974, he has continued to write, to lecture, and to broadcast with apparently undiminished enthusiasm.

Fr Copleston's achievement can most obviously be measured by the fact that his name has come not merely to stand for his monumental *A History of Philosophy*, but to represent a standard by which any history of philosophy will be judged. In the sheer breadth of his scholarship and his ability to treat such a diversity of writers with sympathy and accurate appreciation he has few, if any, rivals. His monographs, on Nietzsche, on Schopenhauer, and on Aquinas, perhaps reveal more of his personal interests; his *Religion and Philosophy*, *Religion and the One* (his 1979—80 Gifford Lectures) and his *Philosophies and Cultures* (the Martin D'Arcy Lectures of 1978) are a testimony to the fact that he was constantly in demand as a lecturer, in places as diverse geographically and culturally as Aberdeen, Rome, California, and Hawaii.

I remarked that the breadth and diversity of his published works is perhaps the most obvious measure of Fr Copleston's achievement. But it is far from being the only measure. Fr Copleston has also through his works made a major contribution to Roman Catholic attitudes to the teaching of philosophy itself. It would not be unfair to say that the teaching of philosophy, in seminaries and to a large extent in Catholic institutions generally, while admirable in intent, was in practice often little more than disguised religious apologetics. There was almost no sense that the students might have something to learn from the variety and richness of the great philosophers of the past, and small appreciation of philosophy as a disciplined search for a truth as yet only partially attained. Fr Copleston was a pioneer in exorcising such attitudes, and in communicating to generations of students a respect for philosophical scholarship as an essential part of their religious training. His own personal, religious, and philosophical integrity have provided an unforgettable example to those of us privileged enough to have him as a teacher or a colleague.

A volume such as this cannot hope to represent all those who have known or worked with Fr Copleston, still less to do justice to the breadth of his interests. So we have tried to centre upon the complex relationships between philosophy and theology, and within that area to concentrate somewhat upon philosophy of religion. Basil Mitchell's essay raises in a modern setting many of the issues which underlie Fr Copleston's entire work. The next four contributions, David Hamlyn on 'Aristotle's God', my own piece on Aquinas, Richard Swinburne's on 'Analogy and Metaphor', and Janice Thomas's essay on the alleged univocity of terms used of God, form a group with a common focus — the meanings of terms we use to speak of God — but without a common view. Anthony Levi and P.J. FitzPatrick contribute essays which at once discuss the history of mediaeval scholasticism, with which Fr Copleston has so long been associated, and raise questions of continuing philosophical and theological interest about the nature of the study of the history of philosophy, and the ways in which philosophy can contribute to, and on occasions disrupt, the received orthodoxies of theology. Hugo Meynell offers a critique of the views of one of the most prominent contemporary atheists. His contribution will serve as a reminder of the background of controversy against which Fr Copleston conducted much of his own writing. Stewart Sutherland, on the other hand, writes about the providence of God from a standpoint which exemplifies the more constructive approach of many contemporary philosophers of religion. And Garth Hallett, who followed Fr Copleston at the Gregorian University, writes on the relationship between moral philosophy and Christian ethics.

I would like to thank all the contributors for their most willing cooperation in the production of this volume. The book, and these remarks, are all too brief to do justice to a man whose ready wit, encouragement, learning, and warmth we have learnt to appreciate. The contributors and Professor Copleston's former colleagues at Heythrop College offer it to him with gratitude and our most sincere good wishes.

1
PHILOSOPHY
AND
THEOLOGY

by BASIL MITCHELL

Professor Emeritus of the Philosophy of the Christian Religion, University of Oxford

In his *Philosophies and Cultures* Father Copleston has occasion from time to time to remark on the relationship between philosophy and theology at different periods and, where the comparison is appropriate, in different cultures. Such reflections lead one naturally to consider what the relationship between them is, or should be, in our culture today.

It would be in the spirit of Father Copleston's own procedure to start not from abstract definitions but from actual practice. If one looks at degree syllabuses, for example at Oxford, philosophy and theology would appear to be very different. A student of theology engages for much of the time in the study of the Bible from a historical and critical point of view, and also of the languages in which it is written, especially Greek. In addition he studies the Fathers and as much of the history of the Christian church and of Christian doctrine as he can manage. Then there is Christian doctrine as a subject in its own right, together, perhaps, with some philosophy of religion. A student of philosophy studies logic and theory of knowledge, moral and political philosophy, with, perhaps, the philosophy of mind or philosophy of language. To this is added a certain amount of the history of philosophy from Descartes to the present day, together with Greek and Latin, if ancient and mediaeval philosophy are included.

Apart from studying the history of philosophy — and even then to quite a large extent — the student of philosophy spends all his time actually philosophising. The differences in subject are differences in what he philosophises about. If by theology we mean systematic theology, it is not true in the same way that the theologian spends most of his time theologising. Much of his work is a variety of literary or historical criticism, devoted to a strict study of the Biblical text; and the same is true of patristics.

The contrast between the two disciplines is sharpened if one concentrates upon the 'rigorous core' of each subject — that part of it which undergraduates are required to do for the good of their souls when, often, they would rather be doing something else. In theology it is New Testament criticism; in philosophy it is philosophical logic. Philosophical logic is basic to philosophy in that it concerns the philosophical analysis of key concepts such as those of meaning and truth which are involved in any kind of philosophy; and, when engaged in philosophical logic, one is, paradigmatically, philosophising. Biblical criticism is basic to theology, but in a recognisably different way. One can be a Biblical critic without being a theologian at all.

By comparison with philosophy, theology looks like a collection of disparate disciplines. What, then, makes it a single subject? Taken as a whole, if one goes on the evidence of degree syllabuses, theology would seem to be identical with hermeneutics (in a broadly intelligible sense of that word), *viz.* with the attempt to answer the question: what ought the Christian now to believe, given that the Biblical writers and their successors in the Christian tradition believed what they did? It is essential to the hermeneutic task, so understood, that the meaning of the original documents be ascertained as accurately as possible — hence the enormous investment in linguistic and historical study — but more than that is needed, since the theologian is concerned with what is to be believed today, and this is affected by much that we know now and was not known to the Biblical writers.

On the face of it philosophy is not related in the same way to a set of foundation documents. A philosopher who read Greats at Oxford may feel that a philosopher who does not read Greek and has not studied Plato and Aristotle must be a rather ill-equipped philosopher, but he does not deny him the title of philosopher; and he himself does not feel inadequate because of his ignorance of, say, Aquinas or Hegel. *Some* acquaintance with the great philosophers of the past is necessary, but it need not be systematic or comprehensive. And the contemporary philosopher is, it would appear, in no way committed *qua* philosopher to the thought of any of his predecessors. If he is interested in Plato and impressed by him, he can practise hermeneutics upon him and endeavour to express certain key Platonic doctrines in terms that are acceptable today, but it is a task that is in no sense laid upon him. As a rule philosophers tend to distinguish between philosophical scholars, concerned with the exegesis and interpretation of Plato, and philosophers proper who are interested chiefly in whether what Plato said is true, and who are often content to treat him as if he were a contemporary and not to mind interpreting him anachronistically.

The contrast may, however, be somewhat overdrawn. As Father Copleston has pointed out,[1] in the ancient world, especially in the Hellenistic period, philosophy was looked upon as a guide to life, and to be a Stoic, Epicurean or Neoplatonist was to place oneself within a recognised tradition. It was in the mediaeval period that theology superseded philosophy in that function. The modern analytic philosopher's absence of commitment may simply be a historical oddity. And even within this modern movement (as the word 'movement' itself suggests) it is possible to exaggerate the individual philosopher's degree of detachment. There exists a tacit, if informal, canon of historical and contemporary works with which he is expected to familiarise himself and certain topics that are to be taken more seriously than others. Moreover, even today a philosopher can identify himself with a tradition which goes back to a particular thinker. He may declare himself a Thomist or a Kantian or a Humean, convinced that these philosophers had the root of the matter in them and no less concerned to express the thought of these philosophers in contemporary terms than any practitioner of Biblical hermeneutics.

Nor do all contemporary theologians conform to the pattern I have sketched. Professor Maurice Wiles has suggested that all that is required of the theologian is that he should attend to 'the theological agenda'; he need not be committed in advance to any particular interpretation of it or to its defence. A possible example of such a theologian is Professor Dennis Nineham. He is a New Testament critic who repudiates the hermeneutic task (in the sense I have given it) as impossible of fulfilment. The meaning of the New Testament writers is so bound up with the thought forms of their age and so remote from anything we can understand, let alone believe, today that there is no point in our trying to find an interpretation of it which can be made accessible to our contemporaries. We must endeavour to understand God in terms of modern categories alone and be content to derive from the Bible and the rest of the Christian tradition only the assurance that a relationship with God can be sustained at any period, no matter how it is conceptualized.[2]

Nevertheless the existence of these variations from the norm is not enough to call the norm itself seriously in question. They are recognizably uncharacteristic. That this is so can be seen from the particular case of Marxism. Marxist thinkers are often classed with theologians rather than philosophers, precisely because in their case it is not just that, as individual thinkers, they have found something to admire in a historical philosopher and chosen to develop his thought. They have associated themselves with a broad social and political movement which has its origins in the philosophy of this one thinker and which, in the Communist Party, possesses an organised institution, analogous to a Church, to which allegiance is owed. The movement is attended by such characteristically religious phenomena as conversion, apostasy and sectarianism. The attitude of Marxists to the works of

Marx and Engels is closer to that of Christian theologians to the New Testament than is that of contemporary philosophers to any of their predecessors.

Having, provisionally at least, made these discriminations, let us now consider to what extent the theologian is or ought to be a philosopher. My initial suggestion is that much of what the systematic theologian does just *is* philosophy. He seeks to interpret the Christian tradition, and the Biblical writers in particular, in such a way that they can be seen to provide answers to the major questions about life. That they can do so is a presupposition of the whole enterprise, as is the conviction of its existential relevance. How the process operates can best be seen in somewhat unorthodox theologians. Bultmann, for example, is concerned to interpret the significance of the New Testament for today. That it represents, or contains, fundamental truth he does not doubt. The question to be answered is under what interpretation its message can be both true and relevant to the modern world. Taken at its face value most of what it says must now be rejected as false, since it is bound up with a mythological view of the world which has been rendered obsolete by the development of modern science. It must, therefore, be demythologised and the original *kerygma* expressed in terms acceptable today, *viz.* in those of the philosophy of Heidegger.

Bultmann's procedure is philosophical throughout and not only in his use of existentialist language. It is a *philosophical* assumption, derived perhaps from Kant, that modern science exhausts the realm of objective fact and that the world as we experience it is a closed nexus of cause and effect, within which God cannot be supposed to be active. It is by contrast with *this* that the world view of the New Testament is held to be mythological. In his treatment of this mythological language of the New Testament Bultmann relies upon a dichotomy, philosophical in character, between fact-stating and expressive uses of language. The mythology of the New Testament appears at first sight to be fact-stating but, so understood, it must stand condemned as obsolete science. Therefore it must not be so understood. That it might conceivably be both mythological (i.e. metaphorical) *and* fact-stating is a possibility that Bultmann's philosophical assumptions do not allow him to entertain.

The philosophical character of Bultmann's procedure is apparent if we compare him with Professor D.Z. Phillips, who writes specifically as a philosopher. Phillips accepts from the New Testament and from the Christian tradition as a whole the doctrine of Eternal Life. Like

Bultmann he is committed to holding it in some sense true. But, taken at its face value, it is obviously not true. Dead people stay dead, and we have learnt from Hume that the notion of survival of bodily death is logically incoherent. Eternal life must therefore mean something else and what it means, Phillips tells us in *Death and Immortality*, is that it is open to us now so to live as to render death irrelevant.[3]

The examples of Bultmann and Phillips may provoke the objection that the hermeneutic task, as they exemplify it, is not so much that of interpreting the Christian tradition as of radically reinterpreting it. If, in deference to philosophical principles, the theologian is forced to such extremes as these in order to discover in the Bible a message that can be received as true for us today, would it not be wiser and more honest, we may be inclined to say, to give up the attempt altogether? And this is what Nineham in effect does. There is *no* way of interpreting the message of the New Testament writers in terms that are acceptable today. Myth *and kerygma* are equally beyond recall. What the tradition preserves for us, and all that we can or need rely upon, is not a message at all but an institution, the Church, which is able to make available to believers today the same fullness of relationship with God as the primitive church experienced in the first century. In developing his argument Nineham relies heavily on another philosophical theory, a variety of conceptual relativism, which leads him to assert that, even if we can by an exercise of historical imagination come to have some inkling of what, for example, Paul meant, there is no possibility of our believing it today.

I have introduced this discussion of Bultmann and Nineham in order to support the suggestion that, to a large extent, theologians are philosophers, with the tacit implication that other theologians, less radical than they, differ from them only in the sort of philosophy they employ or the use they put it to. But an entirely natural response to these examples would be to take them instead as illustrating the ill effects upon theology of tangling with philosophy at all. The proper lesson to be learnt from them, it might be said, is that theologians should eschew philosophy and conduct their thinking throughout in purely Biblical categories. This was, indeed, the programme of the Biblical theology movement, which was largely a reaction against the tendency to identify the doctrines of Christianity with those of some preferred philosophical system, in particular Hegelian idealism (or, worse still, to regard them as provisional approximations to truths that had been finally revealed in Hegel). But however understandable that reaction was it was bound eventually to encounter the hermeneutic problem and with it the need to come to terms with philosophy. For what *were* the biblical concepts which were to be normative for theology? And how were they to be understood in a context different from that in which they had originated or developed? The concept of sin, for example, is central to Christianity as traditionally understood. Without it there is no need of salvation and no room for grace. But is it to be identified with ritual uncleanness or with moral wrongdoing or with something other than and more fundamental than either of these? How has it been related to moral responsibility at key points in the history of Christian doctrine, e.g., in the thought of Augustine and Aquinas; and to what extent do current developments in psychology and sociology require that relationship to be understood differently today? To answer the historical questions demands all the resources of literary and historical scholarship, together with a critical study of these thinkers in their philosophical context. To answer the contemporary ones calls for familiarity with moral philosophy and the philosophy of mind.

Philosophy enters in also at a further remove from the present discussion. The hermeneutic task, as I have represented it, presupposes an essential continuity in the Christian tradition. The theologian, as he engages in it, is trying to express in contemporary terms truths which were first enunciated in the past in languages different from our own and in terms of different views of the world. It is, as we have seen, Nineham's conviction that this can scarcely be done and, even if this extreme view is rejected, it remains clear that some defensible theory is needed of the continuity or development of doctrine. There is, that is to say, a philosophical problem of the identity of doctrine as between successive historical periods, which bears some resemblance to the familiar problem of personal identity. (Nineham adopts in relation to it something very much like Hume's scepticism about the self.) Philosophers have paid little attention to it because they are not themselves, as a rule, concerned to maintain an unbroken historical tradition; but it is a philosophical problem nevertheless.

If, as the argument suggests, a theologian is bound to be for much of the time, whether he likes it or not, a philosopher, what other equipment does he need? Would the best way to get a good theologian be to take a good philosopher and set him to work on the 'theological agenda'? Not unless he also receives the training needed to enable him to cope competently with that agenda, which involves being well grounded in the disciplines mentioned earlier as comprising the theological syllabus: the critical study of the Bible, patristics, the history of Christian doctrine, etc.

Suppose him, however, to have been through all this successfully, will he now *be* a theologian? This is a question to be answered to some extent by stipulation. One may wish to stipulate, as Wiles does, that so long as he directs his attention to the 'theological agenda' and forms some conclusions about it, making use of the theological skills he has developed, then he is a theologian, no matter what those conclusions are. He may have reached largely sceptical conclusions about the historicity of the Gospels, decided that the Fathers were preoccupied with philosophical distinctions that are now entirely obsolete, and been persuaded by Hume and modern Humeans that the concept of God is logically incoherent. There would, then, for him be no point in trying to interpret the Christian message in terms intelligible and acceptable today. The most that he could offer in this direction would be to do his best for Christianity, to allow it the benefit of the doubt in certain important respects and, by an effort of sympathetic imagination, to state its contentions as persuasively as he can. It sometimes happens that atheistic philosophers do this very well — one thinks of J.L. Mackie's treatment of theological ethics[4] — but it is, nevertheless, an essentially parasitic activity, which would not be engaged in unless there were others who actually believed in what they were doing. Hence Wiles' stipulative definition has at best only a secondary use, and it is these latter thinkers who, standing within the tradition and concerned to explicate and defend its fundamental truths, are to be regarded as theologians properly so-called.

The theologian, then, the argument so far suggests, is a philosopher with the requisite training in the other disciplines needed who addresses himself to the hermeneutic task and is committed to defending the Christian tradition. In so doing he will not expect to find total coherence and completeness in the tradition but as much coherence and completeness as is needed in order to understand and appropriate the Christian scheme of salvation. This means giving sufficient weight both to the historical texts and to the contemporary constraints upon belief. The sort of balance demanded can best be seen by considering extreme cases of the failure to achieve it. Fundamentalism fails because it is insufficiently critical in its approach to the Bible; it ignores or denies the relevance of what can be discovered by rational methods about the language and historical context of the Biblical writers and the meaning of what they wrote. Radicalism often fails because it is equally uncritical of what passes for modern knowledge, assuming too readily that, where there is some conflict between the Christian tradition and what is accepted as true by contemporary secular intellectuals, it is the former that must give way. The hermeneutic task, which I have taken as central to theology, involves interpreting the Biblical message in terms that are, so far as possible, intelligible and defensible today, but this does not mean 'in terms that are already understood and accepted today', quite independently of the Christian tradition. The theological task presupposes − and this was the truth in the Biblical theology movement − that the dominant concepts of the Christian tradition do actually possess an enduring power to interpret and illuminate human experience. It follows that, when they are confronted with other conceptual systems which we have some warrant for accepting on scientific or philosophical grounds, some modification is to be expected on one side or the other or on both. To return to the example used earlier, that of the theological concept of sin, considerable light may be cast on it by the Freudian doctrine of the unconscious, but it would be rash for the theologian simply to identify sin with the unconscious. Modern psychology may dictate greater caution in attributing guilt than was customary in past ages, but contemporary notions of guilt may themselves be judged superficial when contrasted with the Christian understanding of sin. If the tradition possesses the sort of intellectual vitality which is presupposed by the practice of theology, it will exhibit this capacity for reciprocal interaction with secular trends without, however, being entirely exhausted by them. A possible analogy, though a controversial one, is with the production of Shakespeare's plays. A creative director will discover in Shakespeare contemporary resonances which, it is reasonable to suppose, would not have been present to the minds of his original audience. Given today's obsession with sex and violence, they may well have to do with these. Shakespeare's inexhaustibility is such that a reciprocal movement actually occurs. We are led to discover more in Shakespeare than we realized was there; and our current preoccupation with sex and violence is given an extra dimension of meaning. This is what a good director will achieve. A poor director may instead impose upon Shakespeare's play a fashionable and wholly ephemeral interpretation which succeeds only in depriving it of much of its original significance. He will have interposed his own personality between his audience and Shakespeare, whereas the other had enabled Shakespeare to engage and enlarge our contemporary vision.

If a process of this kind occurs when our theologically equipped philosopher turns to systematic theology, it will follow that in bringing his philosophy to bear on the 'theological agenda' he is not just using philosophical methods or applying philosophical conclusions which have answered well in other branches of philosophy. It is a well worn theme in the philosophy of religion that meanings require to be stretched when terms are applied to God that have their regular use in other contexts – and all theological terms bear some relationship to God. So it will not do for the philosopher to argue, for example, that, because our ordinary concept of causality cannot be applied to God, there can be no concept of causality applicable to God; or, that since some concept of causality is applicable to God, and this is the only concept available, this must be the one that is applicable to God. Philosophers and theologians are constantly tempted in one or other of these directions. Of course it may turn out, in a particular instance, that no stretching is needed, but the presumption must always be otherwise.

But how is the theologian to tell what modifications are needed among all those that would achieve consistency, and what sort of reasoning does he employ in reaching a decision? What warrant, indeed, has he for accepting, in the first instance, the basic assumption which I have taken to be essential to the practice of theology, *viz.* that it is possible to identify and interpret the teaching of the Bible so that it is intelligible and acceptable today? An objector might complain that, according to my account, the theologian has *carte blanche* to reach any conclusions he likes, for it can only be a matter of subjective judgement how a particular individual achieves the balance I have argued for.

Personal judgement no doubt, but by no means purely subjective. The theologian's judgement is constrained by all the disciplines that are relevant to his task. He has, for instance, to run the gauntlet of Biblical criticism (or give adequate reason why he should not). I have talked hitherto somewhat vaguely, as if using an admissible shorthand, about 'the Biblical message', but it is a commonplace of Biblical criticism that, even if we confine ourselves to the New Testament, the different writers have their characteristic points of view, and that leading individuals like Paul do not always speak with one voice. In the patristic period and later the diversity of voices is influenced by philosophical and political considerations of an arguably extraneous kind. With the Reformation even the formal unity of the Western Church is no longer maintained and, after the Enlightenment, reason and religion are increasingly at odds. At each stage the theologian is confronted by a chorus of 'buts'.

'But the New Testament has no unified doctrine.' 'But the doctrine of the Trinity owes more to Greek philosophy and imperial policy than to the New Testament.' 'But the theology of the Reformation resists all attempts to found faith on reason.' These have either to be rebutted or accepted in whole or in part; they cannot simply be ignored, and reasons have to be given for the line that is eventually taken. In no case is it enough for the theologian simply to legislate. There are linguistic, historical, philosophical and other considerations to be assessed on their merits. These are not entirely determinate, but neither is the theologian free to decide them just as he wishes. The range of possible meanings of a Greek expression as used in the first century A.D. is limited and the views of reputable scholars have to be respected. One cannot simply choose to override them. But it may on occasion be legitimate to employ some later usage as a clue to what was originally meant, if the context will bear it. When a single individual says one thing at one time and another later, it is a reasonable procedure to look for an interpretation of both utterances which will render them consistent. A principle of charity operates – a writer is presumed to be consistent unless it is clear that he is not. And if a reading that is slightly less probable on the other available evidence would render him consistent, there is reason to prefer it. If consistency cannot be saved at all, or only at the cost of undue special pleading, it is reasonable to ask which of the alternatives best coheres with the author's overall view, and what this is has to be determined on the evidence of these and other relevant passages. Here again charity dictates that, *ceteris paribus*, one prefer the view which makes the better sense.

Where a number of people are linked as a group, formally or informally, in maintaining an overall position, and they sometimes differ, an analogous situation arises, but only analogous. That A and B, who are associated in some way, should nevertheless have independent views which may conflict is not surprising, so that one cannot invoke the principle of charity to quite the same effect. Yet, if they do agree considerably in fact and if they see themselves as part of the same movement, it makes sense to try to reconcile their divergent utterances so far as possible and to look for common assumptions that underlie them. Moreover there is the possibility, even the likelihood, that they are trying to get at the same basic contention without entirely succeeding. There is a possible instance of this in Sir Alfred Ayer's televised conversation with Bryan Magee[5] where, after admitting that most of what the Logical Positivists said was false, he went on,

'Nevertheless, I think the approach was right'. Here was a loosely defined group of philosophers who undoubtedly had certain important assumptions in common and who often disagreed with one another on particular points. Yet they were all looking for a formula which would distinguish definitively between science and metaphysics and so enable them to dispose finally of the claims of theology. If there had existed such a formula, it is entirely possible that many of their differing utterances could plausibly have been construed as inadequate and approximate attempts to articulate it.

The Logical Positivists were contemporaries, but in many respects they were the philosophical heirs of David Hume. It would not be wholly misleading to describe them as endeavouring to bring Hume up to date. They illustrate, then, the tendency already alluded to for philosophical doctrines to have histories which endure through several generations. Such doctrines characteristically offer solutions to enduring problems of a kind that require more than a single lifetime to explore. It is to be expected, on this ground alone, that the same should be true of theological doctrines whose transcendent subject-matter precludes definitive interpretation.

Along these lines I should want to argue that the presumption underlying the theological enterprise is defensible — that it is, in principle, possible to identify and interpret the Biblical message in such a way as to render it intelligible and acceptable today. It is entirely compatible with this claim that the history of Christian doctrine should be one of dilution and corruption as well as of reform and regeneration. What is needed to validate the use of this model of continuing identity is not the absence of change or controversy, but the persistence of a recognisable something of which one can intelligibly say that it has been diluted and corrupted, reformed and regenerated.

The words 'in principle' often betray the philosopher at work, and it is arguable that they mark the boundaries of philosophical involvement in theology. No doubt it is appropriate for the philosopher to draw attention to the kind of identity through time that a doctrinal tradition might possess and to suggest the criteria that need to be satisfied for a particular claim to be made good. More generally, it is for the philosopher to distinguish and elucidate the conceptual possibilities between which a choice has to be made. 'Does God act in the world or reveal himself in the words of prophets and evangelists?' The philosopher can assist the theologian by offering alternative ways of explicating the concepts of 'divine action' and 'revelation' respectively, perhaps showing that there are more, and more fertile, possibilities available than the theologian had previously thought. But eventually the theologian has to decide not just whether 'in principle' God could have acted or revealed himself, but if, when and how he did so — given the Judaeo-Christian tradition and anything else that may be relevant. To be able to do this he has to draw not only on the specific capacities of a linguistic, literary and historical kind which are developed by a theological education, but also on a broader capacity to interpret and weigh the various types of specialised evidence in order to achieve an overall account which is theologically illuminating and rationally defensible. The requirement that it be rationally defensible means that the exercise of philosophy is not, so to speak, actually transcended at this stage. Philosophical criticisms would still remain in place, and meeting them would be a philosophical exercise, but the total activity of the systematic theologian would seem to demand qualities of imagination and judgement in spiritual matters which do not belong to philosophy as such.

And yet, if a thoroughly prepared adversary were to go through the argument, step by step, contesting some or all of the specialist moves and concluding, for reasons given, that the cumulative case the theologian had developed and sought to defend was less persuasive than an ultimately atheistic interpretation of the entire 'theological agenda', what else could we call him but a philosopher or a metaphysician? Which seems to make the systematic theologian a philosopher and a metaphysician too. But not only that, for the theologian has put forward a coherent interpretation of the world, informed by a tradition to which he stands committed and which presupposes certain spiritual realities and calls for spiritual discernment. Since they are philosophically controversial (although, he believes, philosophically defensible) neither the commitment nor the discernment belong to him simply *qua* philosopher. The philosophical critic's systematic rebuttal of Christian claims takes the form it does, of a re-ordering of 'the theological agenda', only because there already exists a continuing tradition of thinkers committed to the hermeneutic task.

NOTES

1. *Philosophies and Cultures*, Oxford University Press, 1980, p. 9.
2. See J. Hick (ed.), *The Myth of God Incarnate*, SCM, 1977, p. 202.
3. *Death and Immortality*, Macmillan, 1970. See especially page 50.
4. J.L. Mackie,*Ethics*, Penguin, 1976, pp. 46—8.
5. Bryan Magee, *Men of Ideas*, B.B.C., 1978.

2
ARISTOTLE'S GOD

by D.W. HAMLYN

Professor of Philosophy and Vice-Master, Birkbeck College, University of London

When I was engaged recently in writing a history of Western philosophy (so following the great example of F.C. Copleston, whom we are honouring), Miss Maureen Cartwright, who helped me both by typing the typescript and by offering many invaluable stylistic suggestions, asked why I referred to Aristotle's God with a 'he'. She did not mean by that what one might somehow expect these days; she was not asking why it was appropriate to use the masculine pronoun rather than the feminine. She was asking why I did not use the word 'it'. An easy (too easy) answer to that question in relation to Aristotle would be that the Greek word for 'God' (*theos*) is masculine. It would be too easy because, apart from the fact that the Greeks accepted the existence of goddesses, they were quite happy from time to time to use the phrase '*to theion*' (the divine), which is a neuter construction. A better answer, perhaps, would be to note what Aristotle gives his God to do, what indeed he thinks is the main and probably only function of God — to think. Whatever Aristotle allows God to think about in a way that distinguishes him from ordinary mortals with material bodies — something that is not beyond controversy[1] — it is uncontroversial that according to Aristotle God engages in pure thought, pure *nous*. Surely anything that can do that must be in some sense a person.

It is equally uncontroversial, however, that in many ways, perhaps in most ways, Aristotle's God is *not* a person. Not that Aristotle could have put the matter in that way, since, as far as I can see, the concept of a person was not one that was available to him; certainly there was no Greek word for 'person' at his disposal to express that concept. But the only example of a thinking being on which Aristotle could have based his conception of God as such was a human being. I have argued elsewhere[2] that Aristotle, like Descartes, thought that human beings were distinct from the rest of nature. Whatever Descartes' reasons for that conclusion, Aristotle's seem to have been that the possession of thought or intellect by human beings distinguished them from other beings, and from animals in particular. This was because the workings of the intellect could not, in the light of the consideration that there are no restrictions on what can be thought, be explained in the terms that apply to the rest of his dynamics and to biology.

I shall not rehearse that argument again here. The details of it have, in any case, been subjected to a certain amount of criticism by Howard Robinson,[3] although not, I believe, in a way which demands an abandonment of the general thesis. One might indeed argue that *De*

Anima III, 4 and 5 provides some justification for the Aristotelian claim, made frequently elsewhere, that there is something of the divine in each of us, to the extent that we have and exercise reason. But so to argue would beg the question as far as my present issue is concerned. For what justification is there for the claim that the essence of the divine lies in *nous*? To the extent that Aristotle's argument concerning the intellect leads to the conclusion that there is an aspect of human beings which separates them from the rest of nature, it leads only to something parallel to the Cartesian conclusion that the intellect or mind is in nature distinct from anything material. It leads, that is, to a form of dualism. It provides no reason for asserting that one side of the divide that the dualism comprises is occupied by something divine, however much it raises philosophical questions about the status of that thing in other respects.

What Aristotle seems to insist on at the beginning of *De Anima* III, 5 is an analogy between nature in general and the human soul. Just as there must be in nature something the relation of which to the material of which nature is composed is that of an art to its material, so, by analogy, must there be something in the soul standing in that relation to its material, the body. The implication is that in each case that something works on its material. The big question in the case of the soul is why the something has to be *in* the soul, since most of the potentialities associated with the material body that living things have may be actualized by external agencies or causes and need nothing for their actualization beyond that. The answer must be that the situation is different with regard to thought, for reasons which I have tried to spell out elsewhere.[4] Otherwise there would be no point in going on to say that in the case of thought the agency in the soul takes the form of an intellect. Aristotle does not say in *De Anima* III, 5 that the intellect so construed, the so-called active intellect, is divine, although he does say in what remains of the text (for it is clear, in my opinion, that there is a lacuna of undecidable length in what we have of the text, which has been filled in with other material) that it is immortal and eternal.

Nevertheless, if the analogy is taken seriously, the function of the active intellect seems, at any rate at first sight, to be like that of a God similar to Plato's *demiourgos* — one who is responsible for the existence of objects in the way an artist is responsible for his objects, by giving form to a pre-existent matter. But if Aristotle's God is simply the prime mover, he is not quite like that. Aristotle's argument for the existence and nature of the prime mover in *Physics* VIII is not an argument for a demiurge as such. A craftsman, which is what the demiurge is, originates his objects in a temporal sense, and although Plato's *Timaeus* does not technically subscribe to quite that principle, since time as a moving image of eternity exists in his view only when certain aspects of creation already exist, it is much easier to construe Plato's demiurge as a creator than it is to do the same of Aristotle's prime mover. For, as Aristotle makes clear at the beginning of *Physics* VIII, when he tries to establish, as the first premise of his argument, the eternity of change without beginning or end, the prime mover cannot be construed as a *temporally* first mover; for there is nothing which is temporally first. The possibility of that is not ruled out by Plato's theory, even if time as such does not exist until the creation of the heavenly bodies to provide measures of time. For that creation is, nevertheless, a temporal event. That is presumably why *in general* Plato's philosophy has had a greater appeal for those wishing to provide a philosophical basis for the doctrine of creation.

What, then, does Aristotle mean when he says that in nature as a whole there is something related to matter as an art to its material, and which thereby produces things? The first thing to note is that, in spite of what I may have seemed to be suggesting up to this point, he does *not* say that this something is related to matter as an *artist* to his material, but as an *art* to its material. If an art produces its objects it is not exactly as an artist does. One might indeed say that the relation of an art to its objects is not so much to be their efficient cause as to be their formal cause, while the artist is certainly an efficient cause of those same objects. The prime mover is of course related to nature at large, in Aristotle's view, by being the final cause of the movements of the spheres carrying heavenly bodies, which thereby and indirectly function as an efficient cause, in some respects at least, of the movements of and changes in other things. But we are also told in effect[5] that the eternal revolution of the heavenly spheres comes as near to the nature of the divine as it is possible for a material body to do. That may seem a somewhat limited likeness, given the nature of the activity of the heavenly spheres, and it is true that it is that. But to the extent that the likeness holds good at all, one might say that the prime mover is not only the final cause of the movements of the spheres, but their formal cause too. Here, as elsewhere, the final and formal causes are the same, although their being is not the same; the same thing is both final and formal cause, but it is a different thing to be the final cause from what it is to be the formal cause. The divine gives form to the movements of the spheres as well as being their *telos* or end, inspiring them with love and desire, but what it is to be their final cause in this way is not the same as what it is to be their formal cause.

An art is the formal cause of its objects, and in a sense produces them, in that the objects of an art would not exist as such if there were no such art. There is no other way in which they could be art-objects, or to the extent that there is, as may seem to be the case with *to automaton*, when such objects come about by accident, nature imitates art. We may find, for example, things which look like art-objects which are not the product of any artist (e.g. stones or rocks which look like statues). But art-objects proper could not exist unless the relevant art existed, and things which are like art-objects because nature imitates art are worthy of note at all only because art-objects proper exist. If there were no such things as arts, rocks looking like statues would not be in any way notable. Could one say likewise that if God did not exist, the eternal circular movement of the heavenly bodies would not be notable? And could one go on to say that such a movement is indeed notable, so there must be a God, just as one might say that rocks with certain shapes are often notable, so there must be arts to make them notable as *quasi*-art-objects?

There are too many hidden assumptions behind such an argument to make it likely that it would generally be considered to have more force than the standardly accepted arguments for God's existence. It might indeed be considered to be simply a variation on them. My aim has been to try to give sense to the idea that the prime mover might be both the final and the formal cause of the movement of the heavenly spheres (and thereby, indirectly, of other things too, except that the material of which those other things are composed affects the process and introduces other kinds of causation as well), producing that movement without being its efficient cause in any intelligible way. Is that the relation of an art to its material, i.e. to its objects? Surely only in part, since it is not clear what sense it would make to say that an art was the final cause of its objects. It could, nevertheless, be their formal cause, since, as I suggested earlier, only it gives form to its objects as art-objects; and in that sense, although in that sense alone, those objects are produced by it.

It remains the case, however, that what is said at the beginning of *De Anima* III, 5 provides an analogy only. What is said about the similarity of the positions in relation to their material of arts, the active intellect and whatever produces each kind of thing (ultimately the prime mover) in no way provides any reason for saying that the intrinsic activity of the prime mover is the same as that of the intellect, that it is indeed thought. Indeed the first part of *De Anima* III, 5 offers a whole series of analogies – between what happens in nature and what happens in the soul, between their relationship to their objects and that of an art to its objects, and between what happens in the course of the activity of the active intellect and what happens in the process of light making potential colours actual. Is light, then the formal cause of the existence of actual colours? Perhaps, although this thought is not obvious to us, to the extent that we think that objects are coloured whether or not there is light to see them. In Aristotle's conception of these matters actual colours would certainly have no existence if there were no light, and it would not have been entirely implausible for him to have said, if he wanted an argument for the existence of light, that there are actual colours (i.e. we do in fact see them), so there must be light. But these analogies do not, either separately or in total, justify any claim to the effect that the prime mover's intrinsic activity is thought.

For possible light on this, let us turn to another well-known passage – perhaps *the* well-known passage – in which Aristotle asserts that the divine consists in thought – *Metaphysics* Λ (XII), 7. Unfortunately, 'asserts' is the right word to use, because it is difficult to abstract from this passage an *argument* which has this as its conclusion. After Aristotle has claimed in this section of the *Metaphysics* the necessity of there being a prime mover, and has maintained that the 'first heaven' is moved because the prime mover moves by being loved, the order of thought seems to be that, as the prime mover's existence and mode of existence is necessary, its being is good. Aristotle then goes straight on to assert that its life is such as the best that we enjoy, except that its life is eternal while ours is short. After some sentences setting out the nature of the thought in which that life consists (a matter to which I shall return), he says: 'If, then, God is always in that good state in which we sometimes are, this compels our wonder; and if in a better this compels it yet more. And God *is* in a better state.' (Ross's translation). Oddly enough, he then seems to derive from this what one would have thought he had already maintained – that God has life.

Underneath the thought of the sentences quoted there seems to lie the suggestion that whatever can be an object of wonder and awe *for us* must be in a state at least as good as we are sometimes in, and for preference an even better one. If that is Aristotle's trend of thought, it depends upon a consideration about what is and can be an object of wonder and awe *for us*. Philosophers such as Kant and Hegel, who have written about the sublime, have sometimes appealed, in elucidating the notion, to apparently superhuman forces in nature. One cannot help thinking that for Aristotle such things would have meant very little; for him sublimity lay in a constant, and in that sense superhuman, engagement in philosophical thought, to the extent that this involves contemplation (*theoria*). Whereas Kant appealed to the starry heavens above and the moral law within, Aristotle might perhaps be said to have appealed to the former, although only as secondary to the divine engagement in philosophical contemplation, whatever that entails; he would have had nothing of the moral law within, and might not even have understood the notion. But nothing in the present passage explains why he had such attitudes. The stars were often thought divine by the Greeks, as Plato's example shows. To think of them as divine is certainly to express wonder and awe at their eternal and regular motion. Granted that the prime mover had to be construed as superior to that, why does that superiority lie in its activity in thought and why does that constitute superiority at all? Only if we can answer that question can we understand why God was for Aristotle a 'he' and not just an 'it' as a prime mover *per se* could well be.

Nicomachean Ethics X, 8 purports to provide an argument for the conclusion that the activity of the Gods must consist in *theoria* (contemplation). It is an argument which has as its context the thought that the supreme happiness in human beings lies in *theoria* too; and that is an exercise of the most divine-like part of ourselves. Hence it might be thought that the argument *presupposes*, rather than leads to the conclusion, that the activity of the Gods consists in contemplation. Otherwise there would be no grounds for the thesis that reason (*nous*) is the most divine-like part of ourselves. But the total argument is more complex than that, in that much turns on the criteria of complete happiness; and in this the notion of completeness plays a vital role. In Aristotle's view completeness goes with self-sufficiency, and at 1178a23ff. he argues that the pursuit of contemplation in the philosophical sense is less dependent on external things than the life of moral virtue. Contemplation, *qua* contemplation, therefore, needs no external conveniences or goods; it is only because any human being engaging in contemplation is also a man that these things become relevant. Indeed, as Aristotle says (1178b33), our nature is not self-sufficient for the purpose of contemplation, and we need other things. With the Gods the situation is different, just because they are not human. This becomes crucial when Aristotle asks, as he does at 1178b8ff. what activity we should assign to the Gods. For his premise is that they must be supremely blessed and happy. He rejects as absurd any suggestion that they may engage in ordinary moral and political activity. The virtues that go with these activities are all unworthy of the Gods. Equally, they cannot spend their time asleep, like Endymion! So the only aspect of life that remains to attribute to them is *theoria*. Considered as an argument by elimination it is not one at the highest level. Nevertheless, one can see what is in Aristotle's mind. Perfect and complete happiness involves self-sufficiency, and the only aspect of life that allows that is philosophical contemplation, even if in the case of human beings other aspects of human nature make other demands upon them. What is noticeable, however, is that it is just *presumed* that the Gods are living, and that, for that reason, once given that they are supremely blessed and happy, their activity must lie in the one aspect of life that Aristotle can think of as meeting his criteria.

Nevertheless, the argument is sadly incomplete. Why cannot there be forms of life beyond any that we are aware of in ourselves? Why cannot what we ascribe to ourselves as divine-like, if we so do, be merely analogical on the actual divine nature? To such questions Aristotle has no apparent answer. Even if theology is 'first philosophy', and even if by studying theology one studies 'what is' in its highest form, this is likely to be of little use to us if at the end of the day we can understand the divine nature only by analogy with what we find in ourselves. To suppose that what we understand of the divine nature is exactly the same as what we find in ourselves is to make matters even worse. In that event, the conclusion to be arrived at is not that theology is 'first philosophy', but that psychology is. For in studying one aspect of ourselves we study, on that account, what the divine nature must be like; even if in studying the latter we study 'what is' in its highest form, we can do so only as a result of a study of ourselves. Hence, on that account, psychology or the study of human nature must be epistemologically prior, whatever else is to be said about it.

The crucial step in Aristotle's argument in this passage of the *Nicomachean Ethics*, as with that in *Metaphysics* Λ, 7, is the claim that God or the Gods have life. It is not crucial in the sense that if we accept the validity of the claim all the rest follows. For nothing prevents the possibility that there are forms of life superior to anything that we can contemplate. But it is only the acceptance of the idea that the divine has life that makes possible the attribution to the Gods of happiness, and *ipso facto* (given Aristotle's conception of that) activity in the form of philosophical contemplation. The claim that the divine has life is made in *Metaphysics* Λ, 7 and is presupposed in *Nicomachean Ethics* X, 8, but it is by no means part of the argument for the existence and nature of the prime mover in *Physics* VIII. Nor is it really part of the idea that the prime mover moves the heavenly spheres by inspiring them with love and desire, even if that may be taken as involving the ascription of life to the spheres themselves.

The heavenly spheres move with the only form of movement which is both eternal and possible for a material thing — the constant, regular and sempiternal movement in a circular orbit. The implication is that in inspiring them with love and desire the prime mover inspires them to be as near as possible in character to itself, granted that they are material, whereas the prime mover, as the argument eventually indicates, cannot be. That is not really enough to sustain the inference that if the spheres are capable of love and desire and for that purpose must have life, then the same must be true of the prime mover. At all events Aristotle draws no such conclusion in the *Physics*. The key element in what he has to say is the emphasis on eternal activity.

One might conceivably argue that the only other form of eternal activity known as possible by us is the contemplation, that activity of *nous*, on which Aristotle fastens, if one could give sense to the idea of its constituting an eternal activity, and if, in particular, there were grounds for thinking that nothing in the nature of *nous* prevents that. I have commented elsewhere[6] on the claim of *De Anima* III, 4 that the intellect or reason can think all things. It is a difficult conception. We now seem to be confronted with an analogous claim that nothing prevents the possibility that the activity of *nous* is eternal; it is not only universal in its scope, it has also no natural end. That is to say that there is nothing which of necessity constitutes an external *telos* for it, so that when that is achieved its *kinesis* or process is completed. *Qua* activity, *qua energeia* that is, it must be an activity which is complete in some sense in itself, and is not such that it must be brought to an end by something outside itself. If we have good grounds for thinking that *nous* was like that, we should have reason for thinking also that its activity could possibly constitute that nature which inspires the heavenly spheres with love and desire. But that is all that would follow. It would by no means follow that the divine actually had that nature; that would remain a possibility only. The assumption that the divine has life would make it a little less of a mere possibility; but that, as we have seen, seems to remain an assumption on Aristotle's part.

There are, therefore, at least two questions which remain for us: (1) Is there anything that justifies that assumption? and (2) In what sense can *theoria* as the activity of *nous* be an activity which is eternal? I shall try to deal with the latter question first. It cannot be that *theoria*, as philosophical contemplation, must, or even can, go on for ever; for the activity of *nous* in us is limited, as Aristotle recognizes, by all sorts of bodily considerations, and will, unless freedom from bodily conditions is possible, come to an end. The 'unless' here is of course of some importance, since there are passages in which Aristotle seems to say that the intellect is not destroyed along with the body. There is not only *De Anima* III, 5, to which reference has already been made; there is also the passage at *De Anima* I, 4, 408b18ff., where Aristotle explicitly says that the intellect seems not to be destroyed and is indeed 'something more divine'. Unfortunately, the argument there for that conclusion, involving as it does a parallel with sight, according to which failure of sight in old-age is due to the failure of the eye, not the capacity as such, seems to grant a sort of eternity to the soul in general, not just to the intellect. Moreover, at 408b24 Aristotle seems to allow that 'thought and contemplation decay', even if this is due to the deterioration of the body. It must surely be clear that, whatever be the case with the intellect as such, *we* cannot carry on with philosophical contemplation for ever; the activity of *nous* in us must come to an end with death. There is nothing in Aristotle that suggests that he really believed otherwise on that point.

It is of course similarly true that *what* we can think is limited by various bodily considerations (e.g. the nature of our brains, although, given Aristotle's conception of the brain as the cooling system for the blood, he would have regarded that limitation somewhat differently from the way in which we today would do so). Hence, when Aristotle says that *nous* thinks all things, as he does in the way already noted in *De Anima* III, 4, he cannot have that sort of thing in mind. I have elsewhere[7] described the principle involved as supremely rationalist, but to say that is merely to point to Aristotle's assumption of the omnicompetence of reason. In his view, the reason why *nous* thinks or can think all things must be that because of its nature and functioning nothing can make it otherwise. There can be no limitations on the possibility of its thinking different things in the way that external objects put limits on what can be perceived. It is not, that is, that when it has accomplished one piece of thought, in thinking of one thing, it must come to an end and start again; for there is nothing to bring that about in the way that an external object and the conditions of perception must do. Somehow what is thought and what can be thought is dependent solely on *nous* itself.

It is that same idea which underlies the thought that the activity of *nous* is eternal. That which makes it the case that there are no limits to its possible objects also makes it the case that there are no limits, given what it is, to its activity. But what makes it so? It will not do to try to answer that question simply by saying that thinking is an *energeia*, not a *kinesis*, so that there is no external *telos* the attainment of which puts to an end the changes or movements involved. For perception is an *energeia* according to *De Anima* 431a4ff., and there are certainly limits to its objects and it would not be at all plausible to say that the *energeia* involved is eternal; it does come to a stop. If thought is eternal it can only be because there are no reasons in the nature of thought itself why it should stop; just as there is no reason in the nature of the heavenly spheres why their revolution should stop, given that their motion is circular. That is not to say that they provide their own principle of motion; the prime mover does that, if by 'principle of motion' we mean the ultimate explanation of their motion. It is that their motion does not have to come to a point at which it is necessary that it should stop and start again; there is no *necessary* termination. Analogously, *theoria* does not have to come to a point at which it is necessary that it should stop and start again. In that way it is different from other forms of thinking, such as discursive or inferential thinking, in the course of which there must be conclusions, terminations and changes of direction. In other words, it is not simply the fact that the operation of *nous* constitutes an *energeia* that makes it eternal; it is because of the kind of *energeia* it is, for it is one in which there is no necessary termination at any stage.

What we have to recognize is that in Aristotle's view there is nothing in the nature of *nous* which restricts its activity, *theoria*, either in scope or in time. That says nothing about *our* ability to think everything or for ever. For we are limited by our bodies and their circumstances. As I noted earlier, the relation of the prime mover to the changes in the world is not that of an artist to his material, but that of an art to its material. In all the issues with which we are at present concerned it is the *form* of *nous* which is the crucial matter, not the effects of its embodiment. But what does *theoria* consist in, if it is to be of this kind? The standard translation of the term, which I have myself adopted, is of course 'contemplation', or at all events 'philosophical contemplation'. But, as *De Anima* 412a22ff. makes clear, *theoria* has to be construed as the actualization and exercise of a form of knowledge which is dispositional (the *energeia* of a *hexis*). That makes it impossible for *theoria* to be taken as the activity of finding out something; nor indeed would this be a suitable activity to ascribe to God. One can engage in *theoria* about something, so that *theoria* can in that sense have propositional content. But that does not make *theoria* discursive, a matter of judgment; it is one thing to ascribe propositional content to some epistemic state, it is quite another to suggest that the state itself has propositional structure, as judgment has.[8] If it did, it would come to an end in reaching the end of the proposition, and that is what Aristotle wants to deny of *theoria*. So what is the exercise of knowledge that *theoria* consists in, and in what sense is this ascribable both to philosophers and to God (whether the objects of the *theoria* are the same in both cases, or, as the traditional and, I suspect, correct view of Aristotle's God would have it, the object of God's *theoria* is himself)?

This is a very difficult question. We generally tend to think of the exercise of knowledge as something carried on in relation to other things, other activities, such as practice or the attainment of further knowledge. That is not Aristotle's conception of *theoria*. However one is to construe the *noesis noeseos* of *Metaphysics* Λ, 9, the divine thought in question stands, as it were by itself. If the thought is propositional, it must involve a complete thought of the content of the proposition or propositions, without this bringing in anything else. It is a very difficult conception. On the other hand, there is perhaps a sense in which *understanding* is like this up to a point. Whatever one understands, and whatever the content of the understanding, when one has it one has it (something that Aristotle may be trying to say at *Metaphysics* 1048b24, although the meaning of that passage in general has been much disputed). It does not follow from that that when we have it we have it for all eternity; nor does it follow, on the other hand, that having it is timeless. It is just that, however long it lasts, nothing more is *required* for it to be. That must hold good of *theoria* too. Contemplation is, on the face of it, something that might take or last for a time. But normally we should expect that it is at least possible that it should issue in some further result, such as the drawing of a conclusion. As Aristotle construes *theoria*, the latter possibility is excluded; but the former is not. *Theoria* can take time. It is the intellectual counterpart of savouring something. Presumably, one cannot engage in such intellectual savouring without understanding its object; but understanding might have *theoria* as a consequence, while nothing further follows from *theoria* itself. It is thus complete in a way that has no application to understanding, however much it is similar to it in other ways.

Why should this be the activity of philosophers and God? As far as philosophers are concerned, Aristotle is surely not saying anything very different concerning their goal from what Plato was saying in *Republic* 533–34, where he describes the outcome of dialectic as a contemplation of the Good in a way parallel to a contemplation of the sun, but also as the achievement of an ability to give the *logos* of everything in general and of the Good in particular. When one understands the principles of reality one has nothing else to do, intellectually, but to contemplate them. If the same is true of God, it is because nothing less than this will do for the divine.

With this in mind, let us return to my other question. Is there anything that justifies the assumption that the divine has life? In *De Anima* II, 1, the idea of a hierarchical arrangement of faculties to which Aristotle appeals in explaining life and the soul leads him to say that life consists, at bottom, of the capacities for self-nourishment, growth and decay. Nothing is alive of which at least this does not hold good. But surely that does not apply to God. So, once again, why does Aristotle say that God has life? If he had embraced the sort of view that Plato put forward in the *Phaedrus*, of the soul as a self-moving mover, with 'self-moving' changed in his case to 'unmoved', God as the unmoved mover could be indentified with a soul and could for that reason be said to be essentially alive. Is that the way in which Aristotle thinks? There is a great deal to be found in *De Anima* I concerning the connection between soul and movement, and he denies there, at 408b30, that the soul is moved at all, let alone self-moved. He does allow, however, that the soul can, in some sense, cause movement in a living body (e.g. at *De Anima* II, 4, 415b8ff.). So the unmoved mover could be a soul, as far as that goes. To reach that conclusion, however, we should have to construe the relation of God to the world as similar to that of the soul to a living body. Why should we do that? The identification of the activity of God as that of *nous* might provide an alternative reason for drawing that conclusion, but given the course of Aristotle's argument in *Metaphysics* Λ, 7, we need something the other way round, since the thesis that the activity of God is that of *nous* seems there to be derived from the premise that God has life and not *vice versa*.

As far as I can see, Aristotle provides *no* reason for saying that God has life, so that he can justifiably go on from that to suggest that the activity of God is thought or contemplation. Rather, at *Metaphysics* 1072b25ff. he suggests that God has life because he engages in *theoria*, and life is in some sense the *energeia* of thought (*nous*), and he is that *energeia*. That is a most opaque statement. In what way is life the *energeia*, the actuality or activity of thought? This is not a question that has received much attention from commentators. The point is presumably that here *nous* refers to the faculty of reason or intellect, and its activity or actualization in thinking or contemplation is a form of life. If that is so, however, then, once again, the attribution of life to God is supposed to follow from the attribution to him of *nous* and *theoria*, not *vice versa*. It follows that there is no independent justification of the claim in Metaphysics Λ, 7, that the nature of the divine is to engage eternally in the best activity, i.e. contemplation. It might be quite otherwise for all we know by way of inference from the argument provided.

It is regrettable to have to conclude that Aristotle's argument is sadly defective. The Greek Gods were cast in man's image, and in many ways Aristotle was no rebel against that tradition of thought. Human life is the highest form of life that Aristotle knew of, and he could not conceive of something higher yet radically different. His concern in delineating the nature of God was therefore to find something that holds good of human beings which could be conceived of as holding good of the divine in an exemplary form. For this purpose what is needed is a human activity which is eternal in the sense which I have tried to explain. *Theoria*, in Aristotle's view, satisfied that criterion. Hence he was able to conclude that that was God's activity and that to the extent that we ourselves can manifest that activity in philosophy we must have something of the divine in us — which is merely to say that we must have a capacity, however limited by our bodily conditions, which God is taken to have in an unlimited way.

From another point of view, it may not seem much of a conception of God, since while he exercises that capacity in a way not limited by material conditions, the activity in question is in another sense a limited one. An Aristotelian God has really no more to do with us than the Epicurean Gods, and in a way for a similar reason, even if, unlike the

Epicurean Gods, the Aristotelian God is not made of the same stuff and is not part of the same cosmic arrangement as anything else. It is because the kind of standard of perfection that the Aristotelian God represents removes him from real human concern. In *Nicomachean Ethics* I, 12, Aristotle raises the question whether happiness is praised or prized (or honoured), and he relates this question to our attitude to the divine. We *do* praise the Gods, he says, but there is an absurdity in this, in that praise seems to relate them to *our* standard. Like happiness, he says, the divine is beyond such a standard, and it is by reference to it that other things are praised, in that they are judged by its standard, not it by theirs. It is all too likely that such a conception of the divine will lead to the view that God has nothing to do with us; at all events it is likely to do so when we try to fill out that conception. For it represents simply a standard of perfection which is entirely abstract. If, in Aristotle's view, we approach that standard when we philosophize, what we thereby attain has little to do with the rest of our life. Philosophy, on that view, is not something that has a point or purpose; it is its own point or purpose. That is why there is the difficulty, which I have mentioned, in giving flesh or substance to the idea of contemplation, in a way which might relate it to knowledge and thinking in general while not being those things as we ordinarily understand them. If we fail to obviate that difficulty, we are left with the conception of an activity, attributed to God, which, by certain abstract criteria, represents a standard of perfection, itself abstract and unrelated to anything else that we can understand. If we prize or honour that it is because it is represented as a standard of perfection, and for no other reason. It has nothing else to do with us.

It might be said that in all this I merely give expression to the difficulties that have been experienced perennially in the attempt to set out the nature of the divine. It cannot be denied, however, that Aristotle accentuates the difficulties which in any case exist, and this becomes most obvious when he attributes life to God without, apparently, having any good reason for doing so. Without that attribution of life Aristotle's God could well be an 'it'. With it, his God becomes more than an abstract standard of perfection to the extent that the attribution of life at least makes possible the attribution of other things such as thought, however much we find it difficult to understand what Aristotle has in mind in this. It remains obscure, however, what reasons Aristotle has for ascribing life to God.

In many ways, this simply represents an early chapter in a whole series of philosophical attempts to set out the nature of the divine in philosophical terms and for philosophical reasons. The so-called 'god of the philosophers' is often no more than a 'first cause' in the sense of an ultimate principle appealed to for metaphysical, rather than theological, reasons. In some ways this is at its clearest in Spinoza, where one often has the sense that the name 'God' is being invoked to provide an honorific for what is *causa sui*, the ultimate principle which is its own justification and explanation, and in which is to be seen the explanation of everything else. It would be hard to say that the same is entirely true of Aristotle, given what I have said about his reasons or lack of reasons for attributing life to God and the part that that attribution plays in his subsequent thought; nevertheless, there is that element in his thinking. From a theological point of view it is perhaps to the credit of philosophers that they have so rarely, in their thinking about God, left the matter entirely at the level of a metaphysical first principle; for metaphysics is not theology. On the other hand, it is arguably not to the credit of philosophy if theological issues are introduced under the guise of philosophy. That is, in effect, what I have accused Aristotle of doing. But in putting the matter in that way I raise large issues indeed.

In conclusion, it is only fair to point out that I have not discussed what many have seen as an additional, and perhaps overriding, difficulty in Aristotle's conception of God. This arises from the fact that, as it is commonly said, Aristotle's God is pure form. It is perhaps difficult to find a passage in which Aristotle says that explicitly and in as many words, although he undoubtedly says in *Metaphysics* Λ, 6 that eternal substances are 'without matter' and are such that their essence is actuality. Hence the identification of God with pure form is not unwarranted. It is not clear, however, that this presents so great a difficulty as is sometimes represented. One source of the difficulties that are sometimes seen in all this is the belief that form is always general and that the form of a thing consists either in all or in some of the properties of a thing (in the latter case perhaps those properties that make up its nature or essence). And do not those properties amount to universals? It may well be the case that the form of a thing is determined by the set of properties that belong essentially to that thing; but the form is not just those properties. (It is a further question, yet again, whether in Aristotle's view properties amount to universals; I shall not go into that issue here.)

Aristotle sometimes says that a compound of matter and form

amounts to a 'this' in a 'this'; so that the implication is that the form of
a thing is a particular. Its identification as such is no doubt determined
in material substances by the matter, or rather bit of matter, of which it
is composed. If Aristotle had raised the question of the so-called
principle of individuation (which I do not believe that he did), he might
have dealt with it by answering along those lines. That, however, does
not mean that the form of a thing is merely a set of general or universal
characteristics given particularity by the bit of matter in which they are
to be found. The form is itself a 'this' (as, for example, *Metaphysics*
1017b25 indicates). Hence, what logical objections are there to the
thought that form might be a particular when it is 'without matter'?[9]

It might be objected that we need more than this in the case of God.
Here it must not only be the case that the set of properties determining
the form *happen* to individuate a particular. For in that event there
might, logically, be more than one entity of this kind, even if there is
only one in fact. Must it not be by some kind of necessity that there is
only one God, if he is to function as a metaphysical first principle. The
difficulties that ensue for Aristotle from the need to postulate a number
of eternal substances to account for the observed movements of the
heavenly bodies, as set out in *Metaphysics* Λ, 8, are well known. If we
waive those special difficulties, however, the unique identification as a
particular of God, construed as 'without matter', is secured by the fact
that he is to be characterized *via* superlatives. He is 'best', as Aristotle
said constantly, beginning with the early argument for the existence of
God to be found in the *De Philosophia* (Ross, Frag. 16) — to the effect
that wherever there is a better there is a best, so that, given that things
are such that one is better than another, there must be a best, which is
God. There can be only one best. Given all this, the thought that God
consists of a unique form, without matter, is not so puzzling as it may
seem at first sight. The problems do not lie here so much as in the
question how that form is to be characterized, other than by reference
to honorific superlatives. That has been my great worry about what
Aristotle has to say on these matters, and unfortunately it has not
proved possible to dispel such a worry. One can comfort oneself only
by the thought that on this point Aristotle is in no worse position than
most other philosophers are and have been.

NOTES

1. See Richard Norman, 'Aristotle's Philosopher-God', *Phronesis* 14, (1969), pp. 63–74, reprinted in *Articles on Aristotle*, Vol. 4, eds. J. Barnes, M. Schofield and R. Sorabji (London: Duckworth, 1979), pp. 93–102.
2. D.W. Hamlyn, 'Aristotle's Cartesianism', *Paideia*, Special Aristotle Issue (1978), pp. 8–15.
3. H. Robinson, 'Aristotelian Dualism', *Oxford Studies in Ancient Philosophy, Vol. 1* (1983), pp. 124–44.
4. In 'Aristotle's Cartesianism', *loc. cit.*
5. See e.g. *De Caelo, 286a5ff.*
6. In 'Aristotle's Cartesianism', *loc. cit.*, p. 14.
7. In 'Aristotle's Cartesianism', *loc. cit.*, p. 15.
8. cf. R. Sorabji, *Time, Creation and the Continuum* (London: Duckworth, 1983), ch. 10, although I am not entirely sure that he is saying there quite what I am.
9. For further thought on these matters, see D.W. Hamlyn, 'Aristotle on Form', in *Aristotle on Nature and Living Things*, ed. A. Gotthelf (Pittsburgh and Bristol: Mathesis Publications and Bristol Classical Press, 1985), pp. 55–65.

3

AQUINAS AND THE LIMITS OF AGNOSTICISM

by Gerard J. Hughes, SJ

*Vice-Principal, and Head of the Department of Philosophy,
Heythrop College, University of London*

In recent years, there has been a notable revival of interest among both philosophers and theologians in Aquinas's discussion of the ways in which we can and cannot speak about God. The desirability of getting behind Aquinas's commentators to what he himself says, recognised many years ago by Professor Copleston, is no longer in dispute. But there is plenty of dispute about what Aquinas himself does say. I wish to consider yet again his discussion of what we can expect to say or to know about God, with which the *Summa Theologiae* begins.

There are at least two differences of opinion which have surfaced in recent work upon which I would like to focus. The two questions to which different answers have been given are these:

1. How 'agnostic' is Aquinas's account of what we can know or say about God?
2. Is Aquinas's account correct, or at least defensible?

David Burrell has argued[1] that Aquinas quite consistently adheres to his announced programme, which is to 'consider the ways in which God does not exist, rather than the ways in which he does.' Burrell comments, 'If this be a "doctrine of God", it is a dreadfully austere one'; but he considers that Aquinas is not offering a 'doctrine of God' at all, but rather is 'laying down the universal (or logical) principles governing discourse about divine things rather than establishing a doctrine of God.' Burrell insists repeatedly that Aquinas's whole procedure is metalinguistic, and, while attention to the logical grammar of our talk about God might indirectly 'show' something about God, there is no question of it yielding a positive doctrine whose sense we can establish.

This represents the most 'agnostic' of the recent interpretations, and is one of the more extreme answers which might be given to the first of these two questions. Burrell goes on to defend Aquinas against some possible criticisms, and I take it that he would be willing to give a positive answer to the second question.

Ralph McInerny[2] gives a somewhat more positive picture of Aquinas's conclusions, in that, while he accepts that the emphasis of Aquinas's treatment is on the way of negation, he finds there also a positive account of God's affirmative attributes expressed by terms used analogously. 'The key to the affirmative divine attributes lies in the intelligibility of the claim that perfections found in a limited way in creatures are thinkable while negating these creaturely limitations. If it is not easy to grasp what is being affirmed when this is said to be possible, it is hard to know why its possibility is so often swiftly denied.' In effect this is a denial of the radical agnosticism of Burrell. McInerny believes, as Burrell does not, that Aquinas is giving a positive doctrine of God, however limited, and I take it that McInerny believes Aquinas is correct in so doing.

Patrick Sherry in his article 'Analogy Today'[3] argues for a twofold position: firstly, Aquinas is willing to give a fairly positive account of the way in which analogous terms can be used to describe God (thus agreeing with McInerny against Burrell): secondly, in the light of more modern discussions of meaning, we might well come to hold that some of Aquinas's critics, and in particular Scotus, took a more defensible line in insisting that at least some of the terms we use of God are not analogous but univocal. He criticises Burrell for not really examining Aquinas's theory of meaning, and by implication McInerny for accepting that theory of meaning too easily.

In support of these claims, Sherry argues that since Aquinas clearly wants to say that God 'really is' good and loving in himself, he must admit that God is in these respects somehow like us. It is this likeness which justifies our use of the same words to describe God and ourselves. But in that case, Aquinas cannot really rest content with the classical Aristotelian account of the analogous use of terms. As Sherry puts it:

> The believer does not think that God simply causes perfections in creatures as yoghurt produces good health in people, without there being any likeness between the two; he believes that God really is, somehow, good, loving, just, merciful, and so on in Himself, that there is some degree of likeness between His perfections and ours, and that therefore we use the same terms of both.[4]

Sherry goes on to argue that this very consideration tells in favour of Scotus's view that terms used of God and of ourselves are univocal. Aquinas was prevented from seeing this, despite the fact that his own arguments often led in just this direction, by his mistaken view about concepts.[5]

With much that Sherry and McInerny say I am in full agreement. I agree that more attention needs to be given to Aquinas's theory of meaning than Burrell offers, and that Aquinas does attempt to give something more than merely a set of metalinguistic rules. On the other hand, I think that Burrell's agnostic account of Aquinas, despite these criticisms, is closer to the general thrust of the text, and that a discussion of Aquinas's theory of meaning bears this out. Given this, Aquinas is correct to insist on the analogous nature of the concepts we use to describe God, and that his view can at least be defended against Sherry's Scotist revisionism. The first part of this paper will attempt to disentangle Aquinas's theory of meaning, and to defend the more agnostic interpretation of the meaning of analogous terms used of God.

Compared with the amount of ink which has been spilt on his treatment of terms used analogously about God, comparatively little has been expended in discussing what Aquinas in this same context says about metaphor in theology. Perhaps at some periods in the past it has been felt that the use of metaphor is more properly to be found in the language of prayer and liturgy than in the more serious business of theology. Such was not the view of the early Christian theologians, nor was it Aquinas's. In the second part of this paper, I shall briefly consider what Aquinas has to say on a topic which is of considerable contemporary interest.

I – THE MEANING OF TERMS USED ANALOGOUSLY OF GOD

In the first thirteen questions of his *Summa Theologiae*, Aquinas attempts to lay down the philosophical foundations on which the study of theology must ultimately rest. Two issues above all preoccupy him: the nature of the philosophical legitimation we have for believing that we can successfully refer to God at all: and the relationship between this legitimation and the meaning of the things that theologians might wish to say about God.

It can hardly fail to strike even the most casual reader that the celebrated 'Five Ways' occupy only one of the eighty-five articles in the systematic presentation which comprises the first thirteen Questions of the *Summa*. They are presented in summary, almost cursory, form. Clearly they were not seen by Aquinas, contrary to the impression so often given by later apologists, as the centrepiece of his argument. Aquinas was not here particularly concerned with the details of possible philosophical arguments to establish the existence of God. What was important was rather two things: that such arguments could in principle be formulated; and that the *nature* of the arguments has a major bearing on the practice of theology. It is on these issues that his discussion is focused. The overall strategy is clear enough: it can be shown that a being exists which is in no way potentially other than it is;

this being has therefore none of those properties which involve potentiality; and this conclusion has radical consequences for the meaning of any utterance we make about it.[6] Some of these consequences are drawn in the course of the discussion of God's non-potentiality (his 'simpleness' as Burrell well translates), in which Aquinas repeatedly asserts that various assertions made about God in the Scriptures must be understood metaphorically. In Question 13 he sums up the entire discussion with a more systematic account of the meaning of theological utterances generally. A detailed understanding of this argument depends on getting clear about some issues of terminology, as well as a grasp of its overall strategy.

1. AQUINAS'S TERMINOLOGY

A fruitful point at which to start, since it precedes much of what Aquinas himself says on the matter, is the distinction he draws between two types of *demonstratio*.

> An 'explanation why' starts from a cause, i.e. from what is prior without qualification. A 'proof that' starts from an effect, i.e. from what is prior from our point of view (for, since an effect is more obvious to us than its cause, it is from an effect that we reach a knowledge of its cause). From any effect it can be shown that its cause exists, where the effects are better known to us than the cause, because effects are dependent on a cause, and, given the effect, there must already exist a cause.
>
> When we argue from effect to cause (and especially when we are dealing with God), we must use the effect in the place of the definition of the cause in proving the existence of the cause. In proving that something exists, we must take as the middle term the meaning of a word rather than a strict definition of the thing (since asking about its definition comes after we have established that it exists). Now the words we use of God are derived from his effects, as will be shown later; hence in proving that God exists we can take as our middle term the meaning of the word 'God'.[7]

The distinction Aquinas makes between the meaning of a word and the definition of a thing is extremely important. As in Aristotle, definitions are of things, primarily, rather than of words. But in those cases where we are unable to define things, we have to use working definitions of words instead. In terms of a contemporary example, Aquinas would agree that people might well have used the word 'gold' to mean 'that yellow metal' while still being unable to define gold. To define gold requires that we know its nature. The word 'atom' might once have meant 'indivisible'; but it is certainly not our belief that atoms are by nature indivisible, and our contemporary use of the word reflects that belief. Only when we rework our ordinary usage to reflect our increased empirical knowledge of the natures of things will the meanings of our words and the definitions of things coincide. So Aquinas wishes to distinguish between the meaning of 'God' as we might use the word (he later suggests that we use the word to mean 'what has universal providence for things'[8]) and a definition of God, which we do not have for lack of knowledge of his nature.

A 'proof that' is therefore an argument of the following kind:

'Cancer' means 'what causes malignant growths in the body'
This patient has malignant growths in his body
Therefore this patient has cancer.

The proof that this patient has cancer is derived not from a definition of cancer, but from a working nominal definition of the word 'cancer'. 'The cause of malignant growths' is the meaning (*quid significat*) of 'cancer', formulated in terms of its symptoms; it is not the *definitio* of cancer, which we do not yet know.[9]

Significare

Is it correct to translate *quid significat* here as 'meaning'? The answer to this question is central to a proper understanding of Aquinas's account of the meaning of analogous terms. Aquinas does not have any systematic terminology to distinguish between sense and reference. The term *significare* commonly does duty for both. One must be careful in translating it not to force upon the text a reading which would be anachronistic. On the other hand, in some contexts the force of the argument, if not the terminology itself, justifies translating it by one or the other of the two modern expressions.

Aquinas's most general remark, based on Aristotle's *De Interpretatione* I,1,163a, runs as follows;

'Words are the signs of concepts, and concepts are likenesses of things', so it is clear that spoken words are related through mental concepts to the things to be signified.[10]

Spoken words have the sense they do because they are the conventional signs for concepts; and since concepts refer to things, so, too, do spoken words. *Significare* will thus normally carry the overtones both of 'mean' and 'refer to'. In the case of 'proof that', however, we have already seen that Aquinas can distinguish between the working definition we give to a word ('what causes malignant growths') and the cancer which we refer to when using the word so defined. 'Cancer' *significat* 'what causes malignant growths'; and here we must translate 'means'. But Aquinas is quite clear that we can still use the word in this sense to refer to cancer[11] even though the sense of the word is not a definition of cancer. Again, in his discussion of whether the words we apply to God are synonymous, Aquinas shows himself perfectly able to make what we would regard as a sense/reference distinction.

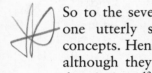

> So to the several different concepts in our mind there corresponds one utterly simple thing imperfectly understood through such concepts. Hence, the words applied to God are not synonymous, for although they refer$_s$ to just one thing, they do so under different descriptions.[12]

I shall henceforth, as in the above passage, flag with a subscript 'S' occurrences of *significare* and its cognates, but will translate them as I think the context requires. Clearly, we cannot take the mere occurrence of *significare* as evidence that Aquinas is talking about meaning.

Repraesentare

Aquinas says that every creature 'represents' God (that is to say resembles him) just to the extent that it has some perfection. We have seen above that he also takes over from Aristotle the view that concepts are likenesses of things. The two points come together in the discussion of synonymy whose conclusion we have just considered:

> Although these perfections pre-exist in God in a unified and simple way, they are received in creatures in ways which are diverse and many. Just as to the diverse perfections of creatures there corresponds one simple source which is represented by the various creaturely perfections in several different ways, so to the several different concepts in our mind there corresponds one utterly simple thing imperfectly understood through concepts of this kind.[13]

It is important that in a context where he most clearly distinguishes between what we call 'sense' and 'reference', the distinction is explained in terms of 'representation', which is used both of the relationship of resemblance between creatures and God, and of the relationship of resemblance between concepts and their objects. His view of this relationship is the clearest indicator of what Aquinas might have said had he been asked modern questions about the meaning of terms.

2. THE MEANING OF ANALOGOUS TERMS

Aquinas follows Aristotle in his view of analogy, as has often been remarked. He mentions two instances of analogous predication:

i) When several things are related to one thing, as when 'healthy' is said of medicine and of urine, both of which are related to health in an animal, the one as cause and the other as symptom;
ii) When one thing is related to another, as when 'healthy' is said of medicine and of an animal, because medicine is the cause of the animal's health.[14]

It is the second of these cases which is relevant to our analogous descriptions of God. Aquinas bases his view that the term 'healthy' is neither equivocal nor univocal on the claim that we can neither say that the *rationes* involved are the same nor that they are totally different, since they are related. Some care is needed, however, in interpreting the next step in the argument:

> When God is said to be good, or wise, the sense$_s$ of what is said is not merely that he is the cause of goodness or wisdom, but that these qualities pre-exist more perfectly in Him. Consequently, we must say that, if we consider what is referred$_s$ to by the word, they (*sic*) are more properly said of God than of creatures, since all such perfections flow to creatures from God; but so far as concerns the application of the words, their primary application by us is to creatures, for it is primarily creatures which we know. And that is why, as we have already remarked, the way in which such words refer$_s$ is proper to creatures.[15]

One cannot take the occurrence of *modus significandi* in the last sentence as decisive evidence for Aquinas's view of the *sense* of terms used analogously of God. The remark takes us back to the first article of the same question, in which Aquinas asks whether any word can be suitably applied to God at all. As appears from the replies, the question is not concerned about the sense which such words have, but about the types of referent they have. Nouns, it is objected, are either abstract nouns, which do not refer$_s$ to substances; or they are concrete nouns which refer$_s$ to composite substances, and neither of these is appropriate for God. Moreover, nouns refer$_s$ to substances which can have qualities, verbs to substances existing in time, pronouns to things in relation to others; and none of these ways of referring is appropriate to God.

> Because it is through creatures that we reach a knowledge of God and draw the vocabulary we use of him, the words we use of him refer$_s$ to him in the way which it is appropriate to refer to material objects . . .

> Because God is both simple and subsistent, we apply to him abstract nouns to express$_s$ his simplicity, and concrete nouns to express$_s$ his subsistence and perfection; and this despite the fact that these words fall short of his way of being, just as the human mind in this life cannot know him as he is.[16]

Still, even if the phrase *modus significandi* cannot be taken as evidence for Aquinas's view of the sense of such statements as 'God is good', the earlier part of that passage does make an important claim. What is being said is not merely that God is the cause of goodness, but goodness pre-exists more perfectly in God. Exactly in what sense are we to understand this? In the next article, and with the same example in mind, Aquinas contrasts such terms as 'goodness' with negative terms and with relational terms (such as 'cause of goodness').

> Instead, we must say that terms of this kind do refer$_s$ to the divine substance, and are predicated of God as of a substance, but fall short of representing him.[17]

The appeal is to the way in which our concepts *repraesentant* God. As we have seen, the relationship of representation is intimately bound up with the *sense* of the terms we use about God. We also have a contrast between the failure of terms to represent God and the unqualified remark that such terms *significant* God, which must surely be translated as 'refer to'. Terms used analogously of God refer to him, then, but in some way or other fail to represent him. There is some defect in their sense when applied to God. Can we discover how serious Aquinas took this defect to be?

To do so, we must bear in mind that God is shown to exist by a 'proof that', which employs a nominal definition of the middle term; and we must recall Aquinas's remarks about the analogical use of 'healthy'.

Consider the following example. A chemist in a veterinary laboratory has to label urine specimens in the light of chemical tests he carries out. Let us suppose that he uses the word 'healthy-U' to describe some of the specimens. He can certainly give a definition of 'healthy-U' in terms of the chemical composition of the urine. The vet has a word 'healthy-A' which he uses to describe animals whose urine is healthy-U. If asked what it was for an animal to be healthy-A, the vet would doubtless reply by speaking of the animal's physical and functional state, and so on. Clearly, then, the proper definition (as Aquinas would term it) of health in an animal is quite different from the proper definition of health in urine. 'Healthy-A' as used by the vet and 'healthy-U' as used by the chemist do not have the same sense; they are equivocal terms. Now suppose that the chemist is told that animals can be decribed as healthy-A, and that those animals can be so described whose specimens are healthy-U. Imagine that the chemist has no other experience of animals which he can use to develop his understanding of health-A. Aquinas would then argue as follows:

a) The chemist knows that healthy-U specimens are causally related to healthy-A animals. He knows that it is possible to refer to health-A in animals.
b) The chemist cannot define health-A, since he does not know in what health in an animal consists.
c) The chemist can produce a nominal definition of the word 'health-A': ' "health-A " is that property in virtue of which an animal produces specimens which are healthy-U'. Similarly, 'health-A' means 'cause of health-U'.
d) Although 'health-A' and 'health-U' are equivocal terms, their senses are not unrelated. Health-A is whatever it takes to produce specimens which are healthy-U. But, unlike the vet, the chemist cannot say any more than this about health-A, since he does not know what it does take to produce healthy-U specimens.

Provided we accept the artificiality of supposing that a chemist has never seen an animal (not even himself!), the example provides little temptation to suggest that the chemist must have at least a vague understanding of health-A. About health-A in itself he is agnostic, though he knows it to be true that some animals are healthy-A.

It will at once be objected that this agnostic account of the use of the analogous term 'health-A' omits two crucial elements in what Aquinas says. He explicitly says that 'God is good' does *not* simply mean 'God is the cause of goodness in creatures'; and he maintains that the goodness of creatures represents the goodness of God, hence resembles the goodness of God. This resemblance, it will be argued, is of central importance for the richer account of the sense of terms used analogously of God. As Sherry puts it, the believer does not believe that God produces goodness in us as yoghourt produces health in people, without there being any resemblance between the two.

We have just seen that Aquinas explicitly says that perfection-terms fall short of representing God. Aquinas offers a comparison which elaborates this point:

> The sense$_s$ of words used of God depends upon the way in which our minds know him. But the human mind knows him through creatures, and hence only to the extent that creatures represent him. We have already shown above that God has in himself all the perfections of creatures, but not distinct from one another, and universally. So any given creature represents him and resembles him to the extent that it has some perfection. But it does not represent him as it might something in the same species or genus, but as a transcendent principle, from whose form the effects fall short while yet bearing some resemblance to it, just as the forms of physical objects represent the power of the sun.[18]

We might, for the sake of argument, concede the principle which Aquinas and Aristotle accepted, that effects in some sense resemble ('represent') their causes. But his parallel with the *power* of the sun and physical bodies should surely caution us against any tendency to overestimate the degree of resemblance. And in any case, Aquinas is careful to note here that when we are dealing with God and creatures, the resemblance cannot be unpacked in terms of specific, or even generic, identity. It seems to me that the consequence of this position is that we are never going to be able to spell out the respect in which the resemblance holds, since any concept we might think of using would suggest at least a generic similarity; and the consequence of that is that we are never going to be able to replace our working definition of God or his attributes with a more adequate one. Just so, the chemist, deprived of any chance of consulting the vet, will not be able to provide any definition of 'healthy-A' which has any term in common with his definition of 'healthy-U'. I therefore think that the notion of representation as Aquinas uses it counts in favour of the agnostic interpretation of his theory of meaning of terms used analogously of God.

What, then, of Aquinas's explicit positive claim about 'God is good' when he says, 'What we call goodness in creatures pre-exists in God in a higher way'?

It is true, as Sherry remarks, that Aquinas does say that 'we know God from creatures which are related to him as to their origin, from a process of extrapolation, and from a process of negation. We can therefore speak of him, but not in such a way that a word which refers to him expresses his essence as it is in itself.'[19] It is also true that it is that perfection which we attribute to God. If asked 'what perfection?' we do have words with which to answer the question — 'wisdom', 'kindness', 'lovingness' and so forth. We know that those are the right words.

But it seems to me that Aquinas insists that, when we apply these words to God, the only sense we can give them is the working causal definition we have for them. Aquinas would agree that we know that God 'really is' good and wise and loving. What we do not know is what it is *for a God* to be these things. It is not simply because of Aquinas's view that the phantasms on which our concepts are based are themselves drawn from our worldly experience that he sees our language used of God as so limited in its cognitive scope. It is because he insists on the divine transcendence.

Sherry's vivid example of the yoghourt is part of an argument to show that the theologian cannot afford to have too big a gap between the divine perfections and the corresponding human perfections. Aquinas is happy enough to insist on the gap, provided he is confident that it is not so wide as to prevent successful reference to God when we use these concepts.

> The words we use of God are indeed derived from his causal activities; for just as creatures, according to the variety of ways in which their perfections are derived, represent God albeit imperfectly, so the human mind knows God in the causal process by which each creature derives from him, and describes him accordingly. Still, these processes do not constitute the sense$_s$ of the words we apply to God (as if to say 'God is living' were simply to say 'Life comes from God'), rather we use these words to refer$_s$ to the origin of all things insofar as life pre-exists in him, although it does so in a way which transcends both our powers of expression and our way of referring$_s$.[20]

The function of the *via remotionis* (assuming that we have identified perfection-terms at all) is to exclude the misleading suggestions of our way of referring. It has nothing to do with stripping away the human or creaturely content of our concept of, say, wisdom or goodness, and then simply applying the purified concept to God, as has sometimes been thought. In so far as we have identified a perfection at all, we *have* identified an attribute which does not by definition include any particular limitation. But it is nonetheless true that the only positive meaning we can give to the term is the meaning it has when applied to creatures; and in *this* sense it is not true of God. The function of the *via remotionis* is to correct the impression given by our ordinary grammar that when speaking of wisdom in God we are speaking either of an abstraction, or of a property which God has. It is not a way of recovering a suitably neutral *sense* of terms used analogously of God.

Similarly, our use of the *via eminentiae* has limited effect. Aquinas does indeed refuse what one might term a narrow verificationist account of the meaning of 'good' when applied to God. To say that God is good is not simply to say that our world is worth living in, or anything of that kind. Neither is 'God is good' synonymous with 'God is the cause of goodness in creatures', if only because God would still be good even had he never created at all. Goodness is said of God *substantialiter* – that is to say, God's goodness is neither a property nor an abstraction, but a subsistent individual. God is whatever it takes to ground the truth of the fact that he is the cause of goodness in creatures. Of course, we can *say* that this ground just is 'goodness', thus signalling that it must somehow resemble goodness in creatures. But though we must use the *word* 'goodness', we are unable to state in what this resemblance consists. It 'transcends our mode of expression' because God transcends our way of existing. He is not a being among others, let alone the supremely good one among the good of this world.

3. DO WE NEED ANALOGY AT ALL?

Thus far, I have been discussing what it is that Aquinas is claiming about the language we use about God in saying that it is analogous. I have been concerned, rightly or wrongly as the reader may judge, to give a rather agnostic interpretation to these claims. To this extent I agree with much of what Burrell says against McInerny and Sherry. Quite a separate question is whether or not Aquinas is correct on what he says. Arguments have been produced which could be used either to question the agnosticism of my reading of Aquinas, or to question the theory of analogical sense which, as I believe, goes with that agnosticism.[21]

Besides taking a slightly more positive view of Aquinas's account of the meaning of analogical terms than I have done, Sherry suggests that if we disengage ourselves from Aquinas's ideational theory of meaning (and I think he is right to criticise Aquinas on this point), we might come to sympathise more with the criticisms Scotus levelled against Aquinas's account of the meaning of analogical terms as such.[22] He rightly points out that Aquinas's criteria for univocity are ultimately metaphysical, and in particular require membership of one genus. Since God is not in the same genus as any creature, no term can be used univocally of God and of creatures. However, Sherry suggests it might be possible to take an alternative approach to univocity, for which the criterion is logical rather than metaphysical. To give but one example of his approach, he argues that the oddity of

Blackpool is healthier than my complexion

is evidence of equivocity, whereas the lack of oddity with

God is wiser than any of us

is evidence for univocity. He concludes that

> Many supposedly 'analogical' terms fall away into the categories of 'univocal' and 'systematically equivocal', and ... most of the traditional attributes of God, especially the moral ones, fall firmly into the univocal class. Certainly there seems to be something slightly odd in the Thomists' claim that we are stretching even terms like 'wise' or 'know' when we apply them to God.[23]

Alston, in his extremely interesting and provocative piece, tries to apply to theology some of the elements of a functionalist approach to human psychological concepts. His crucial point, so far as the present discussion is concerned, is this:

> A *functional* concept of X is non-committal as to the intrinsic nature, character, composition or structure of X. In conceiving of ø in functional terms, we are simply thinking of ø in terms of its function (or some of its functions), in terms of the jobs it is fitted to do. The point is often put by saying that a given functional property or state can have different, even radically different, 'realisations'.[24]

The upshot of this is that there is a common core of sense shared by the terms we apply truly to God, construed functionally, and by those terms as applied to humans, despite the fact that the nature and structure of God is very unlike that of humans. Alston's arguments thus provide additional reasons for Sherry's conclusion that Aquinas is just wrong to think of our uses of 'wise' of God and humans as involving different *senses*, the one primary and the other derived, the one extrapolated and the other mundane.

I do not think that these arguments are at all conclusive. A reasonable test for equivocation is to be found in asking whether the things referred to are of very different kinds. That a cricket ball and a masked ball are such different kinds of thing is surely evidence that 'ball' is used equivocally in the two cases. So too with 'bat' and 'cape'. More difficult, perhaps, is a case like 'choke', where the sense of the verb explains why the part of a car is so called. Engines, like people, can be deprived of some of the air they need to function. But this original connection (even if I am right about it) is hardly involved in our modern use of 'choke' to refer to part of a car. It seems to me that 'choke' and 'choke' are equivocal terms, just because the activity is so different from the pieces of plastic and metal in which a car choke consists. The fact that we can understand the connection between the two senses does not seem to me to militate against saying that the two words now have different senses. Similar considerations would apply to the several senses of 'plane'. If the things picked out by a word are very different, this is evidence that the word has different senses. (I do not suggest that there is always a sharp dividing line between univocal and equivocal uses of words.) Alston's functional analysis does establish, I think, that functional similarity between very different kinds of things *may* be the grounds for our using words univocally of them. Nevertheless, I think that the general point still stands, that ontological differences are in general good grounds for determining differences of sense.

Hence the crucial issue is the ontological transcendence of God. 'God is wiser than any of us' *seems* less odd than 'Blackpool is healthier than my complexion' (or, perhaps more relevantly, 'This cow is not so healthy as its urine'); but on the face of it this is evidence for nothing more than an unwarranted disposition to think of God comfortably in human terms, and consequently to underestimate his transcendence. Were we able to take God's transcendence seriously (as we would did we have access to what his wisdom is like), 'God is wiser than any of us' would seem just as odd. Sherry argues that

> If we link the meaning of terms like 'love' to the truth conditions of sentences containing them, then we are inevitably led back to the

epistemological and ontological questions which I earlier put on one side. It is not just a matter of saying that there must be some grounds for ascribing perfections to God. We must also insist that if we ascribe the same terms to God and creatures, then there must be a connection between the relevant criteria of evidence and truth.[25]

But there is the rub. In the case of God, we do indeed have *evidence* for the legitimacy of describing him as loving or wise. But we do not have a grasp of the *truth-conditions* for so describing him. And while there is, as Sherry argues, 'a connection between the relevant criteria of evidence and truth', the connection is causal, not logical.

Still, the objection might be pressed. Surely at least we know that if God is loving we know too that 'he must desire good for those he loves' (to take one of Sherry's examples)[26]; if God acts, we know at least that he is 'bringing about a change in the world — directly or indirectly — by an act of will or intention' (to take one of Alston's)?[27]

Again, that would be all very well provided we know what it is *for God* to 'desire good' or to 'bring about'. No matter what analysis one tries to offer of these functions, the same problem can be raised again. We know that these terms can be used of God. We know that in some way or other what it is for God to desire or to bring about a change must resemble what it is for us to do these things. But we do not know what it might be in God that makes descriptions true of him. We know something about the truth-conditions for the application of such terms to God; for we know that those truth conditions obtain. But we do not know what those truth-conditions consist in. In other words, we know something *about* the meanings of these terms used analogically of God, since we know that they are related to the meanings of the same words used of ourselves: but we do not know what they mean when used of him.

It does not appear to me that this reply is conclusive. But at least it seems to me defensible, and to be reasonably in line with what Aquinas would be willing to say. It is central to his view to maintain

i) that God is transcendent
ii) that we can prove *that* he exists and has certain attributes without thereby knowing what it is for him to exist or to have those attributes
iii) hence, that we know that terms referring to those attributes in creatures can successfully be used to refer to those attributes also in God

iv) that we know that the senses which those terms have when truly applied to God are in some way like the senses they have when applied to creatures. But we cannot say what senses they do have when applied to God, since we do not know what it is for them to be true of God

v) that we can nevertheless truly say of God that he is good, loving, wise, just; or, in other words, we can truly describe God in these ways. But the *sense* which these descriptions have is limited: to say that God is wise means that God is whatever it takes to ground the fact that he is the explanation of all human wisdom.

It therefore seems to me that Aquinas *is* willing to offer a 'doctrine of God', if that is to be contrasted with merely offering metalinguistic criticisms of doctrines of God. A philosophical critique of the claim that we can refer successfully to God will reveal that the God to whom we successfully refer is radically other than we are. This 'otherness' explains Aquinas's insistence on 'what God is not'; but it does not, in his view or mine, make it senseless to say what God is, it merely places limits to the sense which can be properly given to such utterances. The theory of analogy is metalinguistic, in that it is a theory of sense: but it is a theory of sense which is realist, and is both positive, and critically effective in theology.

II – METAPHORICAL LANGUAGE ABOUT GOD

Knowing that we can successfully refer to God at all is, for Aquinas, dependent on the proofs we can formulate for his existence. The nature of these proofs turns out to place severe restrictions on the sense of the descriptions we can give of God. As he repeatedly points out in his discussion of God's simpleness, certain descriptions cannot be literally true of God – cannot be true of him in that sense. Descriptions of God which are neither negative nor analogous, must, if true of God at all, be metaphorical. What then does Aquinas make of metaphor?

His general position is set out in Ia,1,9, in answer to the question whether it is a good thing that the biblical literature should include metaphors. He answers that it is a good thing, for a variety of reasons (some of which he gives perhaps rather tongue in cheek). Metaphor, he says, fits well with our natural way of arriving at intelligible things from the knowledge of sensible things. It is suited to everyone, especially the simple. It provides work for theologians who must try to discover what the metaphors mean. In particular Aquinas maintains that:

i) The use of metaphor in the Bible is not merely a matter of pictorial embellishment, but is consonant with requirements of the human mind in its attempt to know God.
ii) Metaphorical utterances can be statements, with truth value.
iii) It is easier for us to understand what God is not than to know what he is: the use of metaphor serves to emphasise the transcendence of God, since metaphorical utterances about God mention material things which are far removed from God.

I would like to comment on some of these claims, partly by way of commentary, and partly by way of criticism of what Aquinas has to say.

1.   NATURE AND NECESSITY OF METAPHOR[28]

Aquinas gives a clear criterion for expressions which, if applied to God, must be metaphorical.

> Some words signify the perfections which flow from God to creatures in such a way that the imperfect way in which the creature participates in the divine perfection is included in the definition of the word. (E.g. 'stone' signifies a material object.) Such words can be applied to God metaphorically. Other words signify perfections in an unqualified way, without including in their definition the way in which these perfections are participated in (e.g. 'being', 'good', 'living', etc.) These are said literally of God.[29]

Plainly, the result of this is that comparatively few words can be used to say things literally of God: what Aquinas would have called transcendental expressions (one, good, true, being); some of the expressions which refer to spiritual beings (knowing, loving, willing) provided they do not include by definition any form of potentiality (as, for instance, 'finding out', 'proving', or emotion-terms do). The claim in i) is that the use of such language in the Scriptures is entirely consonant with the content of revelation to human beings. Aquinas is willing to say that the use of metaphor in theology generally is not merely convenient, but necessary – though it is a matter of dispute just how he intended this to be taken.

Nevertheless, whatever gloss Aquinas might give 'necessity', the claim that metaphor necessarily finds a place within theology can be defended in a strict sense. One can make a start by simply pointing to the Creeds, or to the biblical writings, and to the devastating effect of bowdlerising them by omitting all metaphorical expressions in the interests of theological toughness. If, as I shall argue, metaphor is in principle irreducible to literal assertion, then the result of such a purge would be empoverished, unsuited for human use, and doctrinally deficient. It is not simply that the language of religion may properly be metaphorical, but also that the language of *theology* must of necessity contain metaphor (indeed, must consist mostly of metaphor). The critical task is to understand what the languages of religion and theology alike actually mean.

But to do that is no more a simple matter for metaphor than it was for analogy. Discussion of the sense of metaphorical utterances leads inevitably to other highly controversial issues.

2. METAPHOR AND TRUTH

We may return to Aquinas.

> As Denis says, the ray of divine revelation is not cut off by the sense imagery which surrounds it, but preserves its truth, with the result that the human mind which receives revelation is not allowed to remain with imagery, but is elevated to a knowledge of intelligible things. So others too can be instructed by those through whom revelation takes place. Hence things which in one biblical passage are handed on in metaphors are more explicitly set out in other passages.[30]

> Any word which is said metaphorically of God applies primarily to creatures and not to God. Said of God they signify simply some similarities to the creatures in question. For example, 'smiling' said of a meadow simply signifies that a meadow's beauty is related to its being in flower as a person's is to smiling; the similarity lies in the relationship. In the same way, the word 'lion' said of God means simply that God is disposed to act bravely in his deeds as a lion is in its.[31]

These two passages strongly suggest that, in Aquinas's view, metaphors are implicit similes, and further, that the comparisons which they implicitly involve can be literally set out. It may even have been his assumption that the capacity of metaphors to express truths depended on this being the case. There is at least the suspicion that the 'more explicitly' in the first of these two passages is to be understood as 'literally', with the reminder that Aquinas includes analogical discourse within literal discourse, and that literal discourse about God is still far from being *clear* discourse about God.

If this is the train of thought, it seems to me in several respects to be unfortunate. Space does not permit me to argue in detail for the position which I am about to sketch, but it seems to me to be preferable on several counts to that which at least apparently is to be found in Aquinas.

One might, to begin with, distinguish between dead metaphors and living ones. This is not to suggest that there is a clear line of demarcation, but rather that the use of metaphorical language lies along a continuum. At the 'dead' end, metaphors are perhaps not different from idioms, and ought to be considered as literal rather than properly metaphorical. To say that a line of inquiry has reached a dead end is to use a dead metaphor (and perhaps two dead metaphors) which have now become simply idioms of English expression, without any metaphorical force at all. In what follows, I shall be speaking of metaphors which are live.

Aquinas is surely wrong to speak of the metaphorical meaning of *words*. I should have thought it preferable to say that the words used in metaphorical utterances have their normal meanings. In 'God is my rock' and 'Moses struck the rock with his staff', 'rock' is used univocally in both cases, in its normal sense. On the other hand, the force of the two utterances is different; to describe metaphorically is to perform a different speech act from describing literally. Thus, in 'Angus is my shepherd' and 'The Lord is my shepherd', the metaphorical utterance as a whole has indeed a different force, and hence a different sense, from the literal utterance as a whole. Exactly the converse is the case with analogical utterances. Here, on Aquinas's view, to say that Blackpool is healthy and to say that John is healthy is literally to describe in both cases; but 'healthy' has two different, though related, senses. This view of the function of metaphorical descriptions could, I think, be accommodated by Aquinas relatively easily. It remains true that most words, because of their sense, can be used in true utterances about God only if those utterances are metaphorical.

However, the major difficulty in Aquinas's position lies in the analysis he gives of metaphorical utterances taken as wholes. He in fact seems to offer two rather different analyses[32] each of which presents some problems. He deals with

(M) A metaphorically-is B

either as equivalent to

(1) A literally-is B* (where B* differs from B in sense)

or as

> (2) There is some feature F such that A's relationship to A's F is similar to B's relationship to B's F.

Examples of (1) are to be found quite frequently in this section of the *Summa*. For instance, he says

> When scripture attributes three dimensions to God, it refers to the dimensions of his power under the likeness of physical dimensions; thus, 'depth' refers to his power of knowing what is hidden; 'height' to the way in which his power is supreme over all things; 'length' to the enduring nature of his being, 'breadth' to his love encompassing everything. Or, as Denis says, 'depth' to the incomprehensibility of his essence, 'length' to the acts of his power which penetrate all things, 'breadth' to his overarching everything by his providential care.[33]

In the same vein, when people are said to come close to, or depart from, God, 'come close to' and 'depart' refer to movements of the spirit[34]; and God's eternity is described in terms denoting temporal succession although it exists all at once.[35]

The tone of these passages might suggest that the suggested translations of the metaphorical words provide literal equivalents. Plainly, however, they do not do so in every case, though they do in some cases. God literally knows, has power, perhaps cares for things; but his providence is not literally overarching (*superextensio*), nor does his power literally penetrate. Human beings do literally have different spiritual attitudes towards God; but eternity does not literally exist all at once (*simul*). Still, perhaps Aquinas might reply that he was primarily interested in a general point, and not in the precise niceties of the translation. With a bit more care, metaphorical terms could have been eliminated altogether, in favour of terms which could literally apply to a spiritual being.

I have already suggested that it is a mistake to think in terms of the metaphorical senses of individual words. But even were he to concede this, Aquinas seems to be committed to the view that metaphorical utterances can be replaced by literal equivalents. This is certainly the implication of his second pattern of analysis, as the example of the meadow cited above shows. In the same passage, he says that if we speak of God as a lion, we mean that, as a lion is mighty in its deeds, so God is mighty in his. Presumably, 'mighty' is intended to be a literal expression used analogously of God's power. But the metaphorical assertion (M) is reduced, on pattern (2), to a literal assertion that a similarity holds good between the two relationships — lion: lion's deeds, and God: God's deeds.

So at least it is likely that Aquinas's confident assertion that revelation can safely be handed on through metaphorical utterances depends, in his mind, upon the possibility of re-expressing all metaphorical utterances by their literal equivalents. As we have seen, he certainly thinks that the biblical writings *do* offer 'more explicit' ways of setting out these truths. I think Aquinas in saying 'more explicit' means 'literal', and perhaps also that he considers it the task of theology to seek to express literally what is metaphorically contained in the biblical writings from which, in his view, theology takes its first premises.

Be that as it may, one might ask, suppose that metaphors cannot be reduced to literal comparisons, or indeed to any form of literal equivalent, would the value of metaphorical utterances in theology be thereby diminished? And would it still be possible to claim that metaphorical utterances had truth value?

I take it that the claim made by anyone making a metaphorical assertion such as (M) is something like

(3) It helps us to understand A by thinking of it as B.

Note that (3) does not give the *meaning* of (M), but rather gives the meaning of 'metaphorically describe'. It is a meta-remark about the kind of claim being made by someone who asserts that (M), in somewhat the same way as 'P corresponds with the facts' might (on some views) be taken as a meta-remark about the kind of claim being made by someone who asserts that P. (3) tells us what is involved in the speech-act of metaphorically describing. One might produce a kind of pseudo-Tarskian account of truth for metaphorical assertions.

(4) 'A metaphorically-is B' is true in L iff it helps us to understand A to think of A as B.

As with its Tarskian counterpart, we must assume that we already grasp the connection between 'A metaphorically-is B' in L and 'it helps us to understand A by thinking of A as B' in the metalanguage.[36] But at least so far forth, there would appear to be no difficulty in giving a formal account of what it is for a metaphorical utterance to be true. And that is tantamount to claiming that metaphorical utterances can describe things, and can give true descriptions of things. On that score, then, there is no greater difficulty in saying that metaphorical utterances express truths which we have *discovered* about the world than there is about making this claim for literal utterances (including those containing analogous terms).

But two difficulties (at least) still remain.

In the first place, what is it to think of A as B? I take it that the sense of any utterance of the form (M) will depend crucially on the answer to this question. Further, I take it that in the case of any live metaphor (and I am dealing with live metaphors), there will be a variety of ways of thinking of A as B, but not an unlimited variety of ways.[37] Metaphorical utterances, like utterances generally, are embedded in a living linguistic tradition which to some extent controls how they are to be understood. To learn to use metaphor is to learn, among other things, the traditional constraints on how to think of A as B. To think of a skylark as a singer improvising has nothing to do with breath-control. To think of believers as the salt of the earth has nothing to do with the chemical composition of salt. Nevertheless, although some theoretically possible lines of association and reflection are excluded by the tradition, the control exercised by tradition is far from tight. Indeed, it is of the essence of metaphor that it should not be, and that thinking of A as B should be a creative and heuristic activity. For this reason, the sense of 'A metaphorically-is B' is not wholly determinate, and it is essential to the function of metaphorical utterance that it should not be. It is this feature above all which distinguishes metaphorical from literal description, and gives it its specific utility.

Secondly, it might be asked whether it is possible that metaphorical assertions, imprecise and open-ended as they are, are even suitable vehicles for expressing our understanding of things. Can we succeed in referring when we make such imprecise assertions, and can they express an increased understanding?

Much recent work on metaphor has been devoted to just these questions.[38] Many of the positions adopted by Richard Boyd in regard to the function of metaphor in the physical sciences could be used to support what Aquinas wishes to say about the function of metaphor in theology.

Boyd distinguishes between theory-constitutive metaphors, which suggest fruitful lines of further scientific research, and which can be developed, repeated with variations, and elaborated without losing their utility; and literary metaphors which tend with repetition to become trite, hackneyed, and eventually to become dead metaphors which are simply idioms with no metaphorical force at all. Religious and theological language contains both sorts of metaphor (though the boundaries between them are, I think, often rather blurred). Many of the metaphors which Aquinas mentions (especially, for instance, those describing God in terms of the human body) have lost their metaphorical force, and could be replaced (as Aquinas probably intends to replace them) with literal equivalents. Other metaphors have functioned in the history of theology in ways which are very similar to the theory-constitutive metaphors to which Boyd calls attention in the history of science. Thus, Augustine starts from the scriptural metaphor of the Word and develops the metaphorical model of the human soul and its functions to help in understanding the Trinity. Richard of St Victor employed the model of the human family to the same end.[39] Metaphors like redemption led to the elaboration of systematic theological theories based on an understanding of the redemption of slaves. Similar instances could easily be produced from ecclesiology, and sacramental theology. In other cases, metaphors which one might have considered to be dead, such as are involved in seeing God as father, have recently been questioned; their function, it is argued, was much more constitutive than merely literary. They have led to the elaboration of theoretical structures in theology, and, it is argued, to mistaken theoretical structures in theology at that. Boyd says of theory-constitutive metaphors that

> . . the cases of scientific metaphor which are most interesting from the point of view of the philosophy of science (and the philosophy of language generally) are those in which the metaphorical expressions constitute, at least for a time, an irreplaceable part of the linguistic machinery of scientific theory: cases in which there are metaphors which scientists use in expressing theoretical claims for which no adequate literal paraphrase is known. Such metaphors are *constitutive* of the theories they express, rather than merely exegetical.[40]

There are no insuperable problems in saying that we can refer to entities in the world using terms which describe those entities vaguely, open-endedly, (or even, for that matter, falsely). The sense of our expressions is not the only determinant of reference. There is therefore no insuperable problem, whether in science or in theology, in maintaining that the metaphorical utterances which, using a model, we make can genuinely refer, can truly describe the things they refer to. Of course, it is another matter to determine *when* they refer, and more generally when a particular model is appropriate. But such questions about verification should not be settled in advance on the basis of inadequate empiricist views about the nature and cognitive function of metaphorical utterances.

III – CONCLUSIONS

I have tried to argue that the first thirteen questions of the *Summa* are principally concerned with the impact on the nature of religious and theological discourse of the way in which we justify the conclusion that there is a God. The proofs embodied in the Five Ways and the discussion of attributes such as simplicity, eternity, omnipresence and goodness, are introduced not so much for their own sake as because they furnish the necessary foundation for a proper understanding of what can and what cannot be said in theology, and for a better grasp of the meaning of what can be said. What we have here is in part a Prolegomenon, establishing the conditions of possibility, the nature, and the scope of the theological enterprise; and in part an illustration of the positive and negative fruits of such an overall approach.

Secondly, I have tried to show that Aquinas in fact takes a somewhat agnostic view of the sense of analogical terms used to describe God; a view which has much to commend it, and which can perhaps be defended both against some of the Scotist and more recent criticisms which have been brought against it, and against the contention that it has only negative, regulatory, results.

For this reason, though of course not only for this reason, it seems to me to be important to look at the neglected treatment of metaphor which Aquinas also offers in these chapters. Despite what I take to be a false view of the nature of metaphor, I believe that Aquinas is right in some of the central claims he makes about the position of metaphor in theology: that its use is inescapable; that metaphorical utterances can be true or false; that they can be epistemologically helpful. Recent discussion of these issues has, if anything, strengthened these claims, and provides both a support and a challenge to theologians as they reflect on the theoretical implications of their own methodology.

NOTES

All references to Aquinas, unless otherwise noted, are to the *Summa Theologiae*, Part I. References are given to the question and the article (and, where necessary, to the objection being answered).

1. David Burrell, *Aquinas, God and Action* (Routledge & Kegan Paul, London, 1979); the quotations are from p.13 and p.21. See also Nicholas Lash, 'Ideology, Metaphor and Analogy' in B. Hebblethwaite and S. Sutherland (edd) *The Philosophical Frontiers of Christian Theology* (Cambridge University Press, 1982), pp. 68–94.

2. Ralph McInerny, 'Can God be Named by Us', *Review of Metaphysics* 32(1978) pp. 53–73. The quotation is from p. 72.

3. Patrick J Sherry, 'Analogy Today', *Philosophy* 51(1976), pp. 431–46.

4. Sherry, *op.cit.* p. 434.

5. Sherry *op.cit.* p 442.

6. That this being can be identified with the God of Christian belief is asserted, but not proved, at the end of each of the Five Ways. Presumably the justification for the identification is to be gleaned from the ensuing discussion about the properties which must be denied of this being, as well as what can be said positively about it.

7. 2, 2, and also reply 2. *Causa* probably reflects Aristotle's *aitia*, which in general means 'explanation', and cannot in all cases be translated as 'cause' in the modern sense. It might therefore be better to take *effectus* in these passages as 'explananda' rather than 'effects', since the latter would suggest that the kind of explanation being offered is a causal explanation which, in the case of 'explanations why', need not always be the case. I cannot find any one translation of *demonstratio* to suit both the cases Aquinas cites, so had to settle for 'explanation' and 'proof' respectively.

8. 13, 9.

9. 2, 2, reply 2.

10. 13,1. 'Things signified' can include essences (13,1 where *ratio* presumably translates Aristotle's technical use of *logos*), properties (e.g. 13,5 'divine perfections'), indeed items in any of the categories; and also things which exist only in the mind (1,2 reply to 1st objection).

11. At 2,2, reply 2, it is assumed that we are referring to God even when using such expressions.

12. 13,4. *Ratio* here does not have its narrow sense of definition, but its broader sense of 'description'.

13. 13,4.

14. 13,5. A small, but interesting, point is that Aquinas does not seem to commit himself, at least in the way he cites Aristotle, to the view that it is health itself which is healthy in the primary sense; rather it is an animal which is healthy in the primary sense. Contrast *ST* Ia 13,5 with Aristotle *Metaphysics* Γ 2.

15. 13,6. On any interpretation, there is something awkward about Aquinas's syntax in this passage. I am taking the subject of *per prius dicuntur* to be 'words' (supplied from the context) rather than 'perfections' (though it is not impossible that Aquinas could on occasion adopt Aristotle's usage in which wisdom, rather than 'wisdom', is said of God); and I incline to think that the *rem significatam* is not each perfection taken one at a time (to justify the plural 'words'), but rather the one simple God.

16. 13, 1, reply 2.

17. 13, 2.

18. 13,2. I think that my translation of *significant* in the first line can be defended by appeal to the occurrence of the notion of representation in the context, and to the

fact that in the following paragraph Aquinas explicitly deals with the sense (*sensus*) of 'God is good' in the light of the general remarks he makes here.

For other references to the power of the sun, see 4,2 and 13,5. Fr John Russell has pointed out to me that Aquinas might have held that there was a greater degree of resemblance between the heavenly bodies and earthly events than we would find acceptable. On this, see J.L.Russell, 'St Thomas and the Heavenly Bodies' in *The Heythrop Journal* 8(1967) pp. 27–39, which is an extended review of Thomas Litt, *Les Corps Célestes dans l'Univers de Saint Thomas d'Aquin* (Louvain, Nauwelaerts, 1963). If so, my point is less strong, but still, I think, valid.

19. 13,2.

20. 13,2, reply 2. I think *intelligatur vel significetur* at the end of this passage sums up *both* the points he has already made; the point about sense, and the point about the kind of entity to which we refer. In both respects, our use of analogous concepts falls short. Their sense is inadequate; and they appear to refer either to substances with qualities, or to abstract entities. Hence the translation I have offered.

21. Apart from Sherry's article already mentioned, see also William P. Alston, 'Functionalism and Theology', *American Philosophical Quarterly* 22(1985) pp. 221–30. Although it deals with wider issues, its principal strategy could also be applied to criticise Aquinas's position. For a discussion of related issues in Aristotle, see D.W. Hamlyn, 'Focal Meaning', *Proc. Arist. Soc.* 1977/78, pp. 1–18. Hamlyn points out that Aristotle's argument from a thesis about focal meaning does not apply to conclusions in ontology risks being circular. If I am right, Aquinas argues almost in the opposite direction.

22. *Op.cit.*, pp. 438, and 442–4, where Sherry gives a very handy summary both of Aquinas's position and of the principal Scotist objections, as well as an excellent discussion of some modern work which, Sherry argues, might tend to support a broadly Scotist approach. He is also careful to point out that Aquinas and Scotus do not directly contradict one another, since their requirements for univocity are not in fact the same. Nevertheless, he is surely right to point out that there is a substantial difference, and not *merely* one of terminology.

23. *Ibid.*, p. 441.

24. Alston, *op.cit.*, pp. 224–5.

25. Sherry, *op.cit.*, p. 445.

26. *Ibid.*, p. 444.

27. Alston, *op.cit.*, p. 225. Alston is here dealing with functional versions of concepts which involve materiality.

28. By far the best recent treatment of the issues involved is Janet Martin Soskice, *Metaphor and Religious Language* (Oxford: Clarendon Press, 1985), to which I am indebted for much of what follows. For the place of metaphor in Aquinas's view of theology, see also Herwi Rikhof, *The Concept of Church* (London, Sheed and Ward, 1981) pp. 167–91. The rest of Rikhof's discussion is a most valuable account of the problems involved in determining the role of metaphor in theology generally, and extends well beyond the narrow field of ecclesiology with which he is primarily concerned.

29. 13,3, reply 1. This distinction does *not* coincide with that given by Nicholas Lash in his 'Ideology, Metaphor and Analogy' in B. Hebblethwaite and S. Sutherland (edd), *The Philosophical Frontiers of Christian Theology* (Cambridge University Press, 1982) pp 68–94. For Lash, metaphor and analogy are distinguished in that one is anthropomorphic and constructive, the other is metaphysical and critical. Lash accepts too easily Burrell's purely 'grammatical' account of Aquinas's views on analogy. Metaphor and analogy both require some metaphysical backing; but both seem to me to be theories of sense.

The ambiguity of 'sacra doctrina' and unclarity about the precise view which Aquinas takes of theology in the *Summa* make it uncertain whether Aquinas argues for the proper place of metaphor only in the biblical writings and in theology in so far as it must start from the biblical writings; or whether he is willing to admit that metaphor has a central role to play also in expressing the conclusions of theology.

30. 1,9 reply 2.

31. 13, 6.

32. I suspect that (2) is his full-dress analysis, and that (1) is to be regarded simply as a condensed form of it, though it does not seem to me that in fact the relationship is quite so simple as this might suggest. Aquinas hovers between the view that metaphors can be reduced to literal assertions by replacing the metaphorical by the literal sense of the word, and by literally asserting that a similarity exists.

33. 3, 1 reply 1. It is noteworthy that Aquinas is quite happy to give two quite different interpretations of what the metaphorical assertions mean, without, it seems, feeling the need to choose between them. Here, and in the next passage, Aquinas uses the word *designat*, which I have translated 'refers'. I take it, however, that Aquinas intends this to be as much a remark about sense as about reference.

34. 3, 1 reply 5.

35. 10, 1 reply 4.

36. There are of course still further assumptions and refinements which would be needed (for instance about the inadequacy of the biconditional): but these need not concern us here.

37. For the interplay between open-endedness and a controlling tradition, see Janet Martin Soskice, *op.cit.*, pp.154−59.

38. In general, see the invaluable collection edited by Andrew Ortony, *Metaphor and Thought*, (Cambridge University Press, 1979). Of particular interest to my present concerns are the papers by Richard Boyd 'Metaphor and Theory Change: What is "Metaphor" a Metaphor for?' (pp. 356−408), and the replies by T.S. Kuhn, 'Metaphor in Science' (pp. 409−19) and by Z.W. Pylyshyn 'Metaphorical Imprecision and the "Top-Down" Research Strategy' (pp. 420−37).

39. For the relationship between metaphors and models, see Janet Martin Soskice, *op.cit.* pp. 101−103. 'Metaphors arise when we speak on the basis of models'. 'The presentation of a model, its *linguistic* presentation, that is, can take the form of a metaphor, as in the sentence, "The brain is a computer". Metaphors which propose a model in this way are sometimes called "conceptual metaphors", but a more exact if more cumbrous title is "theory-constitutive metaphors".'

40. Boyd, *op.cit.*, p. 360.

4

ANALOGY AND METAPHOR

by RICHARD SWINBURNE

Nolloth Professor of the Philosophy of the Christian Religion,
University of Oxford

It is important to analyse the differences between normal and figurative uses of words. This paper seeks to do that, primarily by distinguishing between 'literal', 'analogical', and 'metaphorical' senses of words. This kind of distinction can be made in more than one way. What I would claim for my way of making the distinction is that it is a fairly natural and useful one and gives these terms a use similar to those which many others have given them in the history of thought. But it needs to be kept in mind that some writers use these words in very different ways from other writers.

I

I begin my task by making two other distinctions. The first is between the meaning of a type sentence and the meaning of a token sentence; let us call them type-meaning and token-meaning. The fundamental kind of meaning is token-meaning; the meaning possessed by a particular sentence as uttered or written in a certain context. (Where the sentence is embedded in a large repeatable context, as a sentence of a book of which there may be many copies or of a play of which there may be many performances, I count all tokens of the sentence in that context as the same token as long as the context remains qualitatively identical in all respects which affect the meaning of the token utterance, e.g. as long as the sentence remains part of the play and is not used for some other purpose.) We derive from token-meaning the notion of type-meaning, the meaning common to all token-sentences of the same type in different contexts. Type-sentences may have more than one meaning, in that tokens of them have different meanings in different contexts. The type sentence 'There is a crook in the next room' will mean in a context of discussion about sheep or fell-walking that there is a stick or staff with a curved end in the next room; in most other contexts it will mean that there is a criminal in the next room. However, type-sentences often have what I call a normal meaning, that is, a meaning which speakers of the language with no knowledge of the particular context of their utterance presume them to have in a context unless special features of that context come to their attention. The normal meaning of 'The King is in the castle' is that there is a hereditary ruler of a country in a large fortified building with thick walls and strong gates. Context alone will reveal which king and which castle. What the token-sentence means involves what 'king' and 'castle' refer to. But that at least what I have just laid out is meant is rightly presumed in the absence of special features of the context – e.g., that the local Town Hall is called 'the castle', although it is nothing like what is normally called a 'castle'. Type-sentences may sometimes have more than one normal meaning, in that independently of context there is no presumption that among several possible meanings they have one rather than the other.

The second distinction is between sentence-meaning and speaker's meaning. This is a distinction often made in the literature, but not always clearly. By 'sentence-meaning' is usually meant the meaning of the token-sentence. 'Speaker's meaning' may then be used in one of two senses in which there is a clear contrast to be made both with token-meaning and type-meaning. But sometimes 'sentence-meaning' is used to mean normal type-meaning, while 'speaker's meaning' is used to mean token-meaning.

The first clear and useful thing which may be meant by 'speaker's meaning' is the meaning which the speaker meant the sentence uttered by him to have. Although speaker's meaning will then of course in general coincide with sentence-meaning, it will not do so in those few cases where the meaning which the speaker meant the sentence uttered by him to have is not the meaning it actually has. There are two possibilities under this heading. First, the speaker may not utter the sentence he intended ('meant') to utter, through a slip of the tongue. I say 'He mumbles a lot', meaning to say 'He grumbles a lot', because I don't take the trouble to articulate my words. Secondly, the speaker may utter the sentence he intended to utter, but in the false belief that the sentence had a different meaning. I say, as students do when discussing Hume, 'There are no casual connections between events', meaning that there are no causal connections, through a belief that 'casual' means 'causal'.[1] The second clear and useful thing which may be meant by 'speaker's meaning' is the information, question or command which the speaker intends to convey by what he says. In this sense too speaker's meaning will normally coincide with sentence-meaning, but sometimes it will not. First, the speaker may intend to convey not merely what he actually says, but something further. I say 'It's cold' and thereby hint that I would like you to close the window. I say to a student who arrives late at a morning class, 'Obviously your alarm clock wasn't working this morning', as a way of pointing out to him that he is late. The token sentence which I utter means one thing, and by uttering it I say and intend to say that thing; but I say it in order to suggest or hint at something else. Secondly, there are cases where the speaker intends to convey something other than he says and not what he intentionally says. I utter and mean to utter a token sentence which I know has a certain meaning but I do not intend to convey to you the information (command or question) contained in that sentence, but something else. One uncontroversial example would be where I intentionally utter a false sentence, intending thereby to convey to you the opposite of what I say, and believing that my sentence will have that effect because I believe that you think I am a liar. Another uncontroversial example would be where there is a private understanding between speaker and hearer (a code, say, for use between secret agents) that a certain sentence will be used to convey information other than that which it contains.

Many examples, however, which are cited under this heading, of alleged cases where speaker's meaning diverges from sentence-meaning, seem to me not to be cases of the above kinds, but rather to be cases where the meaning of the token-sentence diverges from the normal meaning of the type-sentence. They are cases where the conventions for understanding the sentence as being used to convey information other than that contained by a sentence of that type uttered in most other circumstances are public ones (not, as above, private ones for use between secret agents). But then the token-sentence uttered in the particular circumstances does contain that information, because it has the meaning (of expressing that information) which is other than the normal meaning possessed by sentences of that type. For what public conventions about how a sentence is to be interpreted do is to determine what the sentence means.

Metonymy, for example, does not exemplify the required speaker's meaning/sentence-meaning contrasts. Metonymy involves referring to an object by using the name or description of some adjunct. Instead of saying 'a presidential spokesman said', I say 'the White House said'. Here it is not that I say one thing, that a white house talked, in order to convey some other suggestion. I don't say that a white house talked. I use a sentence which, independent of context, would mean that a white house talked (that is the normal type-meaning of the sentence), but in the context of political discussion my token sentence has quite another meaning. I don't mean to convey any information other than I do convey, that is, the information contained in the token-sentence which I utter.[2]

Henceforth I shall use 'speaker's meaning' to denote either of the two useful senses distinguished earlier. In cases where speaker's meaning (in one or other of these senses) is contrasted with sentence-meaning, truth or falsity belong to the token-sentence in virtue of its meaning; and what the speaker meant by uttering it is not relevant.

The meaning of the token-sentence is a function of the meanings of the type-sentence and of the context. The meanings of the type-sentence are a function of the senses of the component words, and the way in which they are combined.

Words of the language have each some one (or sometimes more than one) logicogrammatical status − as noun, adverb, verb or whatever of different kinds (proper name, common name, mass noun, etc.) which logicians have classified. Certain combinations of words are well-formed sentences, and among them are indicative sentences, ones which make claims. Whether a combination of words is a well-formed indicative sentence depends on the order in which words of different grammatical status follow each other. Logicians have formalized many of the possible forms of such sentences. They may for example be of the form 'a is ø', 'a is R to b' or '($\exists$x) (øx)', where 'a' and 'b' are proper names, 'ø' is a (one-place) predicate and 'R' is a relation term. Some words have more than one grammatical status (e.g. 'smiles' as a plural noun or a verb); where the resulting sentence is well-formed only on one interpretation, that is the interpretation. Otherwise it is left to considerations of sense or context as opposed to grammar to disambiguate.

Words have not merely a grammatical status but (within that status) one (or more) senses. Its sense is its context-independent contribution to the meanings of the type-sentence to which the word belongs. Many words have more than one sense − 'lock' as of a door and 'lock' of hair, 'pen' for animals and 'pen' to write with. The frame of the rest of the type sentence often makes clear how an ambiguous word is to be taken. In the absence of special information about the context words are to be taken in the sense which gives the type-sentence its normal meaning. In 'I shut the sheep in the pen', 'pen' is to be taken as an animal pen rather than pen for writing with, because that is the meaning the type-sentence is presumed to have independent of context, because writing pens are not the sort of thing which can contain sheep.[3] However, a token-sentence 'I shut the sheep in the pen' could have a meaning other than the normal meaning of the type-sentence − e.g., in a fairy story about sheep being shut in a giant fountain-pen. Context (of paragraph, speaker, hearer, and environment) selects among the normal meanings of type-sentences and may give to a token-sentence a meaning other than a normal meaning. A token-sentence must be presumed to have among its possible meanings the one which makes it a natural thing to say in the context, if with all other meanings it is not. This may be because only so would it be relevant to the subject of the conversation; or because otherwise it would be obviously (to the speaker) false. If with two or more meanings the sentence is a natural expected thing to say in the context, whereas with all other meanings it is not, then it is ambiguous between interpretations with the former meanings. In a conversation about money hidden in various places including the sides of rivers, 'I put the money in the bank' will be ambiguous (whereas it will not if the conversation has had no reference to hiding money by the sides of rivers). If with no meaning is the sentence a natural thing to say in the context, then the sentence must be taken to have that meaning and the words that sense which makes the sentence the least unnatural thing to say (or, if there is more than one such meaning, to be ambiguous between them).

Among the senses of a word there is often one which it is presumed to have in the absence of information about the sentence frame into which it fits or the context of its utterance. This is the contribution which we presume that it will make to the meaning of any type- and so token-sentence in which it occurs in the absence of information that it does not make that contribution (because with a different possible sense the resulting token-sentence would be a more appropriate thing to say in the context). This presumed sense is naturally called the 'literal' sense. Thus the literal sense of 'cold' is that to say that something is cold is to say that it has a relatively low temperature on a scale such as the Centigrade or Fahrenheit scale. But when people and social environments are said to be 'cold', something different is meant. To say that the sense of low temperature is the literal sense is to say that the presumption with respect to 'x is cold' is that this is what is being said. If there is no presumption between two or more senses or in favour of another sense, then, I shall say, the two or more senses are all literal senses. I distinguish my sense of 'literal sense' from that sense of 'literal sense' in which the literal sense is the historically prior sense; historical priority is not a consideration relevant to philosophical analysis of kinds of meaning.

The sentence frame selects among the senses of words to yield the normal meaning of the sentence type. Context of utterance may fill out the meaning by adding to the intension the reference. It indicates about whom a claim is being made in 'I am old'. Context may also reveal as inappropriate the normal meaning or meanings of the type-sentence, and so force it to be understood in a less usual way, and in the process it may force a less usual sense on the component words. Normally it is right, as the Davidsonian approach supposes, to suppose that the senses of words are there, sentence-frame selects among them to yield possible sentence-meanings, and context selects among these. But, as we shall see in due course, sometimes it is the other way round. Context forces a token-sentence to acquire a meaning which no one would previously have supposed to be a possible meaning of the type-sentence; and that in turn forces a sense on some of the component words which no dictionary would have listed as a possible sense thereof.

When words which have a sense in the language are combined into a well-formed indicative sentence, and the context gives its referring terms a reference, that sentence will generally have meaning. Sometimes it will be indeterminate which of two or more meanings the sentence has, but normally it will be unambiguous. The sentence's having a meaning does not, however, entail that it is coherent. It is coherent if logical considerations do not rule out its being true, i.e., if it does not entail a self-contradiction. 'There is a greatest prime number' has a clear meaning but it entails a self-contradiction. It is the same with 'He is more than six feet tall and also less than five feet tall'; and, I believe, with 'The ball was coloured red all over and also green all over' and 'His pressing the button in England in the Time Machine in 1985 A.D. caused the machine to arrive in Egypt in 1000 B.C.'[4]

II

A given token word 'ø' is sometimes used in the same sense as another token 'ø' of the same type, sometimes in a similar sense, sometimes in a quite unrelated sense. It seems a natural use of the terms 'univocal', 'analogical' and 'equivocal', consonant with their role in the history of comment on language, to mark this difference. So I shall say that a word 'ø' is used on two occasions in a univocal sense if it is used in the same sense, in an analogical sense if it is used in a similar sense, in an equivocal sense if it is used in an unrelated sense. A sense, being a contribution which the word makes to the meaning of the sentence, can be recognised and distinguished from other senses by its meaning-related substitutes, i.e., a word has the same sense if it has all the same synonyms, contraries, determinates, etc., similar sense if it has many of the same synonyms, etc., unrelated sense if it has none of the same synonyms, etc. These relations between senses have been analysed in a careful and sophisticated way by James F. Ross in his *Portraying Analogy*. Ross introduces his category of a predicate scheme. Consider the words which can be substituted for a given word 'ø' in some sentence, while leaving the sentence 'acceptable'. Ross does not define an 'acceptable' sentence, but an acceptable sentence is at least a well-formed sentence of the language which preserves the consistency of the original sentence (p.58); it seems to me that this understanding of 'acceptable sentence' makes for unnecessary complication and that we should understand by 'acceptable' simply 'well-formed'. Thus you can replace 'boy' in 'The boy asked for a job' by 'girl', 'old man', 'plumber' or 'carpenter'. But only some of the substitutes are meaning-relevant, i.e., have with the original word such connections of meaning as being near-synonyms, antonyms, contraries, determinates of the same determinable, determinates of the other, etc. (p.69); as in this example do 'girl' and 'old man', but not 'plumber' or 'carpenter'. The meaning-relevant substitutes for a word form its predicate scheme. Words have the same meaning, are being used univocally, if they have the same predicate scheme (viz., the same near-synonyms, contraries, determinables, etc.); similar meaning, are being used analogically with respect to each other, if they have overlapping predicate schemes; and are equivocal with respect to each other if their predicate schemes do not overlap.

Ross's account of univocity goes back to that given by Aristotle in *Topics* 106a–107b. Thus in 'All bachelors are lonely' uttered on a certain occasion, 'bachelor' has the same sense as when it is used in a large number of other contexts, for in each it has the same synonyms (e.g. 'man who has never married'), contraries ('married man', 'widower', 'divorced man', 'unmarried woman' . . .), is a determinate of the determinable 'man', and has as its determinates such sets as ('bachelor under 20 years old', 'bachelor between 20 and 30 years old' . . . , etc.) and ('bachelor who wishes to be married', 'bachelor who does not wish to be married').

Ross however has applied these notions in a more detailed way to analogy than did either Aristotle or any of his successors. Among the hundreds of examples which he discusses, he considers eighteen examples of different senses of the word 'charged'. Some of these are equivocal with each other, and some analogous (and the extent of analogy varies). Thus (pp.100f.) there is analogy between 'He charged his assistants to watch the financial markets' (in the sense of instructed them) and 'He charged her with information as to her opponents' (in the sense of mentally burdened or loaded her with it). 'For', writes Ross (p.101), 'the former allows as near-synonyms "instructed", "informed", "ordered", "commanded", and "directed", but [the latter] does not allow "ordered", "commanded", or "directed", yet does allow "instructed", "informed" and the like.' Some terms are more analogous than others. An important case of analogy is where a word with its predicate scheme is removed from one context and applied in another — which is the case among others with abstraction (p.108):

> Thus in 'the arch *carries* the weight of the roof', we could substitute 'bears', 'holds', 'sustains', or 'supports'. So too in 'the first premise *carries* the weight of the argument'. The first mentioned near-synonyms for the first occurrence are also near-synonyms for the second.

Yet one set of words (with their contraries, determinates, etc.) is 'a contrast in modes by which one physical object is said to impede the gravitational pull on another', while the other does 'not presuppose physical activity at all'. Hence the implication of the two 'carries' are different, and this will emerge with them or their synonyms having some different contraries, determinates, etc. One 'carries' is a species of 'exerts a physical force on'; the other is a species of 'gives logical support to'.

Analogy is a matter of degree; some words are more closely analogous than others. However, despite Ross's preference for talk of 'near-synonyms' rather than 'synonyms', it seems to me that a token-word in a token-sentence in a given context may have a full synonym, not merely a 'near-synonym' by the test which I have suggested elsewhere.[5] The token 'ø' in a token-sentence p (e.g. 'a is ø') is synonymous with 'ψ' if the substitution of 'ψ' for 'ø' would yield a token-sentence q (viz. 'a is ψ') synonymous with p. p and q are synonymous sentences if (for all A) 'A believes that p' (uttered in the same context as p) is logically equivalent to 'A believes that q' (and if all other replacements of p by q in belief-contexts yield logically equivalent sentences — e.g. 'A believes that B believes that p' is logically equivalent to 'A believes that B believes that q'.[6] By this test there are token sentences 'John is a bachelor' in which 'bachelor' is undoubtedly synonymous with 'unmarried man'.

At the other end of the spectrum is equivocation. Tokens of 'bank' meaning river bank are straightforwardly equivocal with tokens of 'bank' meaning money-shop. Among cases of the equivocal in my sense are words related by what Ross calls denominative analogy. Here the token-word is used because of a relation of objects, situations, etc., to which types of the same word standardly apply. We call things Victorian if they resemble things typically current in the Victorian period (Ross, p.123). One instance of this is where the relation is causal or significative, viz., an object is called 'ø' because it is the cause of things being 'ø' or shows them to be 'ø'. To use the Thomist example, a diet is 'healthy' if it causes a man to be 'healthy' and urine is 'healthy' if it is a sign of a man being 'healthy'. This is the Thomist analogy of attribution. But although there is a connection of meaning, it is not that the two uses of 'healthy' have similar meanings; one is not saying something similar of urine and the diet in describing them both as 'healthy'.

Words which are analogical in my sense are often examples of what Aquinas called analogy of proper proportionality; but, as we shall see shortly, he had some quite different kinds of criteria for when a word was being used analogically from mine. By my criteria 'good', 'wise' and 'powerful' come out as univocal in their use of men and God. 'Wise' is used in the same sense in 'God is wise' as in 'Socrates is wise'. There are the same synonyms – 'knows many things', 'understands many things', same antonyms – 'foolish', same determinates and determinables. Of course there are differences in what wisdom amounts to in God. God's wisdom is essential to him, and it is not the result of learning. But if 'God is essentially wise' is entailed by 'God is wise', the entailment arises either because 'x is God' by itself entails 'x is essentially wise', etc., or because it entails 'If x is wise, then he is essentially wise', which, conjoined to 'x is wise', yields 'x is essentially wise'. A similar point applies if 'God's wisdom is not the result of learning' is entailed by 'God is wise'. These entailments do not arise from 'wise' being used of God in a special sense; the contributions of 'wise' to the meaning of 'God is wise' and 'Socrates is wise' are just the same.

Duns Scotus affirmed, as I do, that such terms as 'good', 'wise', and 'powerful' are used univocally of God and man. He defines a term as univocal if it has sufficient unity in itself to serve as the middle term of a valid syllogism (e.g. 'ø' is univocal in 'a is ø' and 'b is ø' if from the former and 'All ø's are ψ' you can deduce 'a is ψ' and from the latter together with 'All ø's are ψ' you can deduce 'b is ψ') and if it cannot be affirmed and denied of the same thing without contradiction.[7] By these tests 'wise' comes out as univocal with its normal use in its application to God. From 'God is wise', and 'Anyone who is wise knows that man is mortal' it follows that 'God knows that man is mortal'; and the same goes if you substitute 'Socrates' for 'God'. And the same goes for 'good' and 'powerful'. Although it seems to me that Scotus' tests for univocity are not strong enough, they are of the same logical type as mine. Scotus was clearly attempting to elucidate the same kind of understanding of univocity as I am.

Not so Aquinas. Aquinas claimed that predicates such as 'good', 'wise', and 'powerful' were being used analogically of God in comparison with their use of men.[8] Aquinas's reasons for denying univocity arise from various metaphysical and epistemological doctrines which are highly dubious if seen as doctrines about analogy of a kind such as I have been concerned with. Among the former are the doctrine that terms are only univocal if they denote properties in beings which belong to the same genus, or at any rate have the same mode of existence. Among the latter is the doctrine that concepts are abstracted from 'phantasmata' derived from sensible things, and so our language is tied in meaning by its applicability to sensible things.[9] Such claims of Aquinas seem quite inadequately justified if Aquinas's sense of 'analogy' is anything like mine. Trans-categorial terms may be univocal in my sense, and how we derive our understanding of the meaning of a word is not directly relevant to what that meaning is. However, by these doctrines Aquinas may be elucidating a rather different understanding of 'univocal' and 'analogical'.

Even Aquinas seems to have allowed that words denoting a relation between creatures and God are used univocally, e.g., 'cause' in 'God is the cause of the Universe'. That is what gives us a grasp on what God is and, according to Aquinas, enables us to understand what is being said about God by means of analogous terms. For in saying that God is 'wise', 'powerful', etc., we attribute to him the kind of wisdom, power, etc., appropriate to his nature as cause of the Universe.

Further, even if, as I have argued, Scotus is right that 'good', 'wise', 'powerful' are also used in their literal sense of God, there seem to me plenty of words which are used in my sense analogically of God. First, there are words which imply passion. God is said to be 'angry', to 'feel pity', to 'love'. All of these verbs of emotion seem to involve (as part of their meaning) not just belief (e.g., with anger, that someone has done wrong) and a tendency to action (action in the absence of reason against, e.g., with anger, action to hurt the wrongdoer); but also desire (inclination to action despite contrary reason), and even bodily sensation. No one is really angry or feels pity or love unless they feel these things in their stomach or breasts or bowels or behind the eyes;

and have an urge, hard to control, to vent their anger or to show their pity and love. God, according to traditional theology, does not; and the usual use of these terms of God in Christian doctrine and in Christian interpretation of the Old Testament is such that they do not carry these latter elements of meaning. 'Angry' in both 'God is angry' and 'John is angry' has as synonyms both 'enraged' and 'furious' (though in the former these words are of course also only used by analogy with their literal use), but only 'angry' in 'God is angry' has as a synonym 'believes wrong has been done and seeks to right it', and only 'angry' in 'John is angry' has as a synonym 'believes wrong has been done and feels an urge to right it.' Other words used analogically of God are words which imply the use of bodily organs to acquire knowledge or perform actions. God is said to 'see' the wickedness of men, or to 'strike' them down. By using these verbs of God, we discount any implication that sensations or bodily organs are involved. 'Sees' of God is synonymous with 'is aware of'; and of course it is used sometimes of men also in just this sense, as when a man is said to 'see' the connection between the premises and conclusion of an argument. But, more usually of men, 'see' is synonymous with 'is aware of by means of usual sensations (acquired through use of eyes)'. When God 'strikes down' a man, 'strikes down' is synonymous with 'causes to fall' but not with 'causes to fall by means of a blow with the arm'.

Senses of words analogical with the literal sense are often there in the language, ready to be used, listed in dictionaries. Even when a word is used in a certain analogical sense only with reference to God, it may have been used frequently in that sense in the past, and so the sense be available for use in new theological discourse. But sometimes a new analogical sense may need to be introduced into language. This may be done explicitly, by showing its connections to other words (including giving the predicate scheme) and giving examples of its correct application; or it may be done implicitly by using the word metaphorically.

III

When a word is being used in an already existing sense, then mere knowledge of the language in which a token sentence containing it is uttered shows the contribution (or possible contributions) which it is making to the meaning of that sentence. Context of utterance may be needed to fill out the meaning, or discriminate between possible meanings; but that context is not needed for the purpose of generating a possible meaning to start with. Metaphor arises when a word or words are not used in any preexisting senses, but knowledge of a wide context — a lot of information about where the token-sentence containing the word was uttered, by whom, to whom, in what circumstances, against what background of common assumptions — will reveal what is being said. The sense is a new one, generated by the context and by the previous established senses of the word together.[10] The new sense may be analogical with the old one or it may not. (It might, for example, on the contrary exemplify denominative analogy.) If similar metaphors are used frequently, the sense becomes an established one, and the use in that sense is no longer metaphorical. (The metaphor is dead.) When words are used metaphorically the token sentence has a meaning other than a normal meaning of sentences of its type.

I illustrate:

Wittgenstein paints in oils rather than watercolours. . . .(1)
Cynthia proved to be a hedgehog. . . .(2)
Eliot took poetry off the gold standard. . . .(3)
Jane was not so much the last rose of summer, but the first winter jasmine. . . .(4)
No iceberg melts in winter. . . .(5)
Computer failure will often lead to your take-off being aborted. . . .(6)
If you open up a can of worms, you should be able to catch quite a lot of fish. . . .(7)

All of these sentences, except perhaps (3), have a normal meaning with words used in normal senses, taken by themselves with no information about the context of their utterance. But information about the context (e.g. that 'Jane' and 'Cynthia' were used to denote female humans) may rule out all normal meanings. Each of these sentences could acquire a whole variety of meanings and so some of their words have a whole variety of senses according to the context; no dictionary could list the possible senses. (2), for example, may be a description of how Cynthia looks, or how she behaves in her personal relations, and in the latter case it could utilize different features believed to be true of hedgehogs to make different comparisons. It could be saying that in her sexual relationships or in her relationships with employers, or in her relationships with friends, she 'clams up' unless approached with extreme gentleness and tact; or alternatively that she is very 'prickly', takes remarks the wrong way if that is possible, is quick to resent the slightest suggestion that there is anything wrong with her. (6) could be used in the course of a description of a whole variety of human activities; and what corresponds to 'computer failure', 'take off' and 'abortion' will vary in each case. One use, but obviously only one use, is to make the point that getting to know a certain person is difficult, you seem to be beginning to exchange confidences and talk readily when some irrelevant accident outside your control makes your relationship much more formal.

One comes to understand what is being said by noting its obvious inappropriateness in the context if the words are taken in normal senses or other senses indicated by their place in the sentence frame alone. However, we then look for the distinctive features of the objects, activities or whatever denoted by the words in their normal senses (features which belong necessarily to those objects, etc.; or contingently, or are generally believed to belong, or are suggested by the objects) and see which are possible features of other objects, etc., denoted by the words of the sentence.[11] Certain of these connections are more appropriate than others to the context. Words which in their normal sense denote aspects of the discussion in which the sentence occurs are, other things being equal, to be taken in those senses. All of this will throw up many possible meanings for the sentence. If with only one of these is the sentence a natural, relevant thing to say in the context, that is the meaning the sentence has. If on more than one interpretation it is natural and relevant, then the sentence is ambiguous and may be true on one interpretation and false on another.[12]

For example, take (1). Suppose it occurs in a context when Wittgenstein or philosophers generally are being discussed. Then 'Wittgenstein' has to be taken to refer, in accord with normal conventions of reference, to the philosopher Wittgenstein. If the discussion were about which philosophers painted and how they painted, then the sentence could be supposed to have its normal meaning. But suppose, more plausibly, that it occurs in a discussion of Wittgenstein's style of argument. Then it would not be a natural relevant thing to say, and we must look for some other meaning. One distinctive feature of painting in oils as opposed to watercolours is that you dab the paint on to points rather than stroke it on with flowing strokes over a wide area. The work of art is constructed by many separate contributions rather than by fewer connected contributions. What this suggests in the case of writing philosophy is making many separate points which produce a total integrated view, rather than a number of connected arguments in which there is a flow of thought; and that of course is characteristic of Wittgenstein's style. There are, no doubt, also other distinctive features of oil painting as opposed to watercolour painting, but in the absence of any of them having obvious relevance to philosophical style, we take the one suggested. The sentence says that Wittgenstein wrote philosophy by making a large number of seperate points which give a total view, rather than a number of longer connected arguments. The sentence can now be assessed for truth or falsity.

Metaphorical sentences may be somewhat vague; there may be a wide border area of possible states of affairs which are such that in them there is no true answer as to whether the metaphorical sentence is true or false. In a conversation about Cynthia, touching both on her appearance and her personal relations, it is quite unclear just how hedgehog-looking and clamming-up or prickly in her behaviour she has to be in order for 'Cynthia proved to be a hedgehog' to be true. Some details of the conversation and the assumptions of its participants (about Cynthia and hedgehogs) might make the truth-conditions sharper than they would otherwise be; but there would be quite a wide border area, in which it would be as near to the truth to say 'Cynthia proved to be a hedgehog' was true as to say that it was false. However, all sentences have border areas for their truth – when the curtains are blue-green, it is as near to the truth to say that 'The curtains are green' is true as to say that it is false. Metaphorical sentences simply have wider border areas than most other sentences.

Metaphorical sentences may or may not be paraphrasable by other non-metaphorical sentences. Thus some distinctive feature of the objects picked out by the word 'ø' which is being used metaphorically may be one for which the community lacks a word; 'ø' may then be used metaphorically in that context as a name for that feature. Then a metaphorical sentence containing 'ø' used in that sense will not be paraphrasable by a non-metaphorical sentence. Such a metaphor is a 'creative' metaphor, in that it enables us to 'see' things which we had not seen before.[13]

The account of metaphor which I have given is in some ways a very considerable elaboration of comparison theory. This holds that when 'S is P' makes a metaphorical assertion it means the same as the simile 'S is like P', and similarly for sentences of other forms. But this will not do as it stands. In a metaphorical assertion some words are to be taken in their normal sense, some are not. We need a context to show which words are and which words are not to be so taken. Also, everything is like everything else in some respect, and one could not say that either 'Man is a wolf' or 'Man is like a wolf' is either true or false, without taking account of a lot of context to show the kinds of respect in which comparison is being made. Also the comparison is sometimes not with the object or property or activity apparently referred to, but with something associated with it. To reveal what comparison is being made we need, once again, context. Black's 'interaction' account of metaphor claims that a metaphorical assertion forces a system of commonplaces associated with one subject ('wolf') on to another ('man'), 'the metaphor selects, emphasizes, supresses and organizes features of the principal subject ['man'] by implying statements about it that normally apply to the subsidiary subject ['wolf'].[14] Again, this seems on the right lines, but needs to be elaborated to apply to sentences other than subject-predicate sentences, to show how context picks the features for comparison, etc.

Both Black and comparison theory seem to allow that metaphor yields claims which can be assessed for truth or falsity. But both Searle[15] and Davidson[16] claim that the only meaning which metaphorical assertions have is their normal ('literal') meaning; yet by uttering a sentence with that meaning, the speaker manages to convey to the hearer a quite different idea. Man is not a wolf, but saying that he is helps the hearer to see man as a wolf.[17] Searle expresses this view by distinguishing speaker's meaning from sentence-meaning and claiming that metaphorical meaning is speaker's meaning.

The difficulty with this way of putting things is, as Soskice well illustrates[18] and as Searle explicitly points out, the metaphorical statement 'a is ø' and the simile 'a is like ø' will have totally different truth conditions, and that seems very odd when we take a complicated metaphor like:

> Human language is a cracked kettle on which we beat out tunes for bears to dance to, when all the time we are longing to move the stars to pity.

and compare it with Flaubert's actual simile:

> Human language is like a cracked kettle on which we beat out tunes for bears to dance to, when all the time we are longing to move the stars to pity.

Surely the truth conditions of the two statements are the same.

If my account earlier of what constitutes the distinction between speaker's meaning and sentence-meaning is correct, Searle has misapplied it. Metaphor does not involve the speaker saying something other than he means to say; nor does it involve the speaker meaning what he says (in a normal sense) but hinting at something further or hoping that the hearer will come to believe something other than was said as a result of having private criteria for interpreting it. It is rather, as with metonymy, that the speaker uses a sentence which independent of context would mean one thing but which in the context (as shown by public criteria) means something else.

Like literature and science, theology is full of metaphors; sentences and parts thereof which in a particular context of a creed uttered or a book written at a certain time against a certain philosophical, scientific and theological background have a meaning other than a normal meaning, and so constituent words which have a sense other than an established sense. Metaphor flourishes even in creeds, and although some new uses of words in creeds tend to utilize a recently established sense or to create a new sense with which the words are then used in other sentences, this does not always happen. Creeds still contain living metaphors, such as the Nicene Creed's statement about Christ that he is 'light from light'. But metaphor is more obviously rampant in religious works not formulated as creeds. The Bible, for example, is riddled with metaphor. Thus 'he that sitteth on the throne', viz., God, is reported as saying:

> I am the Alpha and the Omega, the beginning and the end. I will give to him that is athirst of the fountain of the water of life freely.
> [Rev.21.6]

No one, however fundamentalist, ever thought that God was literally (!) identical with the Greek letter alpha. Very few people ever thought that in a literal sense God was the beginning or end of some process. And most people never thought that God was here promising a literal drink. Rather, the associations and use in other contexts suggest that alpha being the first letter is the important thing of it, and what is being said about God is that he is the first thing on which other things depend and after which they follow. And the important thing about omega is that it is the last letter in the alphabet, and what is being said about God is that the final purpose of things consists in their relation to God and that he will determine what ultimately happens to them.

There is a wide unclear border between metaphor and analogy as I have defined them. Not all metaphors force analogical senses on words. For a word may be used to designate a property contingently but in no way semantically associated with the property which it normally designates, and in that case there would be no overlap of predicate schemes. And when an analogical sense created by a metaphor passes into established use, that use is no longer metaphorical; but it is vague how frequently and in what circumstances a word needs to be used in a sense for that sense to become established. Yet vague distinctions which coincide more or less with those of many other writers are sometimes more useful than precise ones which do not. And, even so, there are many distinctions to be made among the figurative uses of language, and some writers make distinctions very different from mine. But it remains the case that categories such as analogy and metaphor are of crucial importance for anyone who philosophizes about religion, including Aquinas and Scotus, two philosophers whose thinking Frederick Copleston has helped us to understand, perhaps even more than he has helped us to understand the thinking of so many other philosophers.

NOTES

1. Under this heading comes any case where the sentence makes a reference other than that which the speaker intended to make. Intuitions differ about when a sentence does make such a reference. But an obvious example would seem to be a case such as when a speaker says 'Her husband is kind to her', believing falsely and without the public context suggesting this that Jones is her husband and intending to make a comment about him. Here, as Kripe suggests, the token-sentence refers to someone other than Jones, although the speaker referred to Jones (see Saul Kripke, 'Speaker's Reference and Semantic Reference' in [ed.] P.A. French et al., *Contemporary Perspectives in the Philosophy of Language* [revised edition of *Midwest Studies in Philosophy*, Vol.2], University of Minnesota Press, 1979). There may, however, be cases where the context makes it so clear in a way understood by all participants in the conversation that an object a is 'the ø' that the fact that a is not in fact ø does not have the consequence that a token-sentence 'The ø is ψ' does not refer to a.
2. The source of the sentence-meaning/speaker's meaning distinction is of course the writings of H.P. Grice – 'Meaning', *Philosophical Review* 1957, 66, pp. 377–88, 'Utterer's Meaning, Sentence-Meaning, and Word-Meaning', *Foundations of Language* 1968, 4, pp. 1–18, and 'Logic and Conversation' in (ed.) P. Cole and J.L. Morgan, *Syntax and Semantics* Vol.3, Academic Press, 1975. Grice is well aware of the token-sentence/type-sentence meaning distinction and the difference between it and a sentence-meaning/speaker's meaning distinction, but the way in which he uses the latter distinction seems to me not always satisfactory. The second article puts what is 'conventionally implied' by a sentence in the category of speaker's meaning; and while most examples of 'conversational implicature' in the third article fall, on my account also, into the category of 'speaker's meaning', not

all do — for example, like Searle (as we shall see), Grice regards metaphorical meaning as speaker's meaning.

3. On how the sentence frame selects the sense of a word within it, see James F. Ross, *Portraying Analogy*, Cambridge, 1983, ch. 2 and 3.

4. See my 'Analytic/Synthetic', *American Philosphical Quarterly* 1984, *21*, pp. 31–42; and *The Coherence of Theism*, Clarendon Press, 1977, ch. 2 and 3.

5. See my 'Analytic/Synthetic'.

6. This further clause is a requirement for sentence-synonymy additional to that contained in my 'Analytic/Synthetic', where I gave only the simpler requirement that p and q are synonymous if 'A believes that p' is logically equivalent to 'A believes that q'. It was pointed out to me by Roy Sorenson that it is open to counter-examples, such as that although 'A believes that someone exists' is logically equivalent to 'A believes that A exists', 'A exists' is not synonymus with 'Someone exists'. The additional clause rules out counter-examples of this kind.

   See 'Analytic/Synthetic' also for an account of the meaning of and tests for entailment and so of logical equivalence (mutual entailment); and a defence of the applicability of these notions against Quinean objections.

7. Scotus, *Ordinatio* I. dist.3 q.1; and *Opus Oxoniense* I.iii.2.5–6, translated in A. Wolter, *Duns Scotus: Philosophical Writings*, London 1962, p. 20.

8. Ross also holds that both 'wise' and powerful' are used of God only analogically (op.cit., pp.170f.), but he does not give any detailed argument for this. He allows that other words used in religious discourse are often either univocal or equivocal with normal senses.

9. For elaboration and criticism of Aquinas' reasons for denying univocity, see Patrick Sherry, 'Analogy of Today', *Philosophy*, 1976, *51*, pp. 431–446. See pp. 438 et seqq.

10. The joint generation of new sense by prior sense and context is the theme of Josef Stern, 'Metaphor as Demonstrative', *Journal of Philosophy* 1985, *82*, pp. 677–710. He compares this process to the process of the generation of the reference of a demonstrative (e.g. 'I') by the sense of the demonstrative (e.g. to refer to the speaker of the utterance containing it) and the context (showing by whom the utterance containing 'I' was spoken).

11. Some of these distinctive features may only be believed to belong to the objects, or are suggested by talk about them in immediately previous conversation. If a speaker in a conversation has been complaining about the exhorbitant price paid for a cord of wood, 'That refrigerator is my cord of wood' will then mean in that context that it was too expensive. I take this point and example from Marie Bergmann, 'Metaphorical Assertions', *Philosophical Review*, 1982, *91*, pp. 239–45.

12. My account of how one determines the meaning of a metaphorical utterance owes quite a lot to John R. Searle, 'Metaphor' in A. Ortony (ed.) *Metaphor and Thought,* Cambridge University Press, 1979, especially pp. 113–120. But for Searle, as we shall see shortly, such factors as those described in the text do not determine the meaning of the sentence, but rather what the speaker meant to convey by uttering the sentence.

13. On how metaphors can be 'creative' see Stern, op.cit., pp. 703f.

14. M. Black, 'Metaphor' in his *Models and Metaphors*, Cornell University Press, 1962, pp. 44f.

15. op.cit.

16. D. Davidson, 'What Metaphors Mean' in his *Inquiries into Truth and Interpretation*, Oxford University Press, 1984.

17. Davidson, op.cit., pp. 262f.

18. Janet Martin Soskice, *Metaphor and Religious Language*, Oxford University Press, 1985, p. 92.

5

UNIVOCITY AND UNDERSTANDING GOD'S NATURE

by JANICE THOMAS

Lecturer in Philosophy, Heythrop College, University of London

As a prospective employer I may receive a reference which describes a candidate as knowledgeable, perceptive, of sound judgment, thoughtful, fair minded, trustworthy, creative, articulate, and in his personal life a loyal friend, and loving family man. I will be entitled to doubt the wisdom or sincerity of his referee if time reveals that person to be ignorant, silly, bigoted, irresponsible, unimaginative, disloyal or cruel – if, despite what his reference led me to expect, he makes repeated inept or disastrous decisions, fiddles the books and absconds with secret files.

But what am I entitled to believe if I am told that *God* is wise, just, patient, good, powerful, and loving? Theologians and ordinary believers alike take such terms as 'wise', 'just', and 'loving', to be truly applicable to God but there is considerable and perhaps surprising difference of opinion as to what qualities may be being ascribed to God in these terms and what degree of understanding is imparted with them. This is often presented as a difference dividing defenders of the view that such terms have univocal application to God and to man from those who believe them in some way equivocal, having one sense for humans and a different (though perhaps related) sense when applied to the divine. It will be my contention that quarrrels about the presence or absence of univocity or equivocality in religous language are largely a red herring in attempts to assess the possibility of any degree of human understanding of God.

Consider first the positive side of the debate. Many might feel that there is no point in saying that God is wise or forgiving or loving if what is meant by those terms is something altogether different from what we mean when we apply those terms to people. Indeed if it were claimed that it is true that God is wise in some sense of 'wise' *altogether* different from that in which it is true that Socrates was wise then we. might be right to wonder what it is that we are being told is true, what belief it is that is being endorsed. Even if it is held that God's wisdom far outstrips human wisdom and thus must differ from ours *as wisdom* to some extent, it might be felt that there must be some common core, some shared features, in virtue of which 'wisdom' is the correct term for both the human and the divine characteristic. So Patrick Sherry says: 'The believer does not think that God simply causes perfection in creatures . . . he believes that God really is, somehow, good, loving, just, merciful and so on in Himself, that there is some degree of likeness between His perfections and ours, and that therefore we use the same terms of both'.[1] Like the ethical naturalist who would claim that not just anything at all can be counted as a generous or fair act, a theological naturalist might claim, to take an example of Sherry's that God would not be counted wise, any more than a man or a cat would be, unless he at least pursued long term goals and avoided foolish actions.[2]

If it is felt that there is some unacceptable hubris in holding these terms univocal, in claiming that terms like 'fair' and 'wise' have at least a common core of meaning whether they apply to us or to God, William Alston offers an excellent way of soothing outraged sensibilities, our own or others'. He suggests that we look with favour on the functionalists' interpretation of psychological terms like 'love', 'know', 'intend' and 'will'. To say that divine loving or intending share a common core of meaning with human loving or intending is not to give ourselves airs but simply to recognise that some sorts of attributes can be realized (one and the same attribute) in radically different ways. If a computer recalls a fact 'f' and I recall it also, very different processes may occur in very different mechanisms consisting of very different materials, but in each case the same activity or function is performed – recalling 'f'. I may have one and the same performance of a particular string quartet on tape or compact disc:[4] although the recordings differ greatly in physical realisation the hearer of either will recognise one and the same performance. Alston's approach suggests that divine wisdom, justice, love, may be to human wisdom, justice, love as identical recordings in very different formats are to each other. Perhaps God's otherness is like a recording technology radically in advance of our own or any we could achieve. But we can have some understanding of God – we know he is loving, just, wise and we know what love, justice and wisdom are from human experience even if we don't know what divine states realize these qualities in God. For Alston, 'there are abstract common properties that underlie the enormous differences between divine and human psychological states':[5] thus the otherness of the divine is safeguarded while commonality is maintained.

Opponents of this conclusion point out that God is not just a super man,[6] he is of an entirely different order from man. How can we know what it would be for God to be just, wise or loving? Aquinas would say – or so David Burrell's blunt summary has it – that while we are justified in 'using expressions like wise, good or loving properly of God . . . we cannot hope to know what they mean in that context.'[7] God's transcendence at once puts his nature beyond the reach of empirical enquiry and suggests that no term will mean when applied to him what it means when applied to the non-transcendent.

So Gerard Hughes, also interpreting Aquinas but regarding the view he ascribes to Aquinas as defensible on its own merits, says the most we can know about such terms as 'love' and 'act' used of God is that they do apply to God and that what it is for them to apply to him bears some resemblance to what it is for them to apply to us. We can know *about* the meanings of these terms of God 'that they are related to the meanings of the same terms used of ourselves: but we do not know what they mean when used of him.'[8]

How might one go about resolving this conflict of views or deciding which most merited support? I think the answer to this question one might be tempted to draw from many writings on the subject is that the whole issue turns on the presence or absence of ambiguity and its nature if present. What is needed is a good, foolproof, objective test of univocity or univocality. Armed with such a test we could discover, about 'wise', 'just', 'loving', 'forgiving', 'acting' and any others, whether these terms are univocal or not. If they are univocal whatever they mean of men they must also mean of God and if they are not then what they mean when applied to God is still to a greater or lesser extent mysterious even to one who understands what they convey when said of a man.

It is my contention that if such an independent, objective test of univocality for terms is essential to achieving a resolution of the debate I have outlined, then the hope of resolution must be abandoned. For there is and could be no criterion of univocity which we could use to convict a term of definitely possessing only one sense.

It ought to be said straightaway that this conclusion is not prompted by awareness of the 'sorry state' of the theory of ambiguity of which Israel Scheffler[9] complains at the beginning of his book on the subject — although ample evidence for this verdict is certainly available if it were needed. For it seems to me that, amid much disarray, there are several accounts of the nature of ambiguity (Scheffler's among them) which possess particular virtues and promise well for our hopes of reaching an understanding of the nature of multivocity, or multisignificance as it is sometimes called. Nor do I despair of anyone's ever coming up with criteria of ambiguity which could tell us that some terms are definitely possessed of more than one sense. What I deny is the possibility of exposing as equivocal through such tests each and every term that has more than one sense. By the same token — though this may seem strongly counterintuitive — I hold it vain to hope to gather the univocal terms by collecting terms which criteria of ambiguity do not succeed in proving ambiguous. To fail to prove a term ambiguous is not to prove it univocal.

This last point needs to be distinguished carefully from another which it superficially resembles. In saying that a term found not to display the characteristic qualities (whatever they turn out to be) of ambiguous terms can not automatically be dubbed univocal I am not suggesting that there is some additional, alternative category between univocal and equivocal terms — say a category of analogical terms. We might well want to make further subdivisions within the class of equivocal or multisignificant terms — perhaps, like Richard Swinburne[10] following James F. Ross, we may want to recognize a range of cases from senses very similar to our original term to outright homonyms. However, I take it as a matter of fact about all terms that either they have only one sense or they have more than one sense — whatever relations of resemblance hold among the various senses in the latter case. So in the terminology I am adopting 'ambiguous', 'non-univocal', 'multivocal', and 'multisignificant' are used interchangeably and all refer *inter alia* to terms whose numerous senses are related by analogy.

Richard Swinburne, in his subtle and suggestive essay 'Analogy and Metaphor', defends the view that 'good', 'wise' and 'powerful' are 'univocal in their use of men and God', saying that tests for univocity devised by Duns Scotus, though 'not strong enough',[11] bear out this verdict. Scotus designates

> that concept univocal which possesses sufficient unity in itself, so that to affirm it and deny it of one and the same thing would be a contradiction. It also has sufficient unity to serve as the middle term of a syllogism.[12]

Applying Scotus' second test Swinburne argues:

> From 'God is wise' and 'Anyone who is wise knows that man is mortal' it follows that 'God knows that man is mortal'; and the same goes if you substitute 'Socrates' for 'God'.

Since both the syllogism with 'God' and the same syllogism with 'Socrates' are valid, 'wise' is univocal between God and Socrates.[13]

However, it seems to me that this test cannot be relied upon to separate the univocal from the non-univocal. To begin with, it would show up as univocal those terms with, so to speak, 'nested' senses, terms such as those discussed recently by James D. McCawley where 'there *is* a sense which covers the whole domain of applicability of a word but there are additional more restricted senses'.[14] For example, the term 'Yankee' means 'native of the USA' but also signifies 'native of the northern USA' and also 'native of New England'. From

'John is a Yankee' and
'Anyone who is a Yankee meets one of the requirements for obtaining a US passport' it follows that
'John meets one of the requirements for obtaining a US passport'.

And the same goes if we substitute 'Peter' for 'John' even if John is from Birmingham, Alabama, and Peter is from Boston. Scotus' test fails to reveal 'Yankee' as non-univocal.

It might be argued in reply that terms where there *is* a sense which covers the whole domain of applicability of the word ought to be counted univocal whatever further distinct, narrower senses the term's meaning harbours. Perhaps something like this is what has been meant by those who have said that terms like 'wise' and 'just' are univocal and also that they share a *common core* of meaning when applied to men and God.

To this reply, however, a friend of the view that 'Yankee' is not univocal has at least one ready answer. Imagine someone enquiring whether John is a Yankee. Surely the question could with propriety be answered either 'yes' or 'no'. It would be appropriate to answer 'It depends what you are asking — do you mean "Is he a native American?" or do you mean "Is he from the North?"?' (Compare 'Is Socrates wise?' 'It depends what you are asking — yes he is among the wisest of men but no, even he is not wise as God is.')

In any case, and far more gravely, it also seems to me that the second test proposed by Scotus fails to show up the non-univocal nature even of acknowledgedly non-univocal terms and outright homonyms. Consider

Tom is healthy
Whatever is healthy is free from smallpox
Tom is free from smallpox

Blackpool is healthy
Whatever is healthy is free from smallpox
Blackpool is free from smallpox

and

> Rhinolophus Ferrumequinum is a bat
> All bats are material objects
> Rhinolophus Ferrumequinum is a material object
> The Babe Ruth Special is a bat
> All bats are material objects
> The Babe Ruth Special is a material object

Since all four are valid syllogisms, 'healthy' and 'bat' ought to be univocal but I take it as uncontroversial that they are not.

If we try the other test proposed by Scotus it seems to me it fares no better. This test bears more than a passing resemblance to Quine's well known test for ambiguity. Scotus, remember, says a concept is univocal if ' . . . to affirm and deny it of one and the same thing would be a contradiction'. Quine says 'an ambiguous term such as "light" may be at once clearly true of various objects (such as dark feathers) and clearly false of them'.[15] To return to Swinburne's chosen example of human and divine wisdom, Scotus and Swinburne would presumably say that 'Socrates is wise' contradicts 'Socrates is not wise' and thus 'wise' is shown to be univocal. Yet someone who thought divine wisdom different from human wisdom would deny the contradiction and claim comfort from Quine's test saying that because it can be true at the same time that 'Socrates is wise (as humans sometimes are)' and that 'Socrates is not wise (as God is)', 'wise' is ambiguous. It is hard to resist the conclusion that the two tests yield the 'right' result only if the question whether the term under examination is or is not univocal has already been answered by the person applying the test.

Swinburne's own view of the nature of univocity seems more promising. On this view words

> have the same meaning, are being used univocally, if they have the same predicate scheme (viz., the same near-synonyms, contraries, determinables, etc.)[16]

so

> 'good', 'wise' and 'powerful' come out as univocal in their use of men and God. 'Wise' is used in the same sense in 'God is wise' as in 'Socrates is wise'. There are the same synonyms — 'knows many things', 'understands many things', same antonyms — 'foolish', same determinates and determinables.[17]

This view of the nature of univocity and Swinburne's parallel accounts of analogy and homonymy seem to me to enhance our understanding of the nature of sameness and difference of meaning, of singleness and multiplicity of word sense. However, in the present case of divine attribution I think Swinburne draws a conclusion not licensed by his criteria. If divine wisdom differs from human then 'is wise' has different (perhaps additional) synonyms and antonyms, determinates and determinables in 'God is wise' from those it has in 'Socrates is wise'. We might claim this point to hold whether or not we know what those different synonyms, antonyms, etc. in the divine case are. My conclusion would be that Swinburne's account is very helpful in understanding the nature and degree of the multisignificance of our words to the extent that their meaning, place in the language, usual implications, etc., are known but that it cannot be used to prove univocity. If a person were to know all the synonyms and antonyms etc. of a word then he might well be in a position to say whether or not that word was univocal: the trick is to know that all possible synonyms, antonyms, etc., *are* known.

Put positively, the general point behind the argument of the last paragraph is that we need to know the whole meaning of a term before we can know it to be univocal: incomplete knowledge of a term's sense may still yield knowledge that it is ambiguous if that incomplete knowledge extends far enough. But if I know, say, all about capes that can be worn but have never heard of a cape as a geographical feature I will not think of 'cape' as equivocal and tests of univocity like those of Swinburne, Scotus, and Sherry will seem to confirm my opinion. As so often, we make difficulties for ourselves in this area if we forget the distinction between what may or may not be the case and what we can or can not *know* to be the case. What do I mean by 'the whole meaning' of a term? At the risk of sounding plangent I mean 'all the term in fact means' — whether known to all or any human speakers or not. There may, for all we know, be words of our language which are ambiguous because God gives them different senses over and above the one or more senses known to any of us.

It may be objected that there is considerable oddity in maintaining that our words may have real senses of which none of us is aware. However, the oddity cannot lie simply in the notion of words of my language, in which I count myself proficient, having meanings I do not know. For we would surely all concede that, however large our vocabularies, there are some words whose meanings (or some of whose meaning) we have not yet learned. More than this we are all aware of specialisms other than our own (think of, say, dental technology, motor mechanics, fishing, photography, computing, etc., as well as the many, more academic disciplines) and spheres of life we do not frequent (say, Parliament, Court, theatrical circles, the law courts, high society, the betting shop, etc.) not to mention other countries and cultures (Australia, Glasgow's inner city community) each with its own neologisms, technical terms, jargon. Asked what a term from one of these or myriad other 'realms of discourse' means we would feel that there is a correct answer to the question and that the experts, the users of that discourse, will know it where we do not.[18]

In saying that predicates applied to God may have real senses none of us knows (and thus that the question whether such terms are or are not univocal may be unanswerable for us) I am simply saying that where the sphere of discourse is talk about the divine nature there is the same sort of room for an insider or expert to give to a term a genuine sense which is not known to outsiders. Unpalatable though it may be, for all we know, it may be a fact nonetheless that, where the 'expert' is God, the outsiders include *all* humans.

At this point an objector might wish to press still further on at least two questions. First, without wishing to sound irreverent it might be wondered what is God's standing to make contributions to any natural language. This is not a problem which would only occur to a non-believer. Believer or not, someone might feel that certain doctrines which he held about language and how terms do and can acquire meaning precluded anyone who was not a member of a linguistic community from adding words to that community's language. Moreover, could any natural language really have in it words which were genuinely part of that language though their senses were in part, and always remained, known to only one mind?

The first part of this worry might be met by pointing out that natural languages are forever borrowing and adopting words from one another – French speakers have given English 'gauche': the English have given French 'le weekend'. But then the second part of the worry looms: assuming it is now part of English, 'gauche' became so because English speakers took it up, felt that it was apropos, gave it currency. And that is precisely what is missing where putative additional senses of terms applied to God are concerned – senses additional to any we know. Even if it were to be argued that God, being omniscient, has knowledge and understanding of all natural languages and thus is qualified with any human to count as a member of any linguistic community whatever, can a sense which is never 'released' so to speak into the language, which never gets taken up because no one other than its creator is exposed to it, count as a real sense of a genuine term-of-the-language? Could such a private meaning count as anything more than that?

So the first part of an answer to this two-part worry is that God either *is* a member of our linguistic community or, if he is not thought to be so, he is at worst the sort of outsider who nonetheless could contribute a word to our language.

But what sort of private meaning is the putative additional sense of 'wise' or 'just' which I am claiming may be (if it exists at all) known to God while remaining unkown to any human? What sort of privacy has such a (would-be) sense? Does God alone possess it because God alone knows what his justice consists in or because God alone *could* know what his justice consists in — perhaps because that aspect of his nature is the sort of thing which could not form the content of a proposition a human could entertain or alternatively perhaps because no human could ever, even with divine assistance, be put in a position to obtain such knowledge — if these last two possibilities can be distinguished.

If God alone *in fact* knows what his justice (wisdom, love, etc.) consists in and if it is not, in principle, impossible that humans might learn this, then it seems to me that there is no problem about saying that God may know (right now, while we do not) genuine senses of terms which are (ambiguous) English words for divine attributes. If God has given these terms senses employing exemplars (his own justice, etc.) which are not of necessity private to him and inaccessible to us then it seems to me arguable that he has added to our language in this way — though unbeknownst to us. However, if God's justice, wisdom, etc. are in principle inaccessible to us so that, whatever rules he might employ in deciding that those are applicable we could never learn those rules, it seems to me we cannot describe those terms in so far as they have those extra divine senses, as genuine words of (in this case) English. Just as we would not dub the English word 'green' ambiguous if we discovered that Swahili used the sound 'green' as a word for something quite other than colour,[19] we would not be right to dub our words 'just' or 'wise' ambiguous if some divine language, unlearnable by us, happened to employ the symbols 'just' or 'wise' as words for divine attributes or anything else.

Either way, the moral to be drawn here is that despite what some have thought, linguistic considerations cannot be brought in to tell us how much understanding we have of the divine nature. Far from being able to argue either from the univocity of terms for divine and human attributes to commonality with, and a measure of understanding of, God *or* from the multivocity of terms applied to God and men to the otherness and mystery of God, we could not be in a position to settle the question whether terms applicable to both men and God are or are not univocal unless we could first learn to what degree and in what ways God is unlike us or even beyond our comprehension. Failing a method of acquiring this knowledge we must remain agnostic about whether or not 'just', 'wise' and 'loving' are univocal when applied to God and men.

Some time ago I said that an opponent of the view that for all we know God may have given terms like 'wise', 'just' and 'loving' extra senses of which none of us is aware might wish to press two objections. The first was to question how God could add to words of our language senses which remained unknown to any of us. The answer which I hoped might prove convincing was that God, like any solitary expert, can give extra senses to our terms provided they are in principle learnable by us even if it never falls out that any one else ever learns them. The second objection, which I am raising now, might more readily occur to an unbeliever: is it not frivolous cavilling to advocate scepticism about our capacity to discover univocal terms in our language on the grounds that God may, for all we know, have added senses to our terms of which we are as yet ignorant? If we have canvassed all the senses known to all human speakers is not that rigour enough?

My reply to this objection will be brief. First, it seems possible that the same ground for scepticism might in any case have been put differently, making no explicit reference to God. For how, in trying to establish that any particular term is limited to only one sense can an investigator ever be sure that he is up to date with all the developments in our eternally-evolving language? As we speak, any term whatever may be acquiring, from *someone* qualified to give it one, an additional sense. Second, it seems to me that scepticism about univocity grounded upon the possibility of divine sense-making is at worst no more frivolous than a general scepticism based on the possibility that unbeknownst to me I am a brain in a vat.

In the scholarly and challenging article I referred to earlier Hughes gives the following persuasive reason for believing that terms like 'wise' and 'loving' are equivocal when said of God and men:

A reasonable test for equivocation is to be found in asking whether the things referred to are of very different kinds. That a cricket ball and a masked ball are such different kinds of thing is surely evidence that 'ball' is used equivocally in the two cases. So too with 'bat' and 'cape'.

So we must beware of lapsing into

an unwarranted disposition to think of God comfortably in human terms, and consequently to underestimate his transcendence.

For if we do underestimate God's transcendence we, like Sherry, will fail to see any oddity in 'God is wiser than any of us': we will believe that our apparent ability to make such a comparison is evidence of the univocity of 'wise'.[20]

I have no wish to quarrel with the contention that 'ontological differences are in general good grounds for determining differences in sense'. What presents substantial difficulty is the question how to determine ontological differences. Transcendent God and mundane man certainly seem very different kinds of beings, even more so than a cricket ball and a masked ball. But if both of the latter were described as 'expensive' or 'diverting' or 'colourful' I would not feel required to say that each of these terms applied equivocally to the two sorts of ball. As Susan Haack remarks, 'heterotypical predication is not always equivocal'[21] and we might also here recall Sherry's remarks about 'sound' said of arguments and floorboards.[22]

To prove 'wise' and 'loving' equivocal using his test Hughes would have to contrast not just the ontological status of transcendent God and mundane man but the ontological status of divine wisdom and human wisdom, divine love and human love. But it is a thesis Hughes is at pains to defend that we do not know what God's love is like, what it is for God to act, what God's wisdom is like. To the extent that we agree with this thesis I think we must remain agnostic too about the claim, if it were made, that God's wisdom and human wisdom are different kinds of thing and so about the equivocality of 'wise'. What Hughes' criterion does admirably is to show that attempts (like Sherry's) to prove terms for divine attributes univocal are bound to fail. Only if we have access to divine attributes and can compare their ontological status with that of our own can we answer the question whether God shares any attributes with men.

It might be replied that, although we do not know what God's wisdom and love are like, we do know, knowing God to be transcendent, that his attributes must be wholly or at least significantly unlike any possessed by man. This would be to put forward the view that being divine somehow precludes having wisdom and being loving as these things are had and done by men. I am by no means sure how easily such a metaphysical thesis could be defended but I am concerned to make the point that it does not follow from any theory about the nature of multisignificance that God could not be at the same time wise as wise men are and wise in his *own* sense or senses, perhaps in 'possessing whatever it takes to be the cause of creatures who have wisdom'.[23] Where a term has been shown to have more than one sense nothing precludes one entity from having that term true of it in more than one of the term's senses: tidal waves may be a bore in more than one sense,[24] white feathers are light in both senses,[25] a fresh pot of yoghurt may be at once healthy food for the children and a culture healthy in itself.

Returning at length to the debate between two viewpoints about divine attributes, I hope I have now said enough to show why I said at the outset that the question of univocity was something of a red herring. It has been my contention that agnosticism about the univocity of terms like 'wise', 'just' and 'loving' is in strictness unavoidable. If this is correct, then neither the supporters of the view that God's attributes must be exactly or largely like human attributes referred to in the same terms *nor* supporters of the view that God's attributes must be sharply different from human attributes referred to in the same terms can claim the victory. For all we know, wisdom in God may be very like Solomon's or wholly unlike Solomon's or possibly both. We can get no purchase on the question what the divine attributes are like by referring to some test of univocity to see whether 'just', say, has or has not the same sense when applied to God and man.

In attempting to answer the question how we *are* to get any such purchase, I am strongly inclined to try to stake out a position on the middle ground drawing on a number of very convincing principles advanced by rivals in the debate.

From Hughes we have the pertinent point that it is possible, on some occasions if clearly not in general, to be persuaded of the truth of an utterance while being unsure what statement it is that is true. It may well be that we know from revelation, from biblical authority or from some particular proofs of God's existence which we accept, that 'God is wise' is true. We may still be unsure what sense 'wise' has in this context and thus what exact statement or statements it is whose truth we know. For all we know 'wise' may have the sense 'whatever it takes to ground the fact that he is the explanation of all human wisdom'.

Then from Alston we have the important negative point that psychological terms applicable to men need not fail of application to God simply because God does not consist in the same sort of material we do: nothing in the meaning of psychological terms requires God to have a body and a brain like those of men in order to have psychological properties like theirs. So — again, for all we know — 'God is wise' may mean (in addition to any other statements it may make) that God is like wise men.

From Sherry we have the persuasive reflection that

> discussions about divine attributes and about analogical predication [could profit greatly from consideration] of the Incarnation, which is very important both for deciding what attributes are to be ascribed to God and for considering the relationship between human and divine perfections.[26]

So we *may* gain our knowledge that 'God is wise' is true not from any of the sources of knowledge of God's attributes listed above but rather from reflections on the belief that Jesus was wise.

It may help to return to the notion of an employment or character reference with which I began. If I am asked to write a reference for someone I am unlikely simply to go back to a reference for that person which I have received previously. I will therefore know what statement is being made if I write, say, 'he is trustworthy' for I am making it: I am making a judgment of his character as I think it has been revealed in his actions and those actions are both my evidence for the judgment of trustworthiness and the material I would use if asked what I meant in calling him trustworthy. The point is that it matters what the source of the truth of, say, 'God is trustworthy' is if we are to try and discover what statement is being made in that utterance. Some believers might insist that God intervenes in their lives and that, from the sort of intervention they are aware of, they are able to make a judgment that God is trustworthy which is as well-confirmed as any judgment we might make about the trustworthiness of any man. Here it must be trustworthiness in the human sense that is in question. None of this goes to show that there is no other sort or that God does not possess it as well.

NOTES

1. Patrick J.Sherry, 'Analogy Today', *Philosophy* 51 (1976), p. 434.
2. *Op.cit.*, pp. 443−4.
3. William P.Alston, 'Functionalism and Theology', *American Philosophical Quarterly* 22 (1985), pp. 221−30.
4. Although I am using this example as an aid in summarising Alston's thesis, the example owes more to D.C.Dennet, *Content and Consciousness* (1969).
5. Alston, *op.cit.*, p. 222.
6. F.C.Copleston, *Aquinas* (Penguin Books, 1955), p. 129.
7. David B.Burrell, *Aquinas God and Action* (London: Routledge and Kegan Paul, 1979), p. 10.
8. Gerard J.Hughes, 'Aquinas and the Limits of Agnosticism', p. 51 above.
9. Israel Scheffler, *Beyond the Letter, A Philosophical Inquiry into Ambiguity, Vagueness and Metaphor in Language* (London: Routledge & Kegan Paul, 1979), p. 11.
10. Richard Swinburne, 'Analogy and Metaphor', pp. [72 ff. above]; and James F.Ross, *Portraying Analogy* (Cambridge, 1983).
11. Swinburne, *op.cit.*, p. 76.
12. A.Wolter (trans.), *Duns Scotus: Philosophical Writings* (London: Nelson, 1962), p. 20.
13. Swinburne, *op.cit.*, pp. 75−6.
14. James D. McCawley, *Everything That Linguists Have Always Wanted To Know About Logic* (Chicago: Univ. of Chicago Press, 1980), pp. 7, 9 and 10.
15 .W.V.O. Quine, *Word and Object* (Cambridge, Mass.: M.I.T. Press, 1960), p. 129.
16. Swinburne, *op.cit.*, p. 73.
17. *Ibid.*, p. 75.
18. This is not to say that every bit of jargon which has some currency somewhere has a clear sense − I have doubts about 'realms of discourse'.
19. Scheffler, *op.cit.*, p. 13.
20. Hughes, *op.cit.*, p. 50.
21. Susan Haack, 'Equivocality: A Discussion of Sommers' Views', *Analysis*, vol. 28, April 1968, p. 159.
22. Sherry, *op.cit.*, pp. 440−1.
23. Hughes, *op.cit.*, pp. 48.
24. G.E.L.Owen, 'Aristotle on the Snares of Ontology', in Renford Bambrough (ed.) *New Essays on Plato and Aristotle* (Routledge and Kegan Paul 1965), p. 74.
25. Haack. *op.cit.*, p. 164.
26. Sherry, *op.cit.*, p. 437.

6

THE BREAKDOWN OF SCHOLASTICISM AND THE SIGNIFICANCE OF EVANGELICAL HUMANISM

by A.H.T. LEVI

Buchanan Professor of French Language and Literature, University of St Andrews

It is possible to distinguish in the late fifteenth century between two different developing traditions of educational reform. Both were Christian and heavily moral in their aims. Both built, although in different ways, on intensely experienced religious attitudes. While it is easy to underestimate the facility and regularity with which ideologies mingled and were transmitted across the Alps in a complex process of geographical contamination, it remains possible to say that one type of educational reform, partly characterised by its promotion of 'rhetoric' above 'dialectic' and on the elevation of the study of antique classical literature above the cultivation of scholastic debate, flowered earlier south of the Alps, while the other tradition, predominantly a northern phenomenon, concentrated chiefly on fostering a religious simplicity and piety such as was notably incorporated into the educational ideals of the schools of the Brethren of the Common Life.

It is probable that educational reform in England was generally closer to the Italian model than were the reforms being attempted in France, 'Germany' and the 'Low Countries', whose southern border extended from Trier to Boulogne, and that English influence was particularly strong in north Italy. What suggests that there may well be some geographical basis for the ideological differences underlying the efforts at educational reform, apart from the cultivation of antique Latin authors in the Po valley, are such phenomena as the Italian reaction to Savonarola, Ermalao Barbaro's reaction to Pico della Mirandola's famous defence of the Parisian dialectic as a means of displaying his scholastic debating prowess and his powerfully syncretic mind, the failure of the French member of the papal commission to sign the recommendation to declare thirteen of his celebrated nine hundred *Conclusiones* heretical in 1487, and the insistence of Innocent VII that at least two French theologians in Rome should dissociate themselves from Pico's suspect views.[1]

Both traditions contained strong scholastic affiliations together with strong Biblical and patristic elements. Both were thought of as a return to what was conceived as an earlier educational ideal, and both aspired to a return to a purer religious life. One was to lead towards something we today regard as 'renaissance humanism' and the other towards what we call 'evangelical humanism', although both terms are in fact too inept to define what they signify. The two traditions of evangelicalism and humanism present themselves in strong contrast with one another even when there was no actual conflict between them. On their extreme wings there habitually was one.

Erasmus of course was interested in educational reform, and was stimulated by his schoolboy experiences at both Deventer and 's Hertogenbosch as well as by his experiences in the Augustinian monastery at Steyn. Evangelical humanism grew in part out of the educational ideals to which his early writings testify. Our present concern, however, is not principally with the conflicting ideals for educational reform in the fifteenth century, nor even with the underlying religious, moral and social realities, but with articulation of the ideologies erected to support the different reformatory endeavours, and especially with the fusion of those ideologies into what was to become a new theological tool as well as an instrument for religious renewal, the evangelical humanism of the first decades of the sixteenth century. The fusion of the educational reform movements became a social necessity; the fusion of the ideologies changed the nature of theological debate. The old scholasticism, which had arisen in response to the theological constraints of the twelfth and thirteenth centuries, had by the late fifteenth foundered on the rock of its own internal contradictions. As a theological tool, evangelical humanism came too late to withstand the pressures which Luther and then the Council of Trent were to impose on it, but, although it may be fortuitous, it is not merely symbolic that Erasmus, when he published in 1516 the first edition of the New Testament in Greek, entitled it the *Novum Instrumentum*. He intended it to be a theological tool.

In spite of the heritage of Boethius, what today we regard as 'philosophy' was not, in western European Christian thought north of the Alps, a discipline distinct from theology until at any rate the eleventh century, although it already was for the Muslims and the Jews, whose theologians generally distrusted and opposed their philosophers. The distinction is certainly implicit in Peter Damian (1007–72) and Anselm (1033–1109). Its incipient institutional recognition in the Christian west can perhaps be dated as far back as the itinerant school of Abelard (1079–1142) and the foundation of the cathedral school at Chartres by Fulbert, and in Paris of the monastic school of St Victor by William of Champeaux, during the twelfth century.

The full theoretical basis for the distinction in Christian thought was scarcely elaborated before the thirteenth century, by which time the quasi-totality of the Aristotelian corpus had become available in translations directly from the Greek, having earlier been known only in versions translated into Syriac and then into Arabic. The distinction as it occurs in Roger Bacon, Albertus Magnus and Thomas Aquinas was erected not only on the basis of Aristotle's works but also on that of such of his Arab-speaking commentators as the Persian Ibn-Sina ('Avicenna', 980–1037) the Spanish Moor Ibn-Rochd ('Averroes', 1126–98) and the Spanish Jew Solomon Ibn-Gebirol ('Avicebron', c.1020–70). The Aristotelian basis for the distinction between theology and philosophy was in fact much contaminated by what the nineteenth century, which also coined the substantive 'humanism', termed 'Neoplatonism', and the distinction was inevitably the subject of both exaggeration and reaction. The ensuing controversies involved the polarised positions of Bonaventure (1221–74), Siger de Brabant (c.1240–84), the author of the real distinction between essence and existence in God as it was known to the later middle ages, Giles of Rome (d.1316) and Boetius of Dacia, and culminated in Tempier's celebrated condemnations of thirteen propositions on 10 December 1270 and of 219 on 7 March 1277.[2]

It is necessary here to avert to the fact that the penalties for heresy which were so to constrict theological debate in the sixteenth century were not yet so grave as they were later to become. Abelard, condemned for heresy by the Council of Sens in 1140 or 1141 for holding that intentionality was the basis of sin, that man shares in the punishment but not the guilt of original sin, and that the will can *per se* achieve moral good, was condemned by Innocent II merely to silence and he died on his way to Rome to appeal. Doctrinal positions had equally not yet hardened as they were later to do. Abelard was not condemned for holding that God had revealed Himself to the great pagan philosophers of antiquity and that pagans, enlightened by God's will, were therefore capable of moral goodness and salvation. Bonaventure, a century later, was not condemned for allowing to 'aliqui haeretici' a 'habitus fidei' providing that they held the Trinity of Persons in God (*In Sent*. 1, dist.3, art.i, 304). The thirteenth century saw a perceptible hardening of attitudes in both the definition of orthodoxy and the penalties for deviating from it.

Gratian's *Decretum* of about 1140, a product of papalist thought during the investiture controversy and later to become the first part of the *Corpus Iuris Canonici*, had quoted the infamous 'Lex Quisquis', the most ferocious enactment of ancient Roman law, against the *crimen maiestatis* to which the Theodosian and Justinianian codes had assimilated the crime of heresy (Cod. Theod. xvi,5,3; 5,40 and 6,6; Cod. Just.1,5, 11 and 12; 1,5,8). What was intended as a text-book was interpreted by later glossators as a code and, although Gratian himself, in spite of the severities of Mosaic and Rome legislation, was against the death penalty for heresy,[3] Boniface VIII was to adopt the Lex Quisquis covering heresy into canonical legislation. In Aragon the death penalty for heresy was introduced by Peter II as early as 1197, as later in France under Louis VIII and Louis IX. Between 1234 and 1238 Frederick II imposed the death penalty for obduracy in heresy and in 1231 this legislation was endorsed by Gregory IX whose bull 'Excommunicamus' specified that heretics 'damnati per Ecclesiam saeculari judicio relinquantur animadversione debita puniendi'. The constitutions of Frederick II were extended to the whole Catholic world by Innocent IV in 1252.

In fact the medieval executions appear to have begun by the action of local authorities and by popular lynchings in the eleventh century in the north of France. Heretics were lynched at Cologne in 1144. By the early thirteenth century the burnings had spread to the Albigensian strong-hold in the south of France. In 1210 there were 140 executions at Minerve, in 1211 a large number at Lavaur and 60 in Les Cassés. There were burnings in Troyes in 1200, at Braisne in 1205, at Paris in 1210 and eighty in Strasbourg in 1211. Aquinas concurred in the death penalty for heresy (In IV Sent.,d.13, q.2,a.3, solutio). It had become institutionalised, and was to become even more dangerous when prelates like Wolsey held both canonical and civil jurisdiction.[4]

Before the thirteenth century endowed philosophy with independent, if ancillary, status, the earlier scholastics had used it as an epistemo-logical instrument. The conclusions to which it was allowed to lead were heavily determined by such theological considerations as the necessity of leaving open the possibilities of creation *ab aeterno* as well as *ex nihilo*, of preserving the distinction of Three Persons in one while avoiding both tritheism and a triple Incarnation, of preserving the personal immortality of the individual soul, and of preserving the freedom of the 'voluntas' as a faculty, such as Augustine had conceived it, within the paradoxically named 'liberum arbitrium'. All these doctrinal issues affected such apparently 'philosophical' discussions as those on the principle of individuation, hylomorphism, substantial forms, the distinction between attributes and essence in God, the theory of knowledge, the psychology of the faculties and, of course, cosmo-logical speculation. Scholastic philosophy was created in western Christianity to provide an articulate intellectual substructure for religiously orthodox theological positions.

The most famous theological compendia of the twelfth century, the

Lombard's *Sentences*, Gratian's *Decretum* and Abelard's *Sic et non*, all composed within about twenty years of one another, opposed conflicting, generally Biblical or patristic, authorities, with or without suggesting a resolution. By the thirteenth century the dialectic had developed. Between the authorities with whom the author disagreed and those whose views he accepted, pride of place, and generally of space, was given to the author's reasoning, the 'ratio theologica', as notably in Thomas's *Summa Theologiae*, where the authorities quoted under the heading 'Videtur quod . . . ' are subjected to searching rational criticism.

Thomas's attempted synthesis was a towering achievement, innovative primarily, in spite of the deference it pays to Augustine, in its effort to provide a comprehensive and internally consistent philosophical sub-structure for religious belief. In doing so, it almost necessarily carried strongly naturalistic implications. It drew inevitably on various antique philosophical traditions, but, by making the human reason a derivative reflection of the divine intellect, it made revealed truth necessarily correlative to the mind's search for understanding and, by making God's law a promulgation of his reason, it made that law the necessary correlative to human aspiration to moral fulfilment. There was a danger that God might seem in some way limited by His own creation, and even that truth and the moral order, both derived from the same rational norms, might be ascertainable without recourse to revelation. In fact, much later in the course of European intellectual history, this is exactly what was asserted, notably by Grotius in his 1635 *De iure belli ac pacis*, which founded the whole system of human rights, duties and obligations without recourse to the divine will, and again by Montes-quieu whose 1748 *De l'Esprit des lois* opens with the ringing declaration, 'Les lois, dans le sens le plus étendu du mot, sont les rapports nécessaires qui dérivent de la nature des choses'. Montesquieu underlines his points, 'l'homme a ses lois, Dieu a ses lois . . .'. These statements, however, did not come until after the strong anti-Thomist reaction of the later middle ages had collapsed and until the sixteenth century, correctly perceiving the humanist implications of the Thomist system, slowly replaced the *Sentences* with the *Summa* in every theological faculty in Catholic Europe as the basis for lecture-commentaries which were the staple of theological teaching.

Technically the strength of the Thomist system in the thirteenth century was its moderation between extreme positions on such controverted matters as the abstraction of a 'species intelligibilis' by the 'intellectus agens' in the process of knowledge and on the role of the intellect in the act of choice, a matter on which Thomas was not in fact either entirely clear or entirely consistent.[5] The weakest parts of the system were probably its tendency towards intellectual determinism at the expense of the freedom of the will and its necessarily sharp distinction between the natural and the supernatural orders consequent on assigning different objects to faith and reason. In the sixteenth century Medina's 1577 commentary on the *Prima Secundae* holds that the ultimo-practical judgment of the reason is the efficient cause of the free act (ad q. 9, art.1), so compromising the freedom of the will, while Cajetan interpreted Thomas as holding that nature as it exists aspires only to a 'finis naturalis'.[6]

The dangers of the 'Aristotelianism' of which Thomas was a moderate proponent had early been perceived. Siger de Brabant notoriously went so far as to hold that what was true in philosophy need not accord with the Catholic faith. The university of Paris, which had received its charter in 1200, forbade in a decree of 1210, confirmed in 1215, the teaching, but not the private reading, of the metaphysics and the natural philosophy, although not of the logic and the ethics, of Aristotle. By 1255, however, the whole Aristotelian corpus was prescribed for the first degree at Paris, which swiftly overtook Oxford and Toulouse, where more licence had earlier been given to the study of Aristotle, as the acknowledged theological centre of the scholastic world. The reaction to the influence of Aristotle on what might be termed the Alberto-Thomistic synthesis was nevertheless fierce, particularly among the Franciscans. Bonaventure, who had become a Franciscan in 1238, distrusted from the beginning Thomas's fusion of philosophy and theology. Thomas and he were both appointed to chairs of theology at Paris on 23 October 1256 but, on account of the tension between their teachings, both had the award of the doctorate of theology and the right to occupy their chairs withheld until October 1257. Bonaventure, who carefully distinguished between the realms of faith and reason, protested with increasing stridency against the philosophers who taught the eternity of the world and the unicity of the single human intellect, which implied an Averroistic denial of personal immortality. He was essentially an Anselmian mystic faithful to his teacher, Alexander of Hales (*c*.1185–1245), and to an Augustinian tradition unconcerned with purely philosophical questions.[7] Thomas's own later works betray some irritation with the philosophers whose positions, incompatible with orthodox Christian doctrine, seemed to compromise his own theological achievement.

In 1270 Giles of Rome listed the errors of Aristotle and the 'Aristotelian' philosophers, Averroes, Avicenna, Algazel, Alkindi and Maimonides. Tempier, amply abetted by Robert Kilwardby, the archbishop of Canterbury, was eager to condemn the philosophers' extreme positions and Thomas himself was peripherally involved in the condemned propositions. Even inside the Dominican order it swiftly became impossible to enforce loyalty to his positions, as a series of decrees starting in 1280 makes clear.[8] Historically it can be plausibly argued that the Thomist synthesis was bound to fail to win acceptance on account of the internal compromises of the moderate philosophical positions it contained, themselves imposed by theological constraints. In fact it was Scotus (c.1265–1308) who delivered the coup de grâce by exposing the philosophical compromises and reacting against what was taken to be a menacing theological naturalism.

Scotus was exceptionally conscious of the theological needs of his age, clearly a product of thirteenth-century Oxford in his approach to its problems, and faithful to the Franciscan tradition. His order was enjoined very shortly after his death to adhere to his positions. It seems difficult not to regard his critical acumen as greater than that of any other scholastic teacher, even if in the end it served historically to demonstrate the inherent impossibility of integrating traditional doctrine with a philosophically coherent account of divine activity. Essentially, Scotist criticism of the Alberto-Thomistic synthesis ended up with so pronounced an emphasis on divine transcendence and the absolute freedom of the divine will as to open the way to the notoriously Pelagian implications of Ockham's *via moderna* against which, however, Scotus had himself safely guarded through his doctrine of the absolute predestination of the elect. That doctrine, however, itself depended on the fragile and nominalistically inclined paring away of Thomas's real distinction between God and his attributes to the 'distinctio formalis a parte rei' on which the Scotist system depends, and which Ockham not unreasonably repudiated in favour of the unicity of nature and act in God.

Scotus accepts a distinction between philosophy and theology, which he regards as a practical, affective discipline, contingent on the order that God has chosen to establish and leading to a love as well as to a knowledge of God. The chief point of attack is the danger of

Averroism. Thomas had had difficulty in reconciling his dual view that the soul is the form of the body and that matter is the principle of individuation, although incapable of existing in an undifferentiated state, with the personal survival after death of a soul no longer clearly individuated and incapable of directly knowing any individual as such, since its knowledge depended on the abstraction of a 'species intelligibilis'. Scotus eludes Thomas's major epistemological difficulties, allowing objective validity to concepts by holding a plurality of substantial forms in individual things, basing this view on the formal distinction between the essences of things in the same species. Individuals can be known as such in their 'haecceitas'. The body has its own 'forma corporeitatis', and souls after death are therefore not necessarily reduced to pure forms. The difficulty in this position is to explain how the body's 'substantial' form remains the intellective soul.

Moreover, Scotus's attack on the Averroist elements in Thomas leads him to emphasise divine transcendence to the extent of deriving divine law from a promulgation of the divine will rather than the divine reason, so severing the automatic correlation in Thomas between divine prescription and human moral aspiration. God's law could be other than it is, or other than our reason can fathom. It is limited only in that it cannot be self-contradictory. For Scotus it is the essence of will, divine or human, to be free and to achieve its determination independently of rational constraint. Like Thomas, Scotus distinguishes between God's *potentia absoluta*, by which He is omnipotent, and the *potentia ordinata* which establishes the de facto created order, for Thomas necessarily the product of the divine reason but for Scotus contingent only on the divine will. These positions may be thought to differ scarcely more than in emphasis with regard to the order actually created, but Scotus makes its contingency much clearer, and the consequences of seeing the human will as the sole cause of its own volition, with the presentation to it by the intellect of the object of its act reduced to a mere sine qua non, were to have dramatic implications for the way in which the action of grace in the will could be envisaged.[9]

Tempier had condemned the doctrine that the intellect was the efficient cause of the will's specification. Scotus, strongly influenced by Henry of Ghent, in order to keep the will free after the last judgement of the practical intellect, had to endow the will itself with the power of 'comparatio', thereby giving it an intellective function, and entailing logically a faculty whose dynamism is appetitive or natural rather than free,[10] a conclusion which Scotus rejects. The faculties of intellect and will are distinguished by different sorts of 'habitus' and cannot therefore cooperate in a single act. Although Scotus sometimes concessively allows some partial causality of the intellect in the specification of the will's act, his preferred solution is to reduce the intellectual judgement to a simple sine qua non of the specification of the act of will.[11] The most serious consequence of this position concerns the theology of grace.

Since the introduction of the sharp distinction between nature and supernature it had been axiomatic that man's salvation could be achieved only through the bestowal of a supernatural 'grace' made available to man as the fruit of his redemption by Christ. The early Fathers had used variegated and picturesque metaphors, of which 'redemption' is only one, to describe Christ's salvific activity in the wake of original sin. When the scholastics came to debate the theology of grace, it clearly became necessary to define whether, and to what extent, man's endowments surpassed those of 'pure' nature before the Fall and fell short of them after it, since it was generally agreed, and had been defined since the sixth century, that man could not, by his own natural powers, either merit justification or in any way initiate it, even by accepting proferred grace. He could resist, but not contribute to, the bestowal on him by God of either sanctifying grace, the *gratia gratum faciens*, or 'actual' grace, the *gratia gratis data*. To assume the opposite was at least semi-Pelagian. The problem was to explain how God's initiative in the bestowal of grace was to be reconciled with man's responsibility for his own sin. This was to be the problem with which in the seventeenth century Pascal was to grapple in his unpublished *Ecrits sur la grâce*. Like Jansen, Pascal regards all men as worthy of eternal damnation on account of original sin, a situation which most theologians before and since have regarded as making God responsible for man's sin, even if the guilt was inherited from Adam.

This view was accepted by Gregory of Rimini, who studied in Paris from 1323–9 before teaching at Bologna, Padua, Perugia and Paris, became General of the Augustinians in 1357, and may well have been concerned in the condemnation of Ockham. It was orthodox, but understandably came to be regarded as intolerable, since it deprived all human beings of any power whatsoever to work towards their salvation, leaving those whom God had not predestined to an eternity, conceived as never-ending time, of deprivation and torture. For Pascal, at least, there was no way in which the *viator* could tell whether or not he belonged to the elect, surely the real reason why he never composed his projected apologetic, since it could have served no purpose. It was of course not orthodox, nor other than destructive of any possible form of Christianity, to make God directly responsible for human sin otherwise than by allowing the human race to inherit the guilt of Adam, but this was the view of which Castellio accused Calvin, Calvin accused Zwingli, and More, Fisher and in the end Erasmus accused Luther. It was in the sixteenth century that the dilemma became most acute. Molina, in order to elude it, had to go back to the Scotist quasi-chronology of acts in God and avoided Pelagianism only by holding that God, having by his *scientia media* foreseen whether some particular human being would have *ex puris naturalibus* accepted grace if he had had the power to do so, decreed or withheld justifying grace accordingly. Later Jesuits were not so careful, and generally in fact relied on the theology of Lessius, banned within the Order by Aquaviva, which made no intrinsic distinction between 'efficacious' and merely 'sufficient' grace.[12] This was a clearly semi-Pelagian solution against which the 'congruism' of both Suarez and Bellarmine was a reaction.

It is at this point, before returning to what was the central dilemma in late medieval theology, that we should perhaps draw attention to just how recently scholastic theologians have found a solution which, for reasons which will become clear, neither the later medieval theologians nor the evangelical humanists were able to reach. It is now a matter of theological history that Rome took fright, probably not without reason, at some of the theological speculation which emerged among some of the leading Jesuit theologians in the Lyons region immediately after the second world war, and in 1950 the wide-ranging encyclical *Humani Generis* appeared to implicate some of their positions. Whether or not on account of Roman intervention, Henri de Lubac withdrew the original edition of *Surnaturel: Etudes historiques,* published in 1949 and subsequently reworked into two volumes. Henri de Lubac had appeared, at any rate, to suggest that human nature could achieve its fulfilment only in the supernatural order. In 1950 there appeared also a famous anonymous article in the relatively obscure Swiss theological journal *Orientierung*[13] whose authorship was later acknowledged by Karl Rahner, who finally elaborated his solution in the first volume of the *Schriften zur Theologie* (1954), in an essay entitled *Das Verhältnis von Natur und Gnade* in which he established the concept of 'das übernaturliche Existential'. By 1954 there had been a number of important reactions to the original Swiss article, and in the

English translation of the first volume of the *Schriften*, these are enumerated, together with a number of contributions to the debate made by earlier theologians.[14]

Rahner's view amounted to the contention that man fell into a state of nature that was not only fallen, but also retroactively redeemed, and that he could and must therefore aspire to a 'supernatural' fulfilment not *ex puris naturalibus*, by virtue of natural powers alone, but by virtue of the finality endowed on fallen nature by the redemption. This view clearly avoids any Pelagian implications in a theory of justification which allows man the autonomous power to accept or to refuse grace, but it raises questions about the salvation of pagans, also endowed with redeemed, if fallen, nature, and the role of the Church in their salvation, as also of the nature of any implicit act of the faith without which, as Trent laid down, there can be no salvation. Even comparatively recent theological text-books remain simply agnostic, maintaining the absolute necessity of belief in God as a remunerator after death, and taking advantage of the late medieval principle that if man does what lies within him, what we shall come to know as the 'Facientibus ...' principle, God will provide, 'etiam per miraculum, si opus erit'.[15] The salvation of the pagans was to become one of the great stumbling blocks of the evangelical humanists of the sixteenth century, and Erasmus notoriously provoked the fury of the Paris theologians by putting the invocation 'St Socrates' into the mouth of a character in his colloquy of 1522 *Convivium religiosum*.[16]

Anselm had held that God could not be the ultimate cause of sin, because that would have implied a contradiction in his nature, a solution which refuses to confront the metaphysical issue. Scotus sought to avoid the same difficulty by using a series of distinctions, as between a 'causa efficiens' of the human will's positive action and its sinful 'causa deficiens' which derives from the contingency of the created order, or between God's inefficacious ' voluntas signi et antecedens' by which He wills the salvation of all rational creatures, and His 'voluntas beneplaciti et consequens' by which He does not, or again between God's 'potentia absoluta' by which He could without contradiction condemn the human will to sin, and the 'potentia ordinata' by which He does not. None of these distinctions achieves its purpose or brings any consolation to the *viator*, but it is the last which led straight to the Pelagianism of Ockham's *via moderna*, avoided by Scotus only at the cost of using the 'distinctio formalis a parte rei' to distinguish anteriority and posteriority in God's acts.[17]

William of Ockham (d.1349) and Gregory of Rimini (d.1358) are commonly regarded as having belonged to different and opposed wings of the *via moderna*. What they had in common, apart from certain important epistemological presuppositions, was an emphasis on God's transcendence and on His untrammelled 'potentia absoluta'. Both rejected any real or formal dinstinction in God, so that either man was free to merit his own salvation, and was predestined in accordance with God's simultaneous prevision of merit or God consigned him to damnation 'ante previsa demerita'. For Gregory, in particular, there can be no question of a quasi-chronological distinction of divine acts.[18] Even before his sin, Adam needed grace, the 'adiutorium gratie' to perform a morally good act. Man was therefore created, for Gregory, in a state of 'pure' nature. Ockham on the other hand held that, even after the fall, man was capable of morally good acts to which, in His 'potentia ordinata', God attributed merit. For Gregory, God's will is the sole cause of man's predestination or reprobation. He can attribute grace to pagans and refuse it to those who love Him 'ex puris naturalibus'. Nobody is damned on account of any evil use of free will foreseen by God.[19] Predestination and reprobation are therefore absolute, without any reference to contingent human activity. God's transcendence over contingent creation is thereby safeguarded, as incidentally is the possibility of the salvation of the non-believer, but Gregory accepts God's responsibility for man's damnation as the price to be paid for removing even the formal distinction between Persons in God and between God's nature and His acts.

Ockham embraces the other horn of the dilemma.[20] At Oxford he encountered the opposition of the chancellor, John Lutterell, and both parties appeared before Edward II at York in October 1322. Although Edward II appeared to favour Ockham and removed the chancellor, Lutterell was given a safe passage and permission to argue his case at Avignon for two years, prolonged at the Pope's request. Lutterell drew up a disordered list of fifty-six propositions from Ockham's *Commentary* on the *Sentences*, of which fifty-one were placed before a theological commission appointed by John XXII. The manuscript omits two of them. It seems not unlikely that Ockham rewrote his *Commentary*. In 1326, at any rate, a second commission was appointed, with Lutterell a member, but without Durand de St-Pourçain (d.1334), a Dominican who held that God's general 'concursus' in all human activity is sufficient for merit *de congruo*.[21] This commission considered further propositions and censured Ockham more severely. Although there was no official condemnation, Ockham-ism was proscribed by the Paris arts faculty in 1340. Some of Ockham's views were to be implicated in the condemnations of Nicolaus of Autrecourt, who held a view of divine transcendence such that God could command a rational creature to hate Him, and of John of Mirecourt, who made God the author of all acts of created will in such a way as to make Him also the author of sin, in 1346 and 1347.[22] It is disputed whether Ockham himself went as far as Nicolaus of Autrecourt in the matter of the 'odium dei', but this was certainly the doctrine, too, of the English Dominican, Robert Holcot (d.1349), and Ockham himself certainly held that there was no contradiction 'de potentia absoluta' in the hypostatic union of the divine nature with the symbolically understood nature of an ass or a stone rather than with the nature of man.[23] The difficulty is to know whether Erasmus, for instance, to say nothing of subsequent commentators, really under-stood what Ockham was arguing about, which is that human nature was so assumed at the Incarnation by the second Person of the Trinity as not thereby itself to become a divine Person. What is not in doubt is that the Scotist theory of the will, without the Scotist safeguard of absolute predestination of the elect depending on the 'distinctio formalis a parte rei' rejected by the nominalists, must lead either to a theory of absolute reprobation or to an openly Pelagian theory of grace depending on the prevision of merit, identical with the decree of predestination.

The first proposition condemned by the first commission makes this clear. A morally good act of will *ex puris naturalibus* will be accepted by God as meritorious. The commission thought this tasted of Pelagianism or worse, 'vel peius', and that it was not excused by reference to the 'potentia absoluta'. When Ockham is said to have said in a double proposition that God can accept man as worthy of eternal life in *puris naturalibus*, the commission condemns him, but abstains from comment on the second half, that reprobation must depend on guilt. There are censures for such statements as that God could remit guilt without giving grace, although what was censured was not strictly the statement but the reasoning adduced in support of it, that God could accept as worthy of eternal life someone without 'gratia inhaerens'.

Ockham was ultimately excommunicated by John XXII for his anti-papalist stance in defence of evangelical poverty and against both the temporal power and papal jurisdiction in matrimonial issues. He was clearly not given to compromise, but it may still prudently be doubted whether he actually held all the propositions attributed to him. The point is their logical coherence as certainly one, and probably the only, possible alternative response to that of Gregory of Rimini based on the same 'nominalistic' principles which demanded absolute unicity of essence and attributes in God. Who was actually condemned is sometimes a mere hasard of temperament and historical circumstance. What ultimately was at stake was the apparent impossibility during the thirteenth and fourteenth centuries of finding a metaphysically coherent account of divine and human nature and activity which clashed neither with religious necessity nor dogmatic orthodoxy. In a world in which all rational creatures were still presumed to have access to the gospel message, and in which no solution to the problems of the theology of grace allowed the bestowal of the *gratia gratum faciens* to be independent of credal belief, the impossibility of such a coherent metaphysic was not only apparent, but real. Historically, by the end of the fourteenth century and inside the religious and theological parameters which constrained it, scholasticism had failed. Even if its open rejection by much of European Christendom north of the Alps was to be delayed until the beginning of the sixteenth century, religious commitment necessarily had begun to look for non-scholastic forms of often mystical, metaphorical or in the end humanistic intellectual foundations.

The religious crisis in the Church was already clear from the effects of the preaching and teaching of Wycliffe (d.1384) and Huss (d.1415), although popularist religious movements were not yet capable of toppling either papal authority in its spiritual and temporal claims or scholastic doctrinal hegemony. Not surprisingly the sanctions against doctrinal deviation and evangelically based attacks on ecclesiastical corruption were enforced with increasing severity and, since the scholastic theologians held a virtual monopoly of the instruction of a largely illiterate laity, and developed a vested interest in the benefits accruing from the spiritual dominion and the financial rewards of maintaining a doctrinal status quo, the ultimate religious and theological explosions were contained during the fifteenth century north of the Alps.

By the early fifteenth century God's transcendence was metaphysically sufficiently well assured that it was possible for the scholastic preachers, a body from whom the academic theologians were becoming increasingly remote in Paris, to reassure the hapless *viator* with the celebrated *Facientibus* ... principle, a shoulder-shrugging axiom of hope without foundation on the missing orthodox but religiously tolerable theology of grace. God, naturally 'de potentia ordinata', would not deny grace to those who did what lay within them: 'Facientibus quod in se est deus non denegat gratiam', a principle to which, as we have seen, authors of Catholic theological textbooks could still have agnostic recourse in 1961. But who, in the fifteenth century, could know whether he had done all that lay within him? Pilgrimages, alms-giving, penances, the endless, obsessionally repetitive identical acts made psychologically tolerable by such typically fifteenth-century devotional innovations as the Rosary, the Angelus and the Stations of the Cross, all suggest the religion of moral strain and meticulous observance on which Calvin was to pour such scorn, and which was in search of an assurance and a certainty which could not be provided. Religious accceptability was becoming divorced from the unique criterion of moral stature, and the result was bound to contain elements of popular superstition.[24]

There is, of course, a respectable theology of indulgences, not totally repudiated by the sixteenth-century schismatic communities, but that is not how Tetzel sold them. Worse than the sale of indulgences was the fifteenth-century rise of the chantry bequest. Perhaps a quarter of the population of the British Isles had by the time of Henry VIII become in one way or another dependent on monastic incomes, themselves increasingly derived from legacies and donations in return for which was offered the celebration of rites thought to affect the state of the dead. The corollary of the *Facientibus* ... principle, whether it precipitated or merely reflected the religious crisis, very nearly led to the breakdown of medieval Catholicism as a credible religion. The chantry bequest as a form of religious activity clearly betrays a state of mind which, separating the immediate fate of the dead from the consequences of their own moral choices during life, divorced religious status from depending uniquely on personal integrity and moral probity, to be computed according to a calculus of good works, with the retroactive possibility of changing the outcome by posthumous endowment. It is not surprising that accusations of simony were bandied about, notably by Wycliffe.

On the intellectual level, by the end of the fifteenth century, theology needed a new tool. It had to go back beyond the scholastics and, almost more importantly, beyond Augustine. It had to be evangelical and it had to make the Christian religion correlative to human moral needs.

Efforts to forge it, arising chiefly from a variety of mystical traditions, were already proving powerful, particularly in Florence but also elsewhere, generally south of the Alps. The first generation of northern reformers, Luther and Zwingli, achieved one, but only at the expense of schism and with the necessary sacrifice, in their view, of any autonomous human power of self-determination to good. Erasmus achieved one, perhaps earlier, but partly in reaction to them, and certainly too late, too slowly and too painfully. When forced as near to scholastic debate as he could not avoid, he chose free will as his subject and scriptural exegesis as his tool. Colet had guessed at the form of the new theology. Vitrier in his denunciations of corruption and more particularly in his devotion to Origen, had had intuitions which powerfully influenced Erasmus and helped to find the necessary instrument. Lefèvre d'Etaples and the Meaux reformers were guardedly responsive to it. It was Ignatius of Loyola in the end who transformed it into a practical strategy for non-schismatic reform. The constraints acting on the emergence of evangelical humanism were however formidable. New theological tools are not forged in cold crucibles.

By the sixteenth century it was no longer possible to suppose, as for instance Thomas had supposed, that all rational creatures, at least since the inauguration of the Christian dispensation or very soon thereafter, had had access to the gospel message, a fact which does much to explain the heroic efforts of Christian missionaries to take it to the recently discovered new world as well as to India and the Far East.[25] Erasmus was prompted to urge the possibility of the salvation of the ancient pagans because of the moral elevation he felt on reading them, especially Cicero and Seneca. Lefèvre d'Etaples was more mindful of those whom the gospel message had not reached and who love the 'deum ex operum magnificentia jam cognitum' according to the natural law, keeping his commandments 'excepto ceremoniarum ritu'.[26] Lefèvre, however, does not, any more than Erasmus, offer a scholastic theological justification for this position. The obvious need for a just God to allow for the salvation of those who lived before Christ and for the non-European portion of the human race required a breadth of vision which scholastic theology was in fact unable to achieve after the constraints imposed on it by the Bull *Unam sanctam* of 1302 and the Decree for the Jacobites issued by the Council of Florence in the Bull *Cantate domino* of 1441. The attempts, with which Erasmus was certainly associated, to undermine the authority of these documents by going back beyond Augustine to promote the authority of Origen, firmly committed to belief in God's justice and goodness and in the free will of all rational creatures, and unwilling to believe in the never-ending torment of hell, received setbacks both in the selection for condemnation of Pico della Mirandola's view that it is more plausible to believe in Origen's salvation than in his damnation and in Bédier's later machinations at the Sorbonne against Merlin, the editor of the *editio princeps* of Origen in Latin in 1512.[27]

The history of the interplay of ideas, especially between England, Italy and continental Europe north of the Alps, shows how the different attempts at a resolution of the scholastic impasse slowly emerged. Already by the late fifteenth century the overtly mythologising 'theology' of Marsilio Ficino, especially in the *In Platonis convivium commentarium* and the *Theologia platonica*, had allowed a trust in human moral instinct to lead to complete spiritual fulfilment, a view which emerges cautiously north of the Alps in Erasmus's second *Hyperaspistes* and then in Rabelais, who simply translates the key passage from Erasmus. Ficino had maintained an autonomous human power of self-determination to good, and Pico created a myth inside which to convey it in the first part of the *Oratio de hominis dignitate* intended to preface the 900 *Conclusiones* he had wished to defend at Rome in 1486, so by-passing all questions of God's absolute power and of the metaphysics of the action of grace in the will.[28] Theirs was the doctrine, or feeling, which in spite of the differences which obtained between them inspired Colet and was not without influence on the Netherlandish spirituality which Erasmus in his youth inherited from Rudolph Agricola, Alexander Hegius and Cornelius Gerard before, together with More, putting himself under the religious direction of Colet.

What Colet shared with the *devotio moderna*, and Erasmus with Luther, as well as with Zwingli and, later, Calvin, both of whom started as his disciples, was the conviction that religious fulfilment was essentially ethical in character and had to depend on a commitment that was essentially moral. They all had recourse to the testimony of direct moral and religious experience, an immediate reaction to the word of God as preached in the gospel message, whether or not confined to it, a matter on which they were to dispute. When Luther and Zwingli broke with Rome, the kernel of the dispute concerned the propriety of interposing some authoritative criterion for establishing the authenticity of the religious experience based on the gospel message and the dispute resolved itself into the debate about free will. If man's salvation was achieved by faith and hope in Jesus as a result of direct contact with the gospel message, his salvation did not depend on any act of his own will, although his damnation could ensue from an act of will rejecting the dictates of the word of God. The *claritas scripturae* of Zwingli was directly opposed to any autonomous human power of self-determination to moral good, 'free will' in the sense to be defined by Molina, which both the scholastics, even though in Paris they were chiefly concerned with the defence of devotional practices, and the evangelical humanists, despite the apparently Pelagian implications of their view, were determined in the name of any authentic religious dispensation depending on free personal commitment on the part of all human individuals to uphold. To surrender that power in man resulted for More, Fisher, Erasmus and the others in an impossibly Ockhamist concept of an arbitrary God who might have to be placated but who could scarcely be loved.

The formative influences on Erasmus's early spirituality, and therefore on the theological method he later forged, are not yet the subject of scholarly consensus. His own personal piety, finally to come to rest in seeking support from the *sensus ecclesiae* of which the liturgy was an expression, continued to develop in relationship to his early humanist interests. Both his personal piety and his religious thought were to develop after the composition of the *Enchiridion*. He had already defended Valla's humanism in a letter to Cornelius Gerard of perhaps 1489, and it may have been the discovery in 1504 of Valla's *Adnotationes* on the Latin New Testament, which he published in 1505 on the advice of Christopher Fisher together with another defence of Valla, which alerted him to the possible utility of the technically humanistic tool of textual criticism in pursuit of scriptural studies. Textual criticism was not, however, ever to become the kernel of his theological method, which centred on the dissemination of the moral content of the Christian message. As late as 1507 we know from a letter to Aldus, expressing surprise that Aldus's projected edition of the New Testament had not yet appeared, that Erasmus's own New Testament in Greek, to be provocatively entitled the *Novum instrumentum*, was not yet firmly planned.

It was only slowly that Erasmus came to integrate his evangelical piety with his humanism and humanistic skills. Until 1524 and the *de libero arbitrio*, of which a first draft was finished in February and which finally appeared in September, Erasmus largely contented himself with a negative criticism of what was clearly wrong with the Church, and for that matter in Christendom generally. He attacks whatever he found that was unchristian, superstitious, bellicose or repressive in the Church, in society, in the conduct of the papacy, buttressing the criticisms of the *Enchiridion*, the *Moriae Encomium* of 1511 and the essays of social satire added to the 1515 Froben edition of the *Adages* with a theoretical advocacy of the vernacular dissemination of the moral message of the gospels in the prefatory material to the 1516 *Novum instrumentum* and with the series of *Paraphrases* on the New Testament books. He was clearly happier in such oblique theological genres as satire, commentaries, textual criticism, adages, social criticism, colloquies, editions, paraphrases, exegesis and rhetorical exhortation. When he decided that he had to write against Luther's central position, he announced that it would be preferable to leave the whole question of grace and free will to Christian piety and that he would like to adopt the view that the will needed liberation by grace before it could choose the good. Grace is not earned, but imputed. Erasmus's own inclination, as he acknowledges in a letter to More, was to accept that man can initiate the bestowal of grace *de congruo*, were it not for the authority of Paul and Augustine.[29] Typically, he attempted to keep the limits of the controversy to exegesis, the subject on which Luther, hoping to draw the great humanist to the side of his theological views before schism even threatened, had first consulted him in 1516.

In that year Erasmus had seen More's *Utopia* through the press of Thierry Martens at Louvain. Since the beginning of the century there had been not only close friendship but a virtual unanimity of view between them. Yet their personalities were very different. Erasmus was the more acute and dedicated theologian who increasingly strove to keep clear of political constraints. His personality lacked the strong undercurrent of violence that propelled More into a public life that he must have known was dangerous, and into the frankly vituperative anti-Lutheran polemic of the early 1520's. In his 1523 *Responsio ad Lutherum*, a defence of Henry VIII's *Assertio septem sacramentorum*, More had already claimed that Luther's denial of free will made God the cause of sin.[30] Fisher had made the same accusation in the *Contra captivitatem Babylonicam* and the *Responsio ad Mart. Lutheri epistolam* whose arguments and texts Erasmus was to exploit in the *Hyperaspistes* of 1526 and 1527. Fisher's doctrine of free will scarcely avoids overt Pelagianism, and, in spite of their mutual admiration, by 1529 there is a clear divergence between Erasmus and Fisher on the subject of free will. In a letter of August 22nd 1524 Erasmus repents of having preached 'spiritual liberty'. When the letter was published in 1529, Fisher wrote in the margin, 'Now you are sorry, but too late.'

Erasmus and Luther both accepted a fundamentally scriptural religion and scripturally normative theology. Both accepted the Nicene and the Apostles' Creeds. Not all Lutherans and not all Catholics immediately agreed with Luther and Erasmus about the centrality of the free will issue, although it quickly established itself as more crucial than the disputes about the Eucharist. For Erasmus, man's moral choices had to make him worthy of the bestowal, by imputation, of the *gratia gratum faciens*. For Luther, it was intolerable that man should be saved other than by a direct reaction to the scriptural message without the interposition of any human interpretative authority. It did not make it easier that neither Luther and his followers nor the scholastics regarded the humanist Erasmus as a professional theologian. None of the numerous compromises between Luther's position and Erasmus's did or could ever work, in spite of attempts in both camps, not even the incipient 'duplex justitia' theory briefly thrown out by Erasmus in the 1533 *De sarcienda ecclesiae concordia*, taken by Pflug to Ratisbon in 1541, elaborated by Giles of Viterbo, and presented by Seripando at Trent.

After Luther, the young professor of theology at the new university of Wittemberg, had attempted to enlist the support of Erasmus in 1516, overtures towards an alliance had been made by both Melanchthon and Capito. In March 1518 Erasmus sent Luther's ninety-five theses to More, and by that year his *Epistola ad fratres Germaniae inferioris* had already shown his fear of schism. He tried, at first in vain, to prevent Froben from publishing Luther, partly because he was himself suspected of sympathising too closely with him and feared that the scholastic attack would drag the whole of *bonae literae*, on which the humanist reform of the Church depended, into dogmatic disputes. Repeatedly, Erasmus attempted to calm Luther, with whom at first his dispute seemed only to be the question of discerning the authenticity of the preaching of the gospel message and of the individual's reaction to it. Yet within that difference lay the deeper incompatibilities of thought. If Christian salvation lay in a direct personal response to the divine message, the initiative was entirely God's and man was deprived of any autonomous power of achieving a religiously valid moral dignity. He could not in the full sense have free will. Disputes about the nature of the Lord's Supper, which alone separated Luther doctrinally from Zwingli, however differently they saw the social implementation of

Christian values, took second place, although Erasmus, in spite of his dislike of the term 'transubstantiation', took care to maintain that the Christian consensus obliged him to reject the views not only of Carlstadt and Pellikan, but also of Oecolampadius. As late as 1522, on receiving Zwingli's petition to the bishop of Constance, the *Apologeticus Archeteles*, Erasmus could however write to Zwingli in the middle of the night begging him to be moderate.

Erasmus's break with Luther came earlier than that with Zwingli, to whom he could still write in 1523 of the three Augustinians burned at Brussels 'ob paradoxa Lutheri', among which was an emphatic denial of free will as 'nomen inane'. The first perceptible changes in Zwingli's interior attitude can however probably be traced to a famous letter to Myconius of 1520, at which date he is still in agreement with Luther.[31] But by 1525 the *Commentarius de vera et falsa religione* openly declares the impossibility of avoiding guilt and maintains that a direct response to the scriptural message is the only means to salvation, the 'spes in Deum per Jesum Christum'. Only the individual can recognise the authenticity of the word of God presented to him.[32]

It is possible that during the years 1522 to 1525 Erasmus himself, little concerned with the defence of devotional practices, felt more deeply about the need for an authoritative authentication of the scriptural message, and the personal reactions it provoked, than about man's power to affect his own fate after death. Even when he realised that the central issue was indeed that of free will, as Luther agreed, his technically theological corpus, the *De libero arbitrio* and the two *Hyperaspistes*, reads unconvincingly, although it rises in a crescendo from fastidious distaste to withering scorn. *Hyperaspistes I* was written in a fortnight in 1526, when Erasmus had received a copy of Luther's *De servo arbitrio*, in time to catch the Frankfurt fair. It is only in *Hyperaspistes II*, composed at greater leisure and published in September 1527, that Erasmus, relying on Fisher, tries to find an acceptable meaning for merit *de congruo*. The fusion of evangelical piety with the humanist optimism of the Greek Fathers and the antique classics was never formed into a tight theological synthesis, and it was necessarily a product of the schism and a reaction to it rather than a means of avoiding it. It was however a workable theological tool, perhaps never properly tempered by Erasmus himself, but that which shaped the spirituality of the 'counter-reformation', and Jesuit educational theory.

Zwingli's spirituality grew out of Erasmus's *Carmen alpestre* and

Calvin's, later, in a France in which evangelical humanism had benefited from royal protection until 1534, out of Erasmus's *philosophia Christi*. The break between Erasmus and all three of Luther, Zwingli and Calvin, came over the question of the primacy of interior reaction to the word of God as preached and exemplified in the gospels above the authoritative interpretation of the gospel message. The touchstone became belief in any autonomous human power of self-determination to good, and it grew out of the initial problem of discerning the authenticity of religious reaction, what has come to be called the discernment of spirits.

It cannot be the purpose of this essay to assess the effectiveness after his death, and until the present time, of Erasmus's fusion of humanism, including the study of the antique classics, and evangelicalism. Others perfected the theological tool, rough-hewn as the *Novum instrumentum* of 1516, and the theological method based on its use has set the parameters of theological debate within and between all Christian communities to the present day. It remains however important, now that Erasmus's theological method, perfected too late to avoid the sixteenth-century schism, has been universally accepted among Christians at the expense of all subsequent attempts to revive an inadequate scholasticism, to appreciate that the inchoate method not only served to identify the breaking point in the sixteenth century between Erasmus and the often humanist reformers whose evangelicalism led them into schism, but was also transformed into a powerful spirituality.

There can be little real doubt that the core of the spirituality of Ignatius of Loyola lay in what he called the discernment of spirits. It seems certain that Ignatius's rules for the discernment of spirits, and the chief inspiration for his articulate expression of the spirituality underlying the *Spiritual Exercises*, was Erasmus, and in particular the prefatory 'Appendix' to the *Paraphrasis in Matthaeum* written on January 14th 1522.[33] The important 'topos' is II Cor xi, 13−14, on Satan's ability to change himself into an angel of light, 'ipse enim Satanas transfigurat se in angelum lucis', which is at the heart of the rules for the discernment of spirits in the *Spiritual Exercises* (para. 332). The question is how to recognise 'Satan' in disguise. Gerson touches on it. In 1519 Menot uses it at Tours. It appears the *Tiers livre* of Rabelais where, at the end of chapter fourteen, Pantagruel's view is disconcertingly similar to that of Ignatius. Rabelais was a dedicated, and Erasmian, evangelical humanist. More uses it in defence of Erasmus's Greek New Testament in his celebrated letter *To a Monk* of 1519−

20,[34] and the key text of Erasmus refers to it, saying 'Difficilis est discretio spirituum' before going on to enunciate what are virtually Ignatius's rules for discernment and to maintain the primacy of interior sentiment, the opposition between followers of the world and the followers of Christ, the way in which the good spirit disturbs the wicked, the importance of interior guidance, and the need to approach the scriptures in a spirit of piety. He also proposes the meditative reconstitution of scenes from Christ's life and the use of the interior senses in prayer.[35] Almost more interesting than this direct Erasmian source for the articulate expression of the core of Ignatius's spirituality is the development of Zwingli, who shared with Ignatius the vision of Christ as a military captain, although he interpreted it in less spiritual terms. The letter to Zwingli of 31st August 1523 in which Erasmus had referred to Luther's paradoxes, enumerating some of them, also refers to the topos of Satan appearing as an angel of light, concluding 'Rare is the gift of the discernment of spirits'.

The lines of development are sometimes tantalisingly close. Erasmus, Luther, Zwingli, Calvin and Ignatius all started from a belief in the spiritual power of the fusion of evangelicalism and humanism, traditions which, until Erasmus joined them, had been often in conflict and never entirely joined. It is not by chance that, even when it seemed most dangerous, Ignatius's followers never abandoned a defence of free will. Erasmus's reliance on the *consensus ecclesiae* found its echo in Ignatius's own explicit rules for thinking with the Church. The textual expression of the core of Ignatius's spirituality derives from Erasmus, as does much of the educational theory and theological style of the order he founded, although Ignatius, a contemporary of the second genera-tion of reformers which included Calvin, had to contend with the Council of Trent and could not foresee the form the institutionalisation of his order would take. What he derived from Erasmus was what separated from both of them the reformers who went into schism, the need for an authoritative criterion for discerning the authenticity of the preaching of the scriptural message and of the personal commitment it evoked. However strange traditional perspectives may make it seem, the evidence suggests that Erasmus was the principal instigator of modern theological method, content with parable and metaphor, fidelity to tradition and consensus, and the founder of one of the most powerful spiritualities to have emerged from the sixteenth-century turmoil, in a sense rediscovered in the turmoil of the second world war.

NOTES

1. See James D. Tracy, 'It is a consensus of scholarship both old and new that Renaissance humanism was primarily an educational movement' ('Humanism and the Reformation' in *Reformation in Europe: A Guide to Research* ed. Steven Ozment, St Louis 1982, p. 34). For the aims of the Brethren of the Common Life, see R.R. Post, *The Modern Devotion*, Leiden 1968, and for the interaction of English and Italian humanism, George B. Parks, *The English Traveller to Italy*, vol. 1, 'The Middle Ages to 1525', Rome 1954. Parisian complicity in Pico's attempt to defend his *Conclusiones* at Rome is clear from Bohdan Kiekowski's edition of them, Geneva 1973, and from Raymond Marcel, 'Pic de la Mirandole et la France: De l'Université de Paris au Donjon de Vincennes' in *L'Opera e il Pensiero di Giovanni Pico della Mirandola nella Storia dell 'Umanesimo'*, Florence 1965, pp. 205–30.

2. On these condemnations, their significance, and the means employed to achieve them, see Roland Hissette, *Enquête sur les 219 articles condamnés à Paris le 7 mars 1277*, Louvain/Paris, 1977.

3. 'Hinc apparet, quod mali flagellis sunt cohercendi, non membrorum truncatione vel temporali morte plectendi' (Causa 23, q.5, dict. Grat. post can.7).

4. See Joseph Lecler, *Histoire de la tolérance au siècle de la Réforme*, Paris 1955, vol.1, pp. 107–111, and A. van Hove, *Prolegomena ad Codicem Iuris Canonici*, Mechlin/Rome, 1945.

5. For the texts, see Joseph Lebacqz, *Libre arbitre et jugement*, Louvain, 1960.

6. 'Vires naturales tales secundum se manserunt, quales illas essemus habituri, si in puris naturalibus ad finem tantum naturalem a principio conditi fuissent' (Aquinas, *Summa Theologiae*, ed. Cajetan, Antwerp, 1595, p. 13a).

7. 'Lux ergo intellectus creati sibi non sufficit ad certam comprehensionem rei cujuscumque absque luce Verbi aeterni' (*Sermo*, Anecdota, p. 77).

8. See Ricardo G. Villoslada, *La Universidad de Paris durante los Estudios de Francisco de Vitoria O.P. (1507–22)*, Rome, 1938.

9. Scotus's best known exegete, C.R.S. Harris (*Duns Scotus*, 2 vols., Oxford 1927) sums up (vol. 2, p. 259), 'The inevitable result, therefore, was a vacillating and uncertain effort to keep clear of the more fatal consequences of materialism on the one hand and monopsychism on the other'. On the Scotist theory of the will, see also Walter Hoeres, *Der Wille als reine Vollkommenheit nach Duns Scotus*, Munich 1962, T.E. Davitt, *The Nature of Law*, St Louis/London 1951, H.A. Oberman, *The Harvest of Medieval Theology: Gabriel Biel and Late Medieval Nominalism*, Cambridge Mass. 1963 and E. Gilson, *Jean Duns Scot, Introduction à ses positions fondamentales*, Paris 1952.

10. See Louis Leahy, *Dynamique volontaire et jugement libre*, Paris/Bruges 1964, and the critical review of this work by Lebacqz in *The Heythrop Journal*, V, 4, Oxford 1964, pp. 452–5.

11. The *Opus Oxoniense* is clear on the will's intellective functions, 'non oportet intellectum ante appetere . . . sed sufficit voluntatem comparare hoc ad illud, quia voluntas est vis collativa sicut intellectus, et per consequens potest conferre quaecumque simplicia sibi ostensa, sicut intellectus potest' (d.6, q.1, no.6). Elsewhere, the *Opus Oxoniense* contains a solution of despair (II, d.37, q.2 no.1), 'Exemplum de intellectu, quasi concurrat ad causandam volitionem, . . . non tamen causat nisi voluntate causante, ita quod ejus causatio est in potestate voluntatis'. For Thomas's efforts to solve the same dilemma, see Dom Odon Lottin, *Psychologie et morale aux XIIe et XIIIe siècles*, 6 vols., Gembloux/Louvain 1942ff., vol. 1, pp. 226–43 and 252–62, and E. Gilson, *La Liberté chez Descartes et la théologie*, Paris 1913, pp. 236ff.

12. See X–M Le Bachelet, *Prédestination et grâce efficace. Controverses dans la Compagnie de Jésus au temps d'Aquaviva (1610–13)*, Louvain 1931.

13. Zürich 1950, 14, pp. 141−5. *Humani Generis* was published in the *Acta Apostolica Sedis* for September 2, 1950.

14. The English translation by Cornelius Ernst O.P., *Theological Investigations*, vol. 1, ch. 9, London and New York 1974, notes unfavourable reactions to the original *Orientierung* article in the *Schweizer Kirchenzeitung* of September 7, 1950, pp. 441−4 and in *Civitas*, VI, 1950−1, p. 84, and favourable reactions from Hans Urs von Balthasar, 'Der Naturbegriff in der katholischen Theologie' (in 'Karl Barth', *Darstellung und Deutung seiner Theologie*, Cologne, 1951, pp. 278−335), from L. Malevez, 'La Gratuité du surnaturel', in the *Nouvelle Revue théólogique*, lxxv, 1953, pp. 561−86 and 673−89, and from J.P. Kenny, *Reflections on Human Nature and the Supernatural* in 'Theological Studies', 1953, pp. 280−7. Malevez drew attention to an earlier article by E. Brisbois which had put forward substantially the same view as Rahner's, 'Le désir de voir Dieu et la métaphysique du vouloir selon St Thomas' in the *Nouvelle Revue theologique*, lxiii, 1936, pp. 1103−5. De Lubac's *Le mystère du surnaturel* was published in Paris (Aubier, 1965).

15. So, for instance I.A. de Aldama, 'De virtutibus IV' in the Madrid 1961 *Sacrae Theologiae Summa*, vol. 3, (Biblioteca de Autores Cristianos), pp. 804−5.

16. On the sixteenth-century debate about pagan virtue, see A.H.T. Levi, *Pagan Virtue and the Humanism of the Northern Renaissance*, London, 1974.

17. Thomas's attempt to escape the dilemma (*Summa*, la pars, q.14, articles 9 and 13; q.116, arts. 1−4) is criticised by Scotus in the light of a sharper distinction between nature and supernature. On Scotus's distinctions, see C.R.S. Harris, *Duns Scotus*, vol. 2, pp. 340−5. Scotus explains the absolute predestination of the elect in the *Opus Oxoniense* (1, dist.41, q.1, n.11), 'Ergo primo isti vult deus beatitudinem quam aliquod istorum [gratia etc] et primo vult ei quodcumque istorum quam prevideat ipsum habiturum quodcumque istorum, igitur propter nullum istorum previsam vult ei beatitudinem'.

18. On Gregory of Rimini, see Martin Schuler, *Prädestination, Sünde und Freiheit bei Gregor von Rimini*, Stuttgart 1934 and Gordon Leff, *Gregory of Rimini: Tradition and Innovation in Fourteenth-Century Thought*, Manchester 1961.

19. 'Nullus est reprobatus propter malum usum liberi arbitrii quem deus previdit illum habiturum' (1, d.40 and 41, q.1, a.2). See Leff, *Gregory of Rimini*, pp. 197−201. Gregory continues, 'nec predestinationis nec reprobationis eterne proprie acceptarum ulla est causa'.

20. See especially Robert Guelluy, *Philosophie et théologie chez Guillaume d'Ockham*, Louvain/Paris 1947, and Auguste Pelzer, 'Les 51 articles de Guillaume Occam censurés en Avignon en 1326' in *Revue d'histoire écclesiastique*, vol. 18, Louvain, 1922, pp. 240−70.

21. '. . . in homine absque gratia sunt sufficientia principia bonae operationis moralis . . . meritum verum de congruo innititur libertati divinae quae etiam gratia dicitur' (II Sent., d.28, q.2, Lyons 1562). See Oberman, *The Harvest of Medieval Theology*, p. 143.

22. See Julius Rudolph Weinberg, *Nicolaus of Autrecourt, a Study in Fourteenth-Century Thought*, Princetown, 1948.

23. Oberman, *The Harvest of Medieval Theology*, pp. 90−3 and 255−8.

24. The strong, concise reiteration of formal doctrinal orthodoxy by the Council of Trent in the sixteenth century naturally resulted, especially after reinforcement by the first Vatican Council in the nineteenth, in a continuation among Catholics of devotional practices in accordance with the spirituality of the fifteenth-century Church, even if developed at a much later date. Devout Catholicism, even in the twentieth century, saw the popularity of practices like the cult of relics, candle-lighting, indulgences, and Masses for the dead, and the thirst for religious reassurance assuaged not only by models of moral heroism, but also by sporadic manifestations of the miraculous, as at Lourdes, and by the guarantee of salvation

thought to be afforded by communicating on the first Friday of nine successive months.

25. Thomas at least appears to make this supposition in the *Prima Secundae*, q.19, arts. 5 and 6. Ignatius of Loyola, to whose order belonged some of the most heroic of all the missionaries, himself distinguishes three classes of men, those who lived before Christ, those who were his contemporaries and those who lived after his death (*Spiritual Exercises*, para 71).

26. *Epistolae Pauli*, Rom.2, 14—5, fo 48 v. See J. Dagens, 'Humanisme et évangelisme chez Lefèvre d'Etaples', in *Courants religieux et humanisme à la fin du XVe et au début du XVIe siècle*, Paris, 1959, pp. 121—34.

27. See D.P. Walker, 'Origène en France au Début du XVIe siecle' in *Courants religieux et humanisme. . .*, pp. 101—119. Walker also shows that Luther and Erasmus were agreed that the doctrine of free will was the essential point of difference between them, that Erasmus was inspired by both Origen and Pico in his controversy with Luther and that, as it happens following both Fisher and More, he accuses Luther of making God the author of sin, an accusation against which Luther naturally defended himself, 'licet enim Deus peccatum non faciat, tamen naturam peccato, subtracto spiritu, vitiatam, non cessat formare et multiplicare, tanquam si faber ex ligno corrupto statuas faciat. . .' Erasmus points out that the metaphor comes from Origen, whose exegesis of the 'induravit cor Pharaonis' passage from Exodus he follows.

28. On the interpretation of the Pico's *Oratio*, see W.G. Craven, *Giovanni Pico della Mirandola, Symbol of His Age: Modern Interpretations of a Renaissance Philosopher*, Geneva, 1981.

29. See, for instance, James D. Tracy, *Erasmus, The Growth of a Mind*, Geneva, 1972, especially pp. 230ff.

30. See G. Chantraine, *Erasme et Luther: Libre et serf arbitre*, Paris, 1981.

31. See H. Meylan, 'Zwingli et Erasme', in *Colloquia Erasmiana Turonensia*, ed. J—C Margolin, Paris, 1972, vol. 2, pp. 849—58.

32. 'Hanc rem solae piae mentes norunt . . . Experientia est, nam pii omnes eam experti sunt'. Erasmus had written on reading the *Archeteles* in 1522, 'Obsecro te ut . . . rem seriam agas serio et memineris Evangelie tum modestiae tum prudentiae', but the 1525 text of Zwingli shows that Erasmus's plea was in vain. In 1522 Zwingli was still urging Beatus Rhenanus to do everything in his power to prevent the duel between Luther and Erasmus which was, he had heard, being prepared.

33. See A.H.T. Levi, 'Erasmus, the Early Jesuits and the Classics', in *Classical Influences on European Culture ad 1500—1700*, ed. R.R. Bolgar, Cambridge 1976, pp. 223—38.

34. The monk was John Batmanson, the author of *Contra annotationes Erasmi Roterodami* see *St Thomas More: Selected Letters*, ed. Elizabeth Frances Rogers, Yale 1961, p. 124.

35. For the interpretation of Ignatius's spirituality and references to the literature establishing it, for the probable circumstances in which Ignatius read Erasmus's text, and for the text itself, see *Erasmus, the Early Jesuits and the Classics*.

7

PRESENT AND PAST IN A DEBATE ON TRANSUBSTANTIATION

by P.J. FITZPATRICK

Reader in Philosophy, University of Durham

*F*airness is the quality I have found attributed most often over the years to Copleston's writings on the history of philosophy. Fairness is not a quality that comes by default: it demands a vigilant willingness to let authors be heard on their own terms, and a tireless endeavour to let their distinctive problems be perceived by us in their distinctiveness. My contribution to this volume considers a debate in which these demands were made upon the disputants.

I

The debate was between Filippo Selvaggi of the Gregorian University at Rome, and Carlo Colombo of the Pontifical Faculty of Theology at Milan, later Archbishop of that city, eventually a Cardinal and (the oxymoron is not of my own devising) 'personal theologian' to Paul VI. Their debate was over issues to do with transubstantiation, so I must immediately ask any deterred reader to share my own strictly temporary suspension of disbelief. I shall have occasion to state here some of my reasons for rejecting the Council of Trent's declaration about the eucharistic presence, but have no wish to elaborate what I have argued elsewhere.[1] My purpose, rather, is to estimate the nature and extent of the disagreement, and to draw some morals. The estimation is in one sense made easier by what the disputants had in common – an acceptance of the decrees on the Eucharist made by the Council of Trent, and an adherence to the tradition of scholastic philosophy found in Aquinas. But in another sense, the shared presuppositions of the two writers make the real point of the debate harder to discern. To go by their own descriptions, it concerned the status of what modern science teaches about the constitution of things. In fact – or so I shall submit – it touches the nature of judgments upon the philosophical past, and of shifts between disciplinary boundaries. I begin by rehearsing the stages of the debate.

In 1949, Selvaggi considered the relation between what the Council of Trent had defined about the eucharistic change, and the speculations of theologians in the matter. Trent had used expressions associated with Aquinas, and declared the word 'transubstantiation' to be most fittingly used there. Yet that term was devised in the early Middle Ages, and later formed part of the speculations of theologians such as Aquinas, who used concepts like 'substance' and 'accident' with an Aristotelian ancestry. Today, when natural science has revealed so much more about the nature of things, its language is no longer Aristotelian. What then should be said to those who ask how eucharistic theology stands with respect to recent discoveries? Selvaggi's answer follows the line of argument associated with his colleague at the Gregorian, Pieter Hoenen: he claims that Aristotelian distinctions like those between act and potentiality or substance and accident are not only compatible with modern physics and chemistry but are demanded by them. The findings of modern science call for something more than explanations in terms of extension and motion – the 'mechanical philosophy' associated with Descartes (Hoenen 1945 states and amply elaborates the thesis; an extract in English is Hoenen 1968). There is a place for the Aristotelian notion of substance, because no justice can be done to the unity there is in, say, an atom by treating it as a simple aggregate of particles. The heterogeneity in atoms does not exclude their unity, a unity revealed by the genuine novelty in the behaviour of the particles within the atom compared to their behaviour when outside it (Selvaggi 1949, pp. 28–32). But by this standard, we cannot follow the medievals in their belief that bread is one substance. The materials from which bread is composed retain the characteristics they previously possessed, and the process of baking does not make of them more than an aggregate. Bread lacks the unity which is required if something is to be counted as one substance; it is rather the components of the conglomerate that are substances – atoms, molecules, microcrystals and the rest. In consequence, it is to these components that we must apply Trent's claim that 'the whole substance' of the bread is converted into the Body of Christ. So it is these atoms and the rest that cease to exist and leave only their accidents – that is, the phenomena open to direct experience (Selvaggi 1949, pp. 39–43). Transubstantiation is therefore not a physical change in the sense that it is not 'operatively definable', not open to investigation by any series of physical operations. Any experience deals with appearances, with properties, whereas substance is the object of judgment. But transubstantiation is a physical change in the sense that its starting-point (the substances that compose the bread) and its end-point (the substance of Christ's body) are physical realities (Selvaggi 1949, pp. 43–4).

It is to this talk of 'physical realities' that Colombo took exception in 1955, and to Selvaggi's identification of substance with the particles of modern science. He mentions, as Selvaggi had done, some eucharistic debates from before the war, and aligns himself with the position adopted there by the German theologian Ternus. In 1937 Ternus had replied to the charge (made pseudonymously by a 'Fr. M.') that Catholic eucharistic belief involved accepting a 'dogmatic physics' that remained in the thirteenth century, and so involved rejecting the findings of modern science. Ternus retorted that the challenge had missed the point, because eucharistic theology cannot conflict with physics, owing to their distinctness of subject-matters. 'Substance', 'accident' and the rest are metaphysical concepts, and are not part of what physics deals with, namely reality as a quantity of motion (Ternus 1937, pp. 200–02).[2] It is with this distinction between physics and metaphysics that Colombo aligns himself. Substance is not to be identified with any reality open to physical experience, as Selvaggi would identify it with atomic and sub-atomic particles. When Trent made its declaration on the Eucharist, nothing was known of such things, and so such things could not have concerned it. The 'physical' reality of the bread, the object of modern science, is not affected; the eucharistic change touches realities that are beyond (*al di là*) anything physically attainable, realities that are 'transphysical' and so strictly metaphysical (Colombo 1955, pp. 120–1). An approach like Selvaggi's, while dogmatically orthodox, is theologically inadvisable. It ties theology too closely to the variations that attend upon science, much as did theories that tried to reconcile transubstantiation with Cartesian philosophy (Colombo 1955, pp. 96, 116–7). And it is unfaithful to the general line of development that can be traced over the centuries. The Fathers of the Church, to whom Trent appealed, made no use of physical or philosophical concepts of their time; they accepted a divine intervention analogous to creation; they held the change to be beyond any reality that is open to experience (Colombo 1955, pp. 113–6). What development there has been in the doctrine of transubstantiation has been in the direction of removing it yet further *al di là* from the physical order, making the concepts used ever more metaphysical (Colombo 1955, p. 116).

Given that both sides accepted Trent's decrees, accepted the scholastic tradition in philosophy and theology, and accepted that the eucharistic change, though objective, was beyond experience, we may sympathise with Selvaggi when, beginning his reply, he professed some perplexity as to placing just what the difference between them amounted to (Selvaggi 1956, pp. 17f). It might seem to lie in the expression 'physical reality': but if this be taken to mean nothing more than the data of our senses, or data that can be recorded on instruments, Selvaggi will clearly not dispute Colombo's claim that 'physical reality' does not change (Selvaggi 1956, p. 20). But he insists that to take the phrase in this way is unfortunate, because 'physical reality' suggests what is the object of physical science, and physical science is concerned with more than phenomena; it is an intellectual and experimental activity that is concerned with understanding things as they are. The 'physical reality' of the bread should be taken as what constitutes the stuff that ordinary usage terms 'bread', and it is with this physical reality that common sense, science, and metaphysics are alike concerned. Since we know so much more about bread's constitution than did Trent or the Fathers, we must be prepared to say that its constituents – atoms, molecules and so on – are what is changed in the Eucharist, under penalty of denying the objective character of transubstantiation. In speaking of the substance of the bread, the Fathers never appealed, as Colombo does, to 'realities beyond those that are physically attainable', or to 'realities that are transphysical, that is, strictly metaphysical' (Selvaggi 1956, pp. 20–3).

Selvaggi had in the course of this reply referred to other writings of his, in which he endeavoured to dissociate the notion of substance from a phenomenalism found in Maritain and other neo-scholastic writers, who set it apart from physical science, which, they think, should forswear all ontological claims (see, e.g. Selvaggi 1954). It is such an evaluation of physical science that Colombo explicitly makes in his second contribution to the debate. He cites at some length and with approval an article by the Italian theologian Roberto Masi, concerning the relationship between 'Physics' for Aristotle and 'Physics' in our own time. Physics for Aristotle, though linked with experience, was part of philosophy, and sought to show the ontological causes of real phenomena. Physics today is not concerned with the ontological content of bodies, but only with them in as much as they are subject to experiment and to measurement; it deals with their appearances only, it measures colours and weights without knowing what either is ontologically (Colombo 1956, pp. 263–5). All physics is in the phenomenal order – atoms and other particles as much as colour and weight – and it has nothing to say of the metaphysical order. But that is precisely where transubstantiation occurs, in the substance beneath the appearances; and – Colombo adds – there can be no identifying of substance with what physics reveals about bodies: all that, particles and the rest, lies in the accidental order and so does not change (Colombo 1956, pp. 265–6). In talking of 'physical reality' as the starting-point of the eucharistic change, Selvaggi is separating himself from the scholastic view that the ultimate substantial reality of bodies is unknowable physically, and is knowable, limitedly, only by metaphysical reasoning (Colombo 1956, p. 277). Nor, he contends, is what Selvaggi writes of a piece with the development of theological reflexion on the Eucharist since at least the thirteenth century, which has drawn its distinction in metaphysical terms; it is rather in the line of theories, now abandoned, that sought to accommodate transubstantiation to physical theories that are now outmoded (Colombo 1956, pp. 280–3).

Selvaggi, in the last of the articles in the exchange that I consider, elaborates the scholastic notion of substance, giving references to Aquinas. Its primary sense is that which exists in itself, not that which provides a foundation for the accidents; substance and accidents alike are incomplete, and must not be thought of as two independent realities (Selvaggi 1957, pp. 503–6). Substance is known as the object of an intellectual judgment, working upon sensible properties; it is not – as Kant held – an invariant subject of those properties; nor – as some theologians have held – is it one reality underlying another, and reached only by metaphysical reasoning. To relegate physical science to the order of the accidental, as Colombo does, is to do it no more justice than do empiricism and positivism. Modern physics is more than organized sense-experience. It makes intellectual judgments, in terms of its mathematically expressed theories, upon the whole reality, substance and accidents alike (Selvaggi 1957, pp. 512–14).

Such are the stages in the debate as far as I have followed it here, and the large measure of agreement between Selvaggi and Colombo brings out all the more clearly what they hold to be their points of difference – the ontological status of physical theories, and the nature of the distinctions drawn by theologians in their writings about transubstantiation. I do not want to pretend that these differences are not real, but I submit that they are more complex than they look, and that the disagreements between the two authors raise a group of interconnected questions about understanding the past.

II

I begin with some comments on what Selvaggi holds about the need for Aristotelian distinctions in modern physical science. He faces here the problem that has faced philosophers of the scholastic tradition since the revival or encouragement of that tradition in the last century. How can the philosophy of nature that goes with the tradition be accommodated to the immense progress made by organized investigation of nature since the Middle Ages? The 'new sciences' of the seventeenth century began in conscious opposition to the scholastic tradition that preceded them. Must not the tradition nowadays be even more hopelessly at odds with all that has since come about? The question deserves an answer, and the kind of answer Selvaggi offers, in its insistence on the abiding need for scholastic concepts in physical science, at least respects the claim of that science to make statements about the nature of things. What makes me uneasy here is not any dubiousness in the claim, but rather the exiguousness of it. That the laws of classical mechanics cannot serve by themselves in all parts of physics, is true; that the intuitive clarity in 'pushes and pulls' made some think that the laws might be adequate, is also true; and just as true are claims that an atom is not a 'simple aggregate' of its components. But how much *content* is there in holding that such things prove the need for scholastic concepts?

Consider Selvaggi's claim that there is a substantial unity in those complexes where components behave in a way different from their behaviour in isolation. What does the claim amount to? *How* different is the behaviour to be? Aristotle had an answer, for his concept of substance took a biological paradigm: few things are more obvious than the difference between a living animal and its corpse, and few things more notable than the persistence of a living being over the gradual replacement of its matter. But the biological paradigm is no longer available if it is modern physics to which we want to offer philosophical concepts, so how are we to decide what differences show substantial unities? If an atom is deemed to be substance and bread not, how do we adjudicate among intervening samples? Is a molecule a substance? A crystal? A solution? What could count as a method for answering such questions?

It is not that physics does not raise philosophical questions: it obviously does, and if scholastic distinctions can be of help, they should be used. But they have, if I may so put it, to work their passage. Thus, the difference in behaviour between sub-atomic particles inside and outside the atom is acknowledged by men of science in a setting of mathematical theory and controlled experiment wholly alien to the medieval tradition. How far can concepts that were developed in that tradition be disengaged from it and given the new setting of the activity that has replaced the tradition? Talk of substantial unity can certainly serve to remind us that an atom is not made up from its parts in a way that a clock is. But not only is so exiguous a claim hardly worth the carriage, it draws whatever content it has from the very things in physical science that are subsequent to scholasticism – the mathemat-

ical theory and controlled experiments of particle-physics. What is
there left for the scholastic distinctions to *do* now except let physics
make the running and then turn up to be exemplified? *Sint Maecenates,
non deerunt, Flacce, Marones?*[3] I shall be suggesting that the moral is to
look at the setting in which those distinctions were originally drawn,
but for the present I turn from Selvaggi's attitude to modern physical
theory and consider Colombo's.

If Selvaggi's application of scholastic distinctions to modern physical
science turns out to have less content than it appeared to have,
Colombo's account of the status of that science is vacuous from the
start. Once more, it is a question of philosophical observations needing
to work their passage. Parts of physics notoriously raise questions that
are philosophical − questions to do with determinacy, theories, space,
time, and the rest − and the questions can be and are profitably
debated. But the debate needs to have more in it than talk of
'appearances' and 'substance' if it is to be worth conducting. Modern
science began by abandoning the natural but temptingly over-simple
generalisations of Aristotle's claims about the world, and by means of
controlled experiment and mathematical techniques has devised theories that account for the composition and behaviour of objects; and
presumably it will go further along the road it is travelling on.
Colombo's claim is that whatever is achieved in this way − however
powerful its claims and however resistant to falsification − never gets
beyond the order of appearances. But what more does he want? Science
can blunder in its practice, as anything else can, and one theory can be
succeeded by or subsumed by another. What is supposed to be lacking
to scientific procedure, so that (unlike metaphysics) it never deals with
the substance of things? What is the *'al di là'* of substance *'al di'* of?
What inability have we here that is more than our inability to catch the
horizon?

I said that the moral I should be drawing from the contentions of
Selvaggi is that scholastic distinctions will have to be seen in their
original context. I say the same about the claims made by Colombo
about the status of physical science, but I must make at once an
admission. If Colombo's account of substance here is vacuous, its
usefulness as a piece of *Realpolitik* in eucharistic theology can hardly be
exaggerated. To see why this is so must be our next step, for seeing why
will involve a better understanding of just what is being claimed in
transubstantiation, and so lead us eventually to the questions to do with
past and present.

We saw that Selvaggi has claimed significance for the distinction between substance and accidents even in the context of modern science, and has endeavoured to keep the distinction apart from an attitude that would consign modern science to the accidental order, leaving substance to be the concern of metaphysics. We also saw how he has accordingly stressed that substance and accidents are not to be regarded as two independent realities, as if substance were an impalpable kernel beneath the shell of accidents: the judgment of the intellect about a substance is a judgment working upon sensible properties (Selvaggi 1957, pp. 503–514). Unfortunately, it is this very philosophical coherence of his position that makes it recalcitrant to employment in eucharistic theology, just as it is Colombo's vacuous 'horizon' account of substance that lends it to being easily used in this context. For the eucharistic context is not Aristotelian at all; the complaint made nowadays by some theologians that transubstantiation ties eucharistic belief to the Aristotelian tradition is unfounded. All we have is a nonsensical abuse of terms drawn from the tradition: that Colombo's account of substance lends itself to the abuse is not to its credit. To elaborate my objections to transubstantiation is, as I have said, no part of my present purpose. It will be enough to illustrate what concerns us here: transubstantiation demands that we take the distinction between substance and accidents as a *dissection*, and so treat them as so many *things*. And I will illustrate this contention from the writings of Aquinas himself.

He rightly insists that the eucharistic change is unlike any other (ST 3.75.4); the trouble lies in the way he combines terminology from ordinary change in order to express the uniqueness. Ordinary change, for the medieval understanding of Aristotle, was to be expressed in terms of a potential element successively actualised by two forms. For slighter ('accidental') changes, the potential element is the substance, and the forms are accidental — wine, which was cold, is now warm, but is still wine. For more profound ('substantial') changes, the potential element is matter and the forms are substantial — what was wine has turned into vinegar, it is wine no longer. We can prescind here from all queries we might want to make about the content or worthwhileness of this account. What we must seize on is that the eucharistic change has *no* potential element at all. Natural changes concern the form of a thing, whether accidental (the wine that is warmed) or substantial (the wine that turn into vinegar — or, I would add, the bread that was eaten and digested by Christ during his earthly life). But God's infinite power extends to the whole reality of the bread, matter as well as form, and so the eucharistic change is not substantial (as was the change involved in the digestion of bread) but is transubstantial (ST 3.75.4, 3.75.8).

And it is this 'placing' of transubstantiation that I find unintelligible. Not (obviously) that the eucharistic change should be reducible to changes like digesting bread or warming wine; nor (just as obviously) that the change should be expressible in terms whose ancestry goes back to a Greek philosopher three centuries before Christ. My objection is much simpler — the terms being combined, whatever we think of them, are Aristotelian terms, and we cannot use those terms intelligibly simultaneously denying whatever gives point to them. All we can do — and all that we end by doing — is take the distinctions between substance and accidents or between matter and form, as so many dissections into constituents. Once that is done, transubstantiation becomes an admittedly miraculous reshuffling of entities that compose the bread and the body of Christ. And having thus distorted the distinctions, we shall talk of transubstantiation in terms of omnipotence, when we should be talking of it in terms of intelligibility.

Which is just what Aquinas is obliged to do. When not under theological pressure, he is scrupulous in insisting that we must not treat matter, form and the rest as if they were things. (See his commentary on Aristotle's *Metaphysics*, Z 7, 1033 b 7; *In Arist. Met.*, VII, Lect. 7, Cathala 1423.) But in these questions of the *Summa Theologiae*, his very vocabulary shows something is wrong. In natural changes, he writes, the matter of the starting-point *receives the form* of the end-product, the first form *being laid aside*; in the Eucharist, the *whole substance* passes over, but something does *remain the same* in each case — in natural changes, it is the *matter or subject*, in the Eucharist it is the *accidents*, the appearance of bread (ST 3.75.8). The phrases I have italicised illustrate what I have pointed to — the *reification* of Aristotelian distinctions, the turning of them into dissections of reality into its component parts. Once this is done, the rearrangings of the components become a matter of *power*, and it is in terms of power that Aquinas writes of transubstantiation. Elsewhere, he states lucidly that no question of power can be raised where there is inconsistency (*discohaerentia terminorum*) in the supposed object of its exercise (*De Potentia* I, 3). But in what he writes of the Eucharist, power has priority. God's *infinite power*, as we have seen, is held to extend to the whole reality of the bread, matter and form alike; the *difficulty* of transubstantiation is compared with that of creation (ST 3.75.8). Most revealingly of all, an incisive objection is put by Aquinas himself in terms of intelligibility, and receives an answer that is embarrassingly lame. Not even miraculously, he submits, can something be separated from its definition; but the definition of an accident involves *not* existing in itself; so the accidents in the Eucharist cannot exist without a subject (ST 3.77.1 obj. 2). What answer this gets may strike some readers as a curious inversion of the ontological argument. Definitions do not include the existence of what is defined, they do but state what is proper to it; but the accidents in the Eucharist do not exist of themselves, they are sustained by divine power; so there is no contradiction (ST 3.77.1 ad 2). You had as well argue that, because the definition of a flying saucer does not include the existence of any, there might be some that were not flying saucers at all. The answer, in fact, replies to an objection on grounds of intelligibility simply by talking in terms of power. It makes the accidents be divinely 'sustained'; that is, it assumes that the idea of sustaining accidents makes sense; and it so begs the very question raised in the objection.

I hope it is now clearer why, if we are concerned with theological *Realpolitik*, Colombo is our man, not Selvaggi. When not theologically preoccupied, both Selvaggi and Aquinas insist that we must not regard substance and accidents as separate realities and we have seen how Selvaggi rejects any fantasy of their distinction as that between a kernel and its shell, or anything of the sort. This is philosophically sound, but therefore recalcitrant to doing what theology wants. As we have just seen, it is only the rejected fantasy that gives to transubstantiation any appearance of content it possesses, for it is the fantasy alone that supports the claim that the accidents of bread can survive when their substance has gone, and that the distinctions drawn by Aristotle can be taken as dissections. No legitimately-drawn distinction will do, whether it be between appearance and reality, phenomena and substance, sense impressions and the judgment of the intellect. Distinctions of the sort can make varied and good sense — fools' gold is not gold although it looks like it, whereas vaporised gold is still gold although it does not; sticks look bent in water when they are really straight; water remains water whether hot or cold; the significance of a diagram goes beyond the quirks of the chalk-marks on the black-board. And so on. None of this gets us nearer to the eucharistically required sense of phenomena with no reality, appearances that are appearances of nothing, accidents that have no substance. But if we are determined to believe that such expressions are not just *discohaerentia terminorum*, it is Colombo's account of substance we need, Selvaggi's makes too much sense. By removing substance from anything which experience and investigation can ever discover about things, Colombo isolates it from its proper setting of change and continuity, and makes of it a metaphysical *terra incognita*. What else remains to be done except consider what takes place there in terms of divine omnipotence? Intelligibility has nothing to do with it — what is there left to be intelligible?[4]

I began my account of Colombo's position with his aligning himself with a theologian who rejected the accusation that eucharistic belief involved an acceptance of 'dogmatic physics'. I have to conclude the account by noticing how little he has himself been able to disengage eucharistic belief from medieval thought. Like other scholastic writers (e.g. Selvaggi 1949, pp. 7—17), Colombo has been at pains to keep the eucharistic teaching of the Council of Trent distinct from scholastic speculations (Colombo 1955, pp. 110—12, 119—22). Indeed, his very consigning of physics to the accidental order is intended to allow modern science and scholastic metaphysics to go their separate ways, and so allow (if I may so put it) the scholastic theologian to award himself a philosophical degree *ad eundem* as he elaborates his theories. But his wish to keep dogma and speculations distinct seems to come to very little. He has to say that the definition at Trent presupposes a real distinction between the 'substance' that does change and the 'appearances' that do not; that it is a doctrine '*proxima fidei*' that these appearances are objective, not just subjective; and that it is 'theologically certain' that 'appearances' in the conciliar decree is to be understood in the sense of 'accidents' in scholastic philosophy and theology (Colombo 1956, pp. 278—9). And in so writing, Colombo is not standing apart from what other scholastic theologians do. Whatever be thought of 'dogmatic physics', 'dogmatic metaphysics' seems unavoidable. Indeed, it looks as if talk of philosophical freedom here can never come to anything, precisely because it looks as if the distinctions drawn by Aristotle had been vindicated by the Eucharist — what the pagan had distinguished, God has now put asunder. Appearance and reality, constancy and variation, meaning and its embodiment — these and other contrasted pairs seem to come together, by divine favour, in the theory of transubstantiation. How can Catholic eucharistic belief, whatever its philosophical expression, escape the categories of 'phenomena' and 'ultimate substance'? Are we not forced by the data of revelation to acknowledge here the validity of medieval scholasticism?[5] This line of thought has proved perennially tempting, and proves at least this much: if my strictures on the intelligibility of transubstantiation are well-founded, then the rejection of that ruinous legacy is going to call for some very radical dissent indeed.

III

Our own concerns are more restricted. I have described the debate between Colombo and Selvaggi, and offered an estimate of their respective attitudes to the distinction between substance and accidents, and to the use of that distinction in eucharistic theology. And my adverse judgment upon transubstantiation has gone with an acknowledgement that its abuse of Aristotelian distinctions sits more easily to Colombo's views than to Selvaggi's.

But I have so far taken transubstantiation simply in the sense in which it is offered by Aquinas in the *Summa Theologiae*. I have stated more than once that one moral of the debate I have considered is that we need to see the terms used in it in their historical origins. To trace in detail the development of eucharistic theory in the Middle Ages is an enterprise upon which I do not wish to embark here (or, indeed, anywhere else). What I mean to do rather is to offer a variety of texts that will, in their very heterogeneity, show something of the preoccupations of theologians in those days; and I hope that the texts will throw some light upon the nature of the difference alleged to exist between the two disputants — whether the distinctions drawn and theories then devised were 'metaphysical' and beyond 'physical realities'.

I am glad to acknowledge here my debt to the German scholar Hans-Joachim Jorissen, whose monograph on the development of the doctrine of transubstantiation is remarkable for its judicious clarity, and invaluable for its assembling of sources, many of which are still in manuscript only. I do not share all Jorissen's evaluations, whether of his material or of Roman Catholic belief, but I should like to think that some readers will go to his work for themselves, for I have been concerned with only a few of its many themes. I add that material I know only from Jorissen's book is cited by 'J.' and a page-number; to the rest I refer as usual.

I begin with three earlier examples of how talk of omnipotence replaces talk of intelligibility. Innocent III (Lothar of Segni before his elevation to the Papacy) imagines in his work *De sacro altaris mysterio* (before 1198) the objection of a eucharistic questioner as: 'I am quite sure what God *can* do, but I am not wholly sure what he *has chosen* to do' (J. 36; the Latin corresponding to the words I have underlined is 'valet' and 'velit' — here as elsewhere in medieval theology, questions get begged in a jingle). So Innocent's questioner regards matters of intelligibility as not problematic, and his sentiment is shared by Robert Courson in his *Summa coelestis philosophiae* (about 1207), where accidents existing without a subject are set beside a virgin birth, or of sight being given to the blind; all are exercises of divine power (J. 120). And Baldwin of Ford, in his *De sacramento altaris* (before 1180), expresses the persuasion that underlies these and other appeals to divine omnipotence — 'Jesus is served by every form and matter, by every appearance and substance' (J.20). In other words, distinctions drawn are interpreted as dissections, and to omnipotence it belongs to manipulate the results of the dissecting.

I have already claimed that Colombo's account of substance as *al di là* of all physical reality makes it go easily with the philosophical abuses involved in transubstantiation. But the three texts I have just given exhibit in a crude form the defects I have already claimed to find in Aquinas — a reification of philosophical distinctions, and the replacement of questions to do with intelligibility by questions to do with omnipotence. Do not such texts then, whether these earlier examples or those in Aquinas himself, show that Colombo is nearer to the spirit of medieval scholasticism than is Selvaggi? And are not then his strictures against Selvaggi's talk of 'physical reality' justified?

It is my contention that this is simply not the case, and that Selvaggi — despite appearances to the contrary and despite his own words in one place to the contrary — is nearer to them in spirit. And the first group of texts I cite to prove my submission is from the *Summa Theologiae*; in each, Aquinas reviews some older theory in the theology of the Eucharist.

The first considers the opinion (Abelard's in fact) that after the consecration, when the substance of the bread has been converted into the substance of the body of Christ, the accidents of the bread take the surrounding *air* as their subject. To this very 'physical' account, Aquinas puts two objections that are just as 'physical': air cannot receive such accidents, and, if it did, moving a consecrated host would drive the air away (ST 3.77.1). The second opinion on which he passes judgment asks what becomes of the substance of the bread at the consecration, and suggests that it is resolved into its elements (like the Star of the Magi, some added; J.29). Aquinas objects that, were this the case, the elements would still have to be moved away from under the surviving accidents, for there must be nothing under them except the Body of Christ (ST 3.75.3). A third text of Aquinas surveys and evaluates several earlier opinions about the fate of the water that is mixed with wine in the chalice at Mass. It cannot remain unaltered (nothing must be there but Christ); it cannot be changed into the water that flowed from the side of Christ (that would call for a separate consecration); it seems best to say that it is first transformed into wine, and then transubstantiated into the Blood of Christ (ST 3.74.8). The oddities in these texts should not obscure for us the fact that all three are concerned with the behaviour of recognisable physical objects — air is incompatible with some accidents, and is easily moved; the elements of the bread's substance will need moving away; water undergoes a change into wine before the eucharistic conversion takes place. We are in all three cases in the order of physical reality and of its properties and activities; we are certainly in the order of the miraculous; but there is no talk, whether in the opinions or in the objections, of our being in some order of substance that is set apart from and beyond physical reality.

Other authors cited by Jorissen have just as 'physical' a view of the eucharistic change. The analogies they offer to it reveal their cast of thought — hay into glass, the Egyptian magicians' rods into serpents, water into wine at Cana, Lot's wife into a pillar of salt (J.87, 123, 77 etc.).[6] Indeed, one of the earliest uses of 'transubstantiate' I have seen (it is not mentioned by Jorissen), that by John Belethus (c.1165) in his *Rationale divinorum officiorum*, is in a setting that is even more physical. Some shepherds one day recited the words of consecration over some bread when out in the fields (their 'bait' presumably); it was transformed 'and perhaps transubstantiated, if I may so speak, into the Body of Christ' and they were all struck dead (202 ML 52; the point of the story is to explain why the words of consecration are said inaudibly). That transubstantiation is special is naturally admitted, but the constituents it involves, though miraculously rearranged, are the same as those for ordinary change. Thus, Peter Cantor's *Summa de sacramentis* (between 1191 and 1197), after mentioning hay into glass and wine into vinegar, says that in such changes the *ypostasis* remains while the *forma* goes; whereas in transubstantiation the converse obtains (J. 87). One is as it were a counterpart of the other. Indeed, William of Auvergne in his *De Sacramento Eucharistiae* (about 1223) explicitly describes transubstantiation as opposite (*contraria*) to what philosophy technically terms 'corruption'. In corruption (we could think of wine turning into vinegar), everything goes except what is primary — the matter; while in transubstantiation everything goes except what is ultimate — the accidents (J. 142). In none of these texts is it so much as suggested that transubstantiation takes place at some 'transphysical' level.

Nor is there any suggestion of the sort in a third group of texts, which have to do with the capacity of the consecrated bread and wine to *nourish*. Once more, we must not let the eccentricity of the opinions confuse us as to where they 'locate' the eucharistic change. Nourishment raised problems for medieval scholastics because appearances, it might seem, are incapable of nourishing anything. Indeed, the difficulty was felt all the more because some writers, such as the author of a *Sententiae divinitatis* of between 1142 and 1147, denied any reality whatever to the appearances, and reduced them to the status of the perennial 'bent stick in water' (J. 78). One endeavour to meet the difficulty was made by an author whom we have already met, Peter Cantor: for him, along with the colour, shape and scent of the bread (*panis*) there survives — untranslatably, I fear — '*panitas*'. Peter claimed that, if *panitas* does survive, no further miracle is needed for nourishment to be possible. And how 'physically' he took transubstantiation here is shown by the analogy he offers to support this claim — do not some 'Indians' live off the smell of apples, and has not the smell of wine been known to intoxicate (J. 93)? It is pleasing to notice that the same Indians are invoked by Alan of Lille in his *De fide catholica* (about 1185 to 1190) to prove the direct opposite. For Alan, nothing of the bread survives in the consecrated host except whiteness, roundness, and taste, and so he has to consider what happens if a hungry mouse breaks into a pyx. (Mice come on the scene in more than one medieval treatise on the Eucharist — does this cast a dim religious light on conditions in medieval churches?) Alan contends that, if the mouse is nourished, it is nourished miraculously — and he supports belief in the possibility of such a miracle by the analogies of apple-smelling Indians and intoxication produced through the smell of wine (J. 93). William of Durham introduced some practical element into this word-spinning by claiming that someone had once tried to nourish himself in this 'eucharistic' way, but had failed (J. 153 — the text is probably from the later 1220s, and goes on to wonder whether the failure itself was inevitable or miraculous. As far as I can see, it says nothing of the irreverence in the supposed experiment). Aquinas shows refreshing common sense in rejecting the analogy with the Indians — activities of the sort can give no more than momentary solace, the body needs something more (ST 3.77.6). But once more, neither he nor the other authors here attempt to elucidate the question of nourishment by going beyond the order of physical reality. The question is put and answers are offered in physical terms, just in the way the other suggestions were put and answered. An acknowledgement of the special nature of transubstantiation does not mean that those terms are exchanged for those of some other order.

For Jorissen (pp. 150—4), confusion and disagreement over questions like eucharistic nourishment were first resolved by Alexander of Hales in his *Glossa in quatuor libros sententiarum* (about 1230), where distinctions are drawn in the way Aquinas was to draw them. For Alexander, the substantial form is no longer present in the consecrated host (so it is no longer bread), but the accidental forms survive (so the effects of bread, including nutritive power, survive also). After what I have already written about Aquinas, I can hardly pretend that his senior contemporary produced anything more intelligible than the Indians and mice of the earlier writers Jorissen has been describing. But Alexander had at his disposal the same systematic vocabulary as Aquinas, and so what he does write is at all events less anecdotally picturesque than what was offered by his predecessors. What concerns us here is to recall why the vocabulary was systematic.

Alexander and Aquinas were writing when the effects were being felt of the arrival in Western Europe of the full range of Aristotelian writings, and of the Greek, Islamic and Jewish commentaries upon them. This arrival — surely the greatest culture-shock that Europe has ever endured — had begun in the later twelfth century, and produced a variety of reactions, canonical as well as academic (the second volume of Copleston's *History* gives a clear account, with further references). I point here to one kind of effect only, but a kind that is central to the moral I draw from the debate we have been considering. With the arrival of the texts came Aristotle's comprehensive stock of terminology and distinctions; with those came the interests and questions asked by him; and so the limits of those questions came too.

I regard this effect as central to my chosen theme because it illustrates with peculiar force the complexity of the relationship between past and present. Aristotle's vocabulary, given a Latin dress by Cicero and Lucretius as well as by the schoolmen, lies behind the words we still use when talking about the nature of things. 'Matter', 'form', 'substance', 'category', 'potentiality', 'nature', 'principle', 'physics', 'philosophy': if

Whitehead was right in saying that all European philosophy is foot-notes to Plato, he should have added that the foot-notes are in Aristotle's language. But, inevitably even if not always obviously, the pattern and use of the words has not been unchanging. *Physica* is not 'physics', obviously, but neither is *philosophia* always 'philosophy'. We need to look at what earlier writers did with their words, not just at the words themselves. This is never easy, for as we look we cannot pretend to be unaware of how we now use the words. Just so, while drawing the distinctions we do, we need to admit that others may have been drawn by our predecessors. It is just here that the peculiar difficulty lies in appraising earlier writers, and why there is needed what I mentioned at the start of this essay – a willingness to let the past speak in its own terms. In one sense, the past cannot so speak, for speaking involves a listener too, and here the listener is in the present. Rather, what the willingness must involve is a continuous endeavour to let the otherness and distinctiveness of the past be the object of our appraisal, an appraisal that is part of our own distinctiveness. And that the endeavour is being made will show itself in the effort it demands of us.

I have found fault with Colombo's account of substance and of physical science, and with the claim made by him that medieval writers on eucharistic change situated it at some level beyond or below the reality with which our senses and intellect attempt to deal. I have claimed that Selvaggi's account of substance, precisely because it is philosophically superior to Colombo's, sits less easily to eucharistic employment, and that the uneasiness can be found in what Aquinas writes also. But I must now express a reservation concerning one remark made by Selvaggi himself, in a useful position-paper on the relations between philosophy and physics: that the chief fault of the medievals lay in 'thinking they were doing physics when they were really doing natural philosophy' (Selvaggi 1954, p. 201). I am not concerned to offer a detailed exegesis of this in its context, I simply take it as a starting-point for the remainder of this essay.

IV

We saw earlier how Aristotle proposed, as a general account of change, that a subject was informed (notice the Aristotelian cast of the word!), first with one form, then with another. His own favourite example (found in Metaphysics Z7 for instance, a passage already mentioned) is of a smith working some copper into a ball: the copper remains copper, but at the end of the process has a shape it did not have at the start. Let us attend to one limit of this account — it does not throw light on questions such as why hammering can do this to copper but not to glass. The limit, however, is in my opinion not helpfully described by contrasting 'natural philosophy' with 'physics', as if distinctions drawn nowadays can be applied without more ado to Aristotle or to the schoolmen who read him in the Middle Ages. Still less helpful is the contrast made by Colombo — that the scholastic tradition was concerned with the ontological reality of things in a way that modern physics is not. Any move of this sort fails by being too easy. We must come to terms with the shift in aims and interests there has been, even when the vocabulary itself survived the shift. So let us see very briefly what was involved in the great changes associated with the rise of the 'new sciences' in the seventeenth century.

The rapid growth of opposition in that century to the medieval legacy of Aristotle is notorious. Less well known, but needing to be borne in mind, is that questionings of the legacy had begun further back. Something as central to the change as the struggle for adequate concepts in which to express the movement of bodies — Galileo's *Dialogues* were to give it vivid expression — can be found in the writings of some later scholastics (the third volume of Copleston's *History* has a chapter on them, with further references). I make this point to show why I do not think that the opposition characteristic of the seventeenth century is properly described as between medieval 'philosophy' and modern 'physics' or 'science'. Talking that way puts the cart before the horse, for it draws a distinction that is itself part of the appraisal we make in our own time of what preceded us. The distinction is defensible, but it comes at the end of a process of understanding. We need to begin by letting the schoolmen and their opponents speak for themselves.

Aristotle's distinctions were drawn as part of a general attempt to make sense of the changes and stabilities in the world. The texts of his that became available to the Schoolmen included works concerned with a variety of things, from the parts of animals to the movements of the planets. Of experience of how things behave there was enough, and to spare, but of controlled experiment and observation guided by mathematical concepts and considerations there was virtually none ('virtually' I insert to take account of what was available in the pseudo-Aristotelian *Mechanica*). Moreover, the laws of movement of bodies stand far away from the range of natural observation in which lay one of Aristotle's strengths, and from the theological explanations he favoured. Small wonder that what medieval questioning there was in Dynamics was confined to a few places and people. What sets the seventeenth century apart from earlier times is — among other things — the range and novelty and distribution of the questions asked in it. As the century advanced, ever more topics were being canvassed that had not been raised by the Schoolmen at all, and it is this widening of interest that for us, three centuries later, limits and changes the status of what we now see the Schoolmen to have been doing: the intellectual picture has become so very much wider, such is the way of time with ideas. We should think it odd to say that Socrates has changed on the grounds that, Theaetetus having grown up, the older man is no longer taller than the younger. But odd or not, that is how ideas and creations of the mind change — they are changed by the advent of their successors. That we describe this or that activity of the medieval scholastics as we do is in part the result of how we describe those who came after them. And how we describe either party need not be how it would have described itself.

I illustrate my claim with some texts of the seventeenth century, from scholastics writing at that time when Aristotelian tradition was being widely rejected. The nature of the defence they offer shows that, far from distinguishing between 'natural philosophy' and 'physics', they regarded the scholastic tradition and the new sciences as rivals, and offered evidence in favour of their own views.[7] Consider some texts to do with the need for substantial forms: it would be hard to think of anything more 'physical' than the reasons offered. For the Jesuits at Coimbra ('Conimbricenses', 1625), the grounds are that, since the same inert matter is in all things, the form is needed to account for their distinctive properties (for a man, thinking; for a horse, neighing). When De La Grange, whose work of 1675 is specifically against the innovators, expresses unease about the proofs offered for substantial forms, it is that in his view the proofs fail to show the insufficiency of shape and movement as explanations of things. He then suggests a better example — the production by fire of air and smoke — and (significantly) mentions the persistence in movement of projectiles. Goudin (1692) offers the magnet as a proof of the need for substantial forms, as well as the capacities of jade to cure neuralgia and of jasper to staunch blood. Given proofs of that sort, it is not surprising that the eclectic Du Hamel (1681) supports his own dissatisfaction with substantial forms by the phrase 'chemistry can dissolve out anything'.

From these I turn to a final example that is specifically eucharistic, but just as 'physical'. It comes from the writings of the Jesuit Grimaldi, whose work on Optics was admired by Newton, and who had explained the transparency of liquids in terms of pores in them. An objection derived from transubstantiation was raised to this: what is in the chalice after the consecration is transparent, and yet, since there is no longer wine there, there can be no pores either.

For such authors, the scholastic heritage was concerned with giving an account of physical reality, and for them transubstantiation itself, though miraculous, involved the very same distinctions as had been drawn in order to describe the nature of things. Colombo's 'placing' of transubstantiation is quite alien to all this, as also is the account of substance that he offers and claims to be associated with traditional eucharistic speculation. But what of Selvaggi? Is he not just as alien to the rivalry which those authors saw between Aristotelianism and the innovators of the seventeenth century? For him, as we have seen, Aristotle's distinctions are a necessary complement to science: what difference could be greater?

A difference there is; but it is, if I may so speak, a different kind of difference. Selvaggi is well acquainted with modern physics, and naturally has no intention of reinstating Aristotelian doctrines like the four elements, natural and unnatural motion, and the distinction between celestial and sublunary matter. He contends that distinctions drawn by Aristotle can do justice to an understanding of the composition of things in a way that purely mechanical explanations cannot, and I found fault not so much with the content of this claim as with its exiguousness. I can now complement what I wrote in terms of what we have just seen. Selvaggi, like many other scholastics, filters out from the scholastic inheritance what he regards as obsolete, leaving himself with generic distinctions and terminology that can be a concomitant to any scientific account of the world. What he (and others) ought to make clearer is that the filtering allots to medieval scholasticism a place and status it did not have for medieval schoolmen. Selvaggi is placing it in a much wider setting, where a far greater range of questions has come to be put than then could ever have been put. His phrase, that the schoolmen 'thought they were doing physics when really they were doing natural philosophy' is misleadingly like 'Tom thought he was drinking claret when really he was drinking burgundy', when Tom agrees with us before we start as to what those kinds of wine are. That is not how things are here. What we have here is rather a reappraisal *post factum* of an earlier style of thought, brought on by a consideration of what has taken place in the interval.

But if Selvaggi's phrase can mislead, Colombo's approach is out of true from the start. Not only does he fail to do justice to modern physical science, and to the nature of medieval speculation about the Eucharist, he writes in a way that is speciously and damagingly attractive for those who wish to believe in transubstantiation. His account of substance lends itself, we have seen, to taking distinctions as if they were dissections. But it is precisely 'dissection' at which modern science has been so successful — the constitution of things has become known as never before. What greater apparent boon for an account of transubstantiation than to be construed in 'dissective' terms? The abuse of Aristotelian distinctions involved in any account of transubstantiation receives thereby a curious *aggiornamento*. If the scientist can dissect, so can the scholastic theologian. Indeed, if Colombo's phenomenalistic view of physics be accepted, anything he can do we can do better.

A post-script is hard to resist. Colombo and Selvaggi agree, not only about the status of eucharistic belief, but about the permanence of dogmatic statements. Colombo (1955, p. 110) quotes with approval a statement thereon by Selvaggi: the terms of conciliar definitions have an immutable significance; to grasp their significance, we must revive in us the mentality and circumstances of the definers; we must then translate into modern language the immutable content of the dogma (1949, p. 10). Less than forty years on, the words seem light-years away. So, I would add, do other items in the volumes I have used for this essay. Naming names would be unkind, it is enough to say that each I am to quote comes from a one-time colleague of Selvaggi at the Gregorian. In the volume whence came Selvaggi 1949 I find A.I.H. excluded even more than by recent noises (p. 263), and in the volume for Colombo 1955 a belief that all miracle-stories in the gospels are true (p. 305). And (this is my favourite) the volume that yielded J. Clarke 1951 also yields 'all earnest Catholics have always welcomed papal directives with joy, for they know that the light which enlightens every man is found in the Church' (p. 5). As a compatriot of Selvaggi and Colombo reputedly put it, *Eppur si muove*.

If we are dissatisfied with Colombo's account of substance — still more, if we are dissatisfied with what has to be done with any account of substance to make it eucharistically acceptable — our dissatisfaction should be consistent. The merit of Selvaggi's account was to conceive of substance in the setting of a reality that can be the object of judgment based upon perception. The limitation of the account, I suggest, shows itself in Selvaggi's way of expressing the relation of present to past. It is almost as if, in this context, he favoured Colombo's account of substance. But change, judgment and time we have seen to be essentially involved in questions raised by the debate we have examined. How then can they not be raised in any debate over the inheritance of belief? At all events, debates cannot be silenced by appeals to immutable contents or substantial identities. We have seen too much. Substance was where we came in.

NOTES AND BIBLIOGRAPHY

1. See the exchange of views that appeared in *New Blackfriars* in 1972 and 1973; a collection of essays by Herbert McCabe, forthcoming from Geoffrey Chapman, will reprint them. In a volume to be published by the Cambridge University Press I develop my views on the topic, and material from this essay will be incorporated. I add once for all here that I have taken some themes only from the debate between Selvaggi and Colombo, and that I do not follow its fortunes here after 1957.

2. An account of several articles written on transubstantiation before the War is provided (in lurid Americanese) in J.Clarke, 1951. I have been no more successful than he in getting beyond the liberal extracts printed in Ternus to the original source where 'Fr. M.' wrote – a periodical called *Volk im Werden* for 1937. I gather from Ternus (p. 220) that 'dogmatic physics' was blamed there, not just for the reason given in the text, but because its *a priori* character opposed it (surprisingly) to theories in physics devised by Germans, and (unsurprisingly) to theories devised by Jews. Ternus, incidentally, attributes the 'non-metaphysical' view of science to Husserl among others (p. 222). Neither Colombo nor Selvaggi mentions this.

3. What I wrote will not, I hope, be taken as showing a lack of sympathy for Selvaggi, whose evaluation of science I find both knowledgeable and serious (I find Colombo's neither). My point is that linking what is disparate in time and setting needs a good deal of filling out if it is not to lead to vacuous anachronism. For another example, see Selvaggi, 1949, pp. 34–5, where particle-identity in quantum-theory is philosophically elucidated in terms of what Aquinas writes about mixtures.

4. Newman (always a bad omen for reasoned belief) both anticipates Colombo's view of substance in the *Apologia* ('General Answer to Mr Kingsley') and makes transubstantiation a matter of *power*. 'I cannot tell *how* it is; but I say, "Why should it not be? What's to hinder it? What do I know of substance or matter? Just as much as the greatest philosphers and that is nothing at all."' A good antidote to all this is in the eleventh chapter of Trevelyan's *Life of Macaulay*, where he is seen as distinguishing between belief in transubstantiation and belief in miracles – it is like having Lazarus decomposing in the grave, while being called upon to believe that he is really alive.

5. The phrases in quotation-marks and the drift of the argument are found in an article by Francis Clark, who very honestly makes the distinction be demanded, not only by 'all sane philosophy', but by 'the eucharistic doctrine of the Church' (F.Clark, 1967, p. 40). What he does not make clear is that mere distinctions are not enough for what the doctrine is seen as demanding.

6. Hay into glass *is* natural, whatever some modern authors cited by Jorissen may think. My colleague Dr D.M. Knight tells me that Sir Humphry Davy investigated

the beads of glass found when haystacks burned down (hay contains silicon).
7. I leave references and further details to 'Some Seventeenth-Century Accounts of Transubstantiation', to appear in the forthcoming Festschrift for Herbert McCabe.

Bibliography

Clark, F. (1967) 'The Real Presence: An Appraisal of a Recent Controversy', *Adoremus* 49, pp. 32–48.

Clark, J.T. (1951) 'Physics, Philosophy, Transubstantiation, Theology', *Theological Studies* 12, pp. 24–51.

Colombo, C. (1955) 'Teologia, filosofia a fisica nella dottrina della transustanziazione', *La Scuola Cattolica* 83, pp. 89–124.

—(1956) 'Ancora sulla dottrina della transustanziazione e la fisica moderna', *La Scuola Cattolica* 84, pp. 263–288.

Hoenen, P. (1945) *Cosmologia*. Pontificia Universitas Gregoriana.

—(1951/1968) 'Descartes' Mechanicism', trans. P.J. Crittenden, in W. Doney (ed.) *Descartes: A Collection of Critical Essays*. Macmillan, 1968, pp. 353–368.

Jorissen, H. (1965) *Die Entfaltung der Transubstantiationslehre bis zum Beginn der Hochscholastik*. (Münsterische Beiträge zur Theologie, Heft 28, 1). Aschendorffsche Verlagsbuchhandlung.

Selvaggi, F. (1949) 'Il concetto di sostanza nel Dogma Eucaristico in relazione alla fisica moderna', *Gregorianum* 30, pp. 7–45.

—(1954) 'Fisica, Cosmologia, Metafisica' in *Studi Filosofici intorno all' "Esistenza"*. . . (*Analecta Gregoriana*, vol. 67), Pontificia Universitas Gregoriana, pp. 195–201.

—(1956) 'Realtà fisica e sostanza sensibile nella dottrina eucaristica', *Gregorianum* 37, pp. 16–33.

—(1957) 'Ancora intorno ai concetti di "sostanza sensibile" e "realtà fisica"', *Gregorianum* 38, pp. 503–14.

Ternus, J. (1937) '"Dogmatische Physik" in der Lehre vom Altarssakrament?', *Stimmen der Zeit*, pp. 220–30.

8

KAI NIELSEN'S
ATHEISM

by HUGO MEYNELL

Professor of Philosophy, University of Calgary

When I started getting into philosophy, and meeting other students interested in the subject, the assumption seemed to be widespread that it was impossible both to be a serious philosopher and to be a believer in God. But when one was tempted to despair on the matter, one remembered Fr Copleston, who both believed in God and knew a great deal more about philosophy than those who maintained this assumption. When I first saw him, he was giving a lecture, followed by questions and answers, to a student society which consisted almost entirely of atheists and agnostics; I shall never forget his performance, which, as I have come to realise since, was vintage Copleston — a wonderful blend of courtesy and good humour with philosophical erudition and skill.

From the point of view of the believer, the situation is now rather better, although old attitudes die hard. If one is to take account of contemporary philosophical atheism at its best, one can hardly do better than attend to the work of Kai Nielsen. To investigate Nielsen's arguments is one of the most useful exercises which may be undertaken by those who obstinately continue to believe, in spite of everything, that there is still a case to be made for a rational theism.

In setting out what he takes to be the essence of atheism, Nielsen suggests that it is a more complex matter than a mere belief that it is probably or certainly false that there is a God. The atheist, as he sees it, rejects belief in God for one or more of the following reasons, depending on what sort of 'God' is at issue. If it is a matter of an anthropomorphic kind of God, the atheist does indeed claim that it is with overwhelming probability false that there is such a being. If, however, an anthropomorphic God is not in question, the atheist rejects belief in such a being as 'either meaningless, unintelligible, contradictory, incomprehensible, or incoherent'. If, as in the case of some allegedly 'religious' thinkers, 'God' is being used openly or covertly to refer to love or to moral ideals, the atheist objects to such a use as deceptively masking what is really a kind of atheism.[1]

Where this third use of the term 'God' is concerned, I strongly agree with Nielsen. If all that someone implies by saying that there is a God is that love is an effective force in human life, or that people follow moral ideals, the term is much better dropped. As to the other two cases, Nielsen is in effect setting the theist a dilemma. Either the God is anthropomorphic, in which case the supposition of the existence of such a 'cosmic mickey mouse' is intelligible and coherent, but can be shown to be almost certainly false; or it is non-anthropomorphic, in which case the supposition does not reach the dignity of error, being meaningless, or contradictory, or whatever. Now I believe that Nielsen's apparently exhaustive dilemma, 'anthropomorphic' or 'non-anthropomorphic', does not completely cover the possibilities. While some of the more enthusiastic exponents of the *via negativa* have played into the hands of atheists by qualifying terms applied to God to vanishing-point or beyond, classical theism has by and large balanced the 'negative way' by an 'affirmative way'. And the 'affirmative way' has maintained that *some* of the properties of human beings belong to an infinite or superlative extent to God. 'Anthropomorphism', in the sense that this is a term of abuse for classical theism, is a matter of believing or implying that God literally has other human properties, characterist-ically those which involve embodiment or changeability. Very roughly and summarily, we as human beings know and understand just a little about ourselves and the world, and our will has very restricted scope and power. Further, we are morally frail, and liable to be distracted by desire or fear from doing what we believe to be right. In common with us, God is supposed to have understanding, knowledge, and will; God understands all possible states of affairs, and wills those which actually obtain.[2] In contrast with us, God's will and purpose are not to be swayed by desire or fear as is the human will, and indeed are not subject to change at all;[3] if they are deemed to be so, this is a fair example of anthropomorphism. According to Nielsen, we have no clue to 'what could be *meant* by speaking of an infinite individual transcendent to the world.'[4] I have just tried to show briefly what could be and in fact is meant. God is infinite in that the divine knowledge and understanding are unrestricted, the divine will irresistible; God 'transcends' the world in that there is a distinction between God and everything else that exists, which depends solely on the divine will.

The late J.L. Mackie's *The Miracle of Theism*[5] argues with force and skill for atheism, and is several times commended by Nielsen. But it is remarkable that Mackie's atheism is strikingly dissimilar to Nielsen's in that *he acknowledges that classical theism makes perfectly good sense*; but *denies that there is any good reason for believing that it is true*. To allude once more to Nielsen's list of alleged defects in non-anthropo-morphic theism, Mackie claims that classical theism is perfectly meaningful, intelligible, non-contradictory, comprehensible, and coherent; but that there are many reasons for supposing it false, and none for supposing it true which do not break down under examin-ation. Significantly, he charges those who defend a view like Nielsen's of basing their position upon a theory of meaning which has itself been proved to be false.[6] If the logical positivists did not invent the thesis that theism is senseless rather than false, at all events they made it their own. They defended the thesis on the basis of an articulate theory of meaning, which was roughly to the effect that every meaningful proposition which is not true by definition is such that it can at least in principle be verified or falsified by sense-experience. Statements about God, they maintained, cannot even in principle be thus verified or falsified, and are therefore senseless. But, notoriously, the verification principle turned out to be meaningless when applied to itself. It is certainly not true by definition, unless one stipulates a definition of 'meaningful' which does not correspond with common usage. Nor is there any course of sense-experience by which one could, even in principle, verify or falsify the proposition that all meaningful state-ments which are not true by definition may in principle be verified or falsified by sense-experience.

Nielsen does not expound any general theory of meaning, empiricist or otherwise; but, he says, one does not need to avail oneself of such a theory to show that there is something at the very least highly problematic about the meaningfulness of God-talk.[7] But presumably, to rule out as meaningless in a manner which is not arbitrary a way of talking which is well-established, one must have *some* conception of what makes a statement meaningful rather than otherwise; and if this is spelt out clearly and distinctly, with serious reasons given for accepting it, this would seem to amount to a theory of meaning if anything would. If it is *not* thus spelt out, it is hard to see what is gained except a measure of obfuscation; one is being asked to accept the view that God-talk is meaningless, or at least only very problematically meaningful, in that it fails to meet criteria of meaningfulness which are not, and apparently cannot be, clearly and distinctly set out and justified.

In fact, the criteria which are implicit in Nielsen's ruling-out of God-talk show every sign that they are of that empiricist kind, difficulties in the setting-out and justification of which have just been sketched in the case of logical positivism.[8] In particular, he sets great store by the principle, emphasised especially by Hume and Kant in connection with the possibility of rational arguments for the existence of God, that nothing can be an object of knowledge which cannot be an object of experience. Meister Eckhart comments severely on those who presume that God might be seen with the same eyes with which one sees a cow; but evidently, for philosophers in this tradition, it would be better for

God to be thus visible. But the principle has more to be held against it than the objections of a late medieval Christian mystic. It seems to me, indeed, astonishing that a philosophical doctrine with so little to commend it should have gained such wide currency. Perhaps the best explanation is that it makes life so much more simple for the enemies of rational theism. The doctrine is also, as I shall soon try to show, readily confused with a much more acceptable one, and may be taken on by the unwary as a substitute for it.

The fact is that there are many *prima facie* instances of knowledge where what is said to be known cannot conceivably itself be or become a part of our experience or an object of our observation. Three types of example spring to mind — 'knowledge' of the remote past, of the thoughts and feelings of persons other than ourselves, and of the theoretical entities postulated by practitioners of mature sciences. Nielsen appears to maintain that it is conceivable that one might somehow perceive an electron or an omega particle[9] — I do not think this is so, but will concede the point for the sake of argument. But to 'perceive' the thoughts and feelings of others *is* inconceivable. At a pinch, one can get over both of these problems, of the knowledge of the entities described by nuclear physicists and of other minds, by resorting to operationism in the one case, and behaviourism or physicalism in the other. That is to say, one may claim that statements about theoretical entities in physics are reducible in meaning to statements about observable things and states of affairs, and that statements about other minds are really statements about behaviour or the states of brains or nervous systems. But even granted that these manoeuvres will work — in fact I think it can quite easily be shown that they will not — the application of the underlying principle to statements about the remote past, to statements of the kind made by historians and palaeontologists, will lead to the most manifest absurdities. Who is going to claim that either one can have no knowledge of the past, or statements about the past are reducible in meaning to statements about experiences of the present or future? Nielsen seeks to drive a wedge between statements about God on the one hand, and statements about fundamental particles on the other, by saying that there is no *logical* ban on the notion of perceiving fundamental particles.[10] But even if one accepts this, as there seems little reason to do, Nielsen's position is not much helped unless he either is willing to argue that we could conceivably observe the contents of other minds and the events of the remote past, or will draw the inference, repugnant alike to science and to common sense, that we can have no knowledge of these matters.

In connection with his claim that God is unobservable in principle in a way that fundamental particles are not, Nielsen urges that the manner in which God is supposed to 'transcend' the universe is utterly problematic.[11] (It may be noted in passing that other minds, fundamental particles, and the things and events of the past, themselves in a certain sense may be said to 'transcend' the evidence which we may have for their existence and nature, according to the argument which I have just put forward; in that there is no strictly valid deductive inference either way between the statement of a putative fact in any of these classes, and statements about the evidence with which such a statement may be supported.) To clarify the notion of 'transcendence' at issue in talk of God's relation to the universe, it is necessary to make some distinctions which philosophers and theologians have not always been at sufficient pains to draw; it is an index of the merit and importance of Nielsen's work that he forces them to do so. If one means by 'God transcends the universe', 'God is neither the whole universe nor any part of it', and one assumes, as it is not unnatural to do, that by 'the universe' is meant 'the sum-total of what exists', then a perfectly sound proof is to be had that God does not exist. (In fact, it is an 'ontological proof' in that it follows directly from a conception of what God is; but, like other ontological proofs, it may be suspected of underlying fallacy, as we shall see.) The proof runs as follows. Everything which exists is either the universe or a part of it; God as 'transcending' the universe is neither; therefore God does not exist.

But it seems more fruitful, especially in the light of what has already been said about the positive notions at our disposal for characterising what is meant by 'God', to ask the question of God's existence in another way. Is it possible, or even likely, that the universe in the sense just given (the sum-total of what exists — let us call this 'universe A') includes that which is related to the rest of it (let us call this 'universe B') rather as we as conscious agents are related to what we do and make? A being who conceives and wills the (rest of) the universe, part of 'universe A' but distinct from 'universe B', does not seem inconceivable; we have a model of the nature of such a being, as I have suggested already, in our own conceiving and willing. This is in accordance with a view which has long been held by theists both Eastern and Western — it is as characteristic of Ramanuja as of

Augustine — that it is through consideration of the nature of the human self that we can obtain the clearest idea available to us of the nature of God.

An objection commonly made, and reiterated by Nielsen, is that the universe is not something that we can reasonably or even coherently make statements about as a whole.[12] If the point of this is that it is sophistical to postulate extra entities in order to explain the sum total of what exists, I have just conceded this, but have argued that such postulation forms no proper part of the defence of a rational theism. But taken in any other way, it is difficult to see why one should take this objection seriously. No one objects when scientists inform us that hydrogen is the commonest element in the universe, or that the universe came into existence with a 'big bang' some eighteen thousand million years ago, or that the universe is liable to end in a state of 'heat death'.

I have argued that one cardinal doctrine of empiricism, at least implicitly espoused by Nielsen, leads to intolerable paradoxes when consistently applied. It seems that once such principles for eliminating God-talk as meaningless, incoherent, and so on, are clarified, they break down; if the principles are not and cannot be clarified — if one is operating, as Nielsen admits he is, with no articulate theory of meaning[13] — they ought to carry no conviction. It might reasonably be urged that it is proper to embrace a 'softer' form of 'empiricism', whereby only those entities are to be admitted which must be postulated as providing *adequate explanation* for what may be the direct object of sensation, experience or observation. Such a mitigation of empiricism copes, indeed, with the three classes of knowledge which I mentioned earlier. Though we cannot perceive the emperor Caligula, a positron, or our neighbour's itches or speculations, such entities are properly said to exist or occur as explaining, respectively, say, marks on documents or monuments, patterns in bubble chambers, and sequences of human movement. But it is not quite obvious that so generous an extension of empiricism would be bound to rule out God; Aquinas, among others, thought that while all knowledge was based on experience, one could come to some knowledge of God as 'cause', or ultimate explanation, of the world of experience.

Nielsen properly reminds his readers that he is not claiming that the concept of God 'is unintelligible or meaningless full stop';[14] to claim that God exists, or that God loves us, is like claiming that the square root of two is puce or that the emperor Tiberius is the highest prime number. But I wonder whether his claims as to its unintelligibility and meaninglessness do not *either* prove too much — ruling out ways of talking which he would wish to accept as in order — *or* have to be qualified to death. Might not Nielsen's argument against theism, that it is either crudely false or qualified beyond the limits of significance, be properly applied to his own claim as to the 'meaninglessness' or 'unintelligibility' of theism? To say that the term 'God' is *utterly* meaningless, he concedes, would plainly be wrong; for the excellent reason that one can distinguish between deviant and non-deviant instances of God-talk. Thus 'God loves us' will pass muster, at first sight at least, in a way that 'God lost weight last week' or 'God brews coffee' will not.[15] However, as Nielsen says, 'God' is a referring expression; thus when the believer says, for example, that God created us, 'there is the presumption that the speaker understands "God" and knows or believes in the reality of what is being talked about'.[16] But God cannot be indicated by ostension;[17] and if one cannot point at God, one ought at least to be able to get at God through some description or other. But none of these will do. If one says, for instance, that God is '"that being upon whom the world can be felt to be utterly dependent", nothing has been accomplished, for what does it *mean* to speak of "the world (the universe) as being utterly dependent" or even dependent at all?'[18] The same applies to such phrases as 'creator of the universe out of nothing'.[19] Nielsen concludes that 'the concept of God is so incoherent that there could not possibly be a referent for the word "God"'; assuming that, in accordance with the practice of sophisticated Christians, Jews and Muslims, one has abandoned belief in an anthropomorphic God as a false superstition.[20]

This argument is to be countered by reference to what I have already said about the ambiguity in both the concept of 'anthropomorphism' and that of 'the world' or 'the universe'. If God is conceived *in no way whatever* as anthropomorphic, and if one means by the world or universe simply the sum-total of what exists, then Nielsen's argument is sound. But suppose one means by 'God' the intelligent will on whom all else is supposed to depend, rather as human actions and products depend on intelligent wills; and by the world or the universe all else that exists other than this being. In that case, the objections simply fall to the ground. Incidentally, while God certainly cannot lose weight, strictly speaking God can and does brew coffee, assuming only that coffee is brewed — as follows directly from Aquinas's impeccably orthodox maxim, 'God operates in every operation of nature and will'.[21]

On these and similar arguments against the meaningfulness of religious discourse, one cannot do better than quote Kolakowski: 'Time and again we fall upon the same *petitio principii*: believers are told that their language is intrinsically unintelligible and that they themselves cannot understand it, and this because their language fails to meet the rules of intelligibility established by a philosophical ideology whose main purpose is to shape these rules in such a way as to exclude religious language from the realm of intelligibility'.[22] I would add that the rules cannot be framed in such a way as not to have inconvenient consequences outside the realm of religion, when they are consistently applied.

I would concede to Nielsen that, even if belief in God cannot be shown to be meaningless or incoherent, some positive reasons ought to be available for it to be rational to believe in God. His strictures on all types of 'fideism' seem to me to be very well-taken.[23] If God is in no way required in explanation of what there is, or of any aspect of what there is, then God, as an unnecessary entity, ought to be disposed of by Ockham's razor. Now each of the kinds of examples that I cited exemplify a principle analogous to that of verification; that the real world is no more and no less than what is to be known through the application of intelligence and reason, respectively in the formulation and testing of hypotheses, to experience. By such means we, or rather the scientific community, have arrived at the impressive systems of contemporary physical, chemical, and biological science. What is to be known, apparently, is an *intelligible* which is to be apprehended progressively through inquiry into experience. To deny this is actually self-destructive. Such denial is either based on reasonable judgment of evidence, or it is not. If it is not, it is not to be taken seriously; if it is, it presupposes the very thing that is being denied, that one tends to get at the truth by reasonable judgment of evidence. Science at once presupposes and demonstrates that the universe is intelligible; one may properly ask for the explanation of this very general fact about the world. That the world is not *really* intelligible (on the grounds that what really exists is the phantasmagoria of sense-impressions, as suggested by Hume, or unknowable things in themselves, as maintained by Kant) does not seem a satisfactory way out of the problem; the claim that one should not ask why the world is intelligible should be treated, unless indeed compelling reason can be given, with the same contempt as other attempts to stop people asking questions. An adequate answer seems to be, that the world's intelligibility is ultimately to be accounted for by the fact that it is conceived and willed by something analogous to a human intelligence. Evidently, such an argument could only be adequately set out at much greater length, as indeed I have tried to do elsewhere. The object of this paragraph has simply been to sketch the direction one might move in order to establish that classical theism was not only meaningful, but likely to be true.[24]

Nielsen follows most other modern opponents of rational theism in returning again and again to the authority of Hume and Kant, as destroying the basis for its claims as I have just described them. But it is notable that both of these philosphers also impugn the basic assumptions of science as usually conceived − that by means of mental procedures applied to experience we come to know of a world which exists and is as we find it to be independently of our experience and of our mental procedures. For Hume, all of our knowledge which extends further than our present experience and our memory depends on the holding of the laws of cause and effect; but the laws of cause and effect have no more substantial basis than our psychological habits.[25] In spite of the efforts of his successors, and indeed of Hume himself,[26] to mitigate the rigours of this scheme, its real upshot is a thoroughgoing scepticism which is just as damaging to science as to rational theology. Kant of course appreciates the *a priori* element in human knowledge, and emphasises with unprecedented power the creative activity of the human mind in coming to know the world. But he infers from this that things in themselves are unknowable to us; that 'nature' both as perceived and as explained by the sciences is the result of an inscrutable interaction between such unknowable things in themselves.[27] To put it very simply and crudely, science at first sight yields knowledge of a real intelligible world through inquiry into the sensible; Hume in effect denies this intelligible aspect of reality due to the thoroughness of his empiricism, with scepticism as the inevitable result; while Kant ascribes the intelligibility of nature to the human mind itself, leaving knowledge stranded in an apparent as opposed to a real world. Now it is often supposed that the scepticism of the Humean scheme, and the confining of human knowledge to appearance as opposed to reality by the Kantian one, have nothing to do with the aspersions of these philosophers on rational theism. I believe this to be a mistake. A full-blooded scientific realism presupposes that, by use of intelligence and reason on our experience, we progressively come to know a world which exists prior to and independently of our intelligence or reason or experience. Reflection shows that this world cannot but be intelligible. And the God of rational theism is the intelligent will supposed to ground this intelligible world.

I will conclude with some comments on Nielsen's remarks about the relation, or rather the lack of it, of religion to morality.[28] I strongly agree with his attack on the view that morality should be based entirely on revealed divine commands. On the contrary, our own moral insights have to be used in determining whether any putative divine revelation really is such or not; insofar as this is not done, any moral abomination whatever may be perpetrated on the pretext that it is divinely commanded. Nielsen also attacks the 'natural law' doctrine expounded by many theists, on the familiar grounds that it presupposes an essential human nature which is intrinsically problematic, and that it involves an illegitimate transition from what *is* to what *ought to* be.[29] However, the upshot of his own account of the justification of morality is much more like the 'natural law' doctrine than he supposes. Natural law morality, in common with Nielsen's morality of 'considered moral judgments' in 'reflective equilibrium', is a matter of attending to the preconditions of human fulfilment in general, and of intelligently and reasonably establishing what kinds of action are good accordingly. It is to be conceded that 'natural law' has very often been conceived much more rigidly than this (though Thomas Aquinas is studiously vague on the matter), and if so it is to be rejected or at least substantially modified; but if 'the natural law' is to be thought of as what would be arrived at by a process like that recommended by Nielsen, it still dovetails very neatly into a theistic world view. So far as inferences from a putative divine revelation persistently and seriously conflict with moral judgments in wide reflective equilibrium, one may properly maintain either that the inferences must be unsound, or that the putative divine revelation is not really such.

It might be objected that in that case the notions of God and of divine revelation are morally otiose, since we can in any case determine what is good and right by reason on the basis of experience. But this would be wrong. Nothing is more typical of human affairs than the refusal, due to desire or fear, to apply intelligence and reason thoroughly in determining the general good, or to act in accordance with them given that one has done so. Theistic religion, both through the hopes and fears associated with it, and through its consciousness of companionship and help available in the moral struggle, supplies a motive for thinking out what is really good, as opposed to merely in the interests of oneself or one's group, and for acting accordingly. If some religious persons are apt to overlook the existence and significance of the natural conscience in human beings, secularists are prone to underestimate the strength and ubiquity of the forces which interfere with its operation.

Nielsen admits in passing that 'religion — for some people at any rate, may be of value in putting their *hearts* into virtue';[30] but I do not think he makes anything like enough of this. It is a melancholy fact about the world that many persons are made to suffer not only *although* they pursue the path of virtue, but *because* they do so — like those who resist the unjust prescriptions of a tyrannical government, whether of the right, the left, or the centre. Should one not at least *wish* it to be the case that virtue will ultimately be rewarded with happiness, a thesis which, short of belief both in an afterlife and in God, is certainly false?[31] I admit that these points, if one concedes them, show only the *importance* for morality of God's existence; they do not begin to show *that* God exists.[32] For this other types of argument are needed, the nature of which I have already tried to sketch.

Nielsen mentions the opinion that 'God makes something good simply by commanding it', and adds that this is the view that 'a consistent Divine Command theorist should take'.[33] The trouble here is with the adverb 'simply'; it appears to me that a theist who believes in natural law or related notions will conceive divine commands as of a piece with the whole of divine creation. At that rate, God does not make courage or temperance or fidelity good *simply* by commanding them; God makes them good by creating human beings in such a way that they will flourish in the long run, both individually and socially, by displaying these qualities. I agree with Nielsen that what he would call a 'simple' divine command theory, which takes no account of the nature and needs of human beings and other creatures, is not only erroneous, but thoroughly pernicious; people have claimed that God's authority for doing some pretty frightful things, and the notion of a 'natural law' or a type of morality such as Nielsen's (they come in the last analysis, as I have already argued, to much the same thing) should be used as a check on such tendencies.

As Nielsen sees it, 'natural moral law theorists confuse talking about what is the case with talking about what ought to be the case. They confuse *de jure* statements with *de facto* statements. A statement about what normal people seek, strive for or desire is a factual, non-normative statement.' And one cannot deduce what is normative from any such statement or conjunction of such statements.[34] The link between is and ought, it may be replied, is a matter of happiness and justice. By way of exception, a good action may be one which is unfair, or does not tend to realise the greater happiness of the greatest number — that is what was really proved by Moore in his arguments against 'the naturalistic fallacy'. But someone who did not realise that in general, *ceteris paribus*, a good action tends to promote happiness among those whom it affects, would not know the meaning of 'good'.[35] And how human beings and other animals may attain happiness depends on the sorts of beings that they are. A being programmed (so to say) for using its reason and acting accordingly will not come to fulfilment if it is prevented from doing so, and will be frustrated and unhappy as a result. Whether the 'programming' is due to God or evolution or both does not affect the immediate issue. It should be noted that Nielsen himself convincingly sketches the way in which one may take the needs and feelings of people into account in establishing what is good; but the type of argument exemplified by the beginning of this paragraph is just as fatal to this, if taken to be sound, as to a 'natural law' morality.

For Nielsen, morality is 'a practical . . ., attitude-molding, rule-governed activity, whose central function it is to adjudicate the conflicting desires and interests of everyone involved in an impartial and fair manner. In morality we are most fundamentally concerned with the reasoned pursuit of what is in everyone's best interest'.[36] Well, if what is good, as Nielsen admits implicitly though not in so many words, is what is reasonably to be determined as in everyone's best interest, here the normative does seem to depend on the factual, given that what is in our best interest depends on how we have evolved or been created to be. That a strict logical deduction between the relevant facts and the right prescriptions may not be feasible does not affect the issue. No more is there any relation of strict deduction between the statements of theoretical science and statements about the occurrence of the observational data on which their verisimilitude depends; but it would be a bold man or woman who inferred from this that the sciences do not depend on observational data. It looks as though, on Nielsen's view, the truth of moral statements has much the same relation to people's desires and interests as that of scientific statements does to actual or possible observations. The religious moralist may admit this; and indeed his reflections and arguments are liable to start from it. Both to work out rationally what is really good, when it goes against one's individual and group interest, and to implement that good in practice, are often very difficult. The hopes and fears which go with belief in God, as well as the conviction that one's trials and struggles are witnessed, may be and have been potent factors in overcoming such difficulties. I have already conceded that, even if it can be shown that religion is useful to morality in this kind of way, this does not of itself show that it is true.

Natural law morality characteristically assumes that we are rational beings, as well as beings with other kinds of natural inclination; even, if one may put it in this way, that we are beings with a natural inclination to reason. Nielsen says that if we take into account 'only the inclinations that withstand reflection and examination – careful moral and factual scrutiny – we have already imported into morality principles that are not *simply*[37] derived from or based on human inclinations.' By proceeding in such a way, he suggests, 'we go beyond a natural law morality that tries to discover what we ought to do – on their account what God wills for us – by taking careful note of our natural inclinations.'[38] But it is difficult to see on what grounds Nielsen holds that such a procedure 'goes beyond' a natural law morality; on most traditional accounts of such a morality, for example that of Aquinas, it would exemplify it. No exponent of natural law of whom I have heard would disagree for a moment with the thesis that we have to bring reason to bear on natural inclinations (conceding for a moment Nielsen's apparent assumption that the pursuit of reason is not itself a 'natural inclination') in order to determine what is good. I would readily agree with Nielsen that it is impossible to show that contraception is against 'natural law' as so conceived;[39] indeed, I would say that it is largely attempts to use 'natural law' arguments to support such conclusions which have got the notion itself into disrepute.

And such a note of concession is indeed a proper one on which to end. Reflective theists have every reason to be grateful to Nielsen, for having provided such a skilful and comprehensive series of arguments with which to test their position.

NOTES

1. *Philosophy and Atheism* (Prometheus Books: Buffalo, New York, 1985), pp. 20–1. This work will be referred to as PA in subsequent notes.
2. Certain qualifications have to be made; on Aquinas's view, God *permits*, rather than actively *wills*, the mental refusals underlying the evil acts of finite rational beings. For Aquinas on evil, see *Summa Theologiae* I, xix and xlviii.
3. This is the view of classical theism as exemplified by Aquinas. For process theology, God is subject to change at least in the details of his purposes. See C. Hartshorne, *The Divine Relativity* (New Haven: Yale University Press, 1964).
4. PA, p. 20.
5. Clarenden: Oxford University Press, 1982.
6. J.L. Mackie, *The Miracle of Theism*, pp. 1–3.

7. PA, p. 227 (Note 4).

8. PA, pp. 16, 18, 19 and *passim*.

9. PA, p. 17.

10. Loc. cit.

11. Loc. cit.

12. PA, p. 83.

13. PA, p. 227.

14. PA, p. 21.

15. PA, pp. 82–3.

16. PA, p. 79.

17. PA, p. 81.

18. PA, p. 83

19. PA, p. 85.

20. PA, p. 82.

21. *Deus operatur in omni operatione naturae ac voluntatis.*

22. L. Kolakowski, *Religion: If There Is a God* (New York: Oxford University Press, 1982), pp. 171–2; cited by Charles Davis, *Religious Studies Review* (April 1985), 145.

23. Nielsen has put into currency the admirable expression 'Wittgensteinian fideism', to refer to the view, with which I disagree as much as he does, that religious language is completely autonomous and self-justifying.

24. For similar arguments to God from the 'fit' between human reasoning powers and the cosmos, see R. Taylor, *Metaphysics* (Prentice-Hall: Englewood Cliffs, New Jersey, 1963), pp. 96–101. Also C.S. Lewis *Miracles* (Collins: London and Glasgow, 1960), chapter III.

25. Cf. *Enquiry Concerning Human Understanding* (London: Oxford University Press, 1957), Sect. V, Part I.

26. E.g. *Enquiry*, Sect. XII.

27. '. . . Such knowledge has to do with appearances, and must leave the thing in itself as indeed real *per se*, but as not known by us' (*Immanuel Kant's Critique of Pure Reason*, tr. Norman Kemp-Smith, London: Macmillan, 1978, p. 24).

28. PA, pp. 159–187.

29. PA, 163–6.

30. PA, p. 175.

31. The qualification ought to be made that in some religious systems karma plays a role equivalent to that of God in this respect; happiness is in the long run adjusted to virtue by a kind of inexorable law of nature.

32. This is the defect, I believe, in Kant's so-called 'moral' argument for the existence of God, at least as this is generally understood.

33. PA, p. 175.

34. PA, p. 165.

35. I have argued this at length in *Freud, Marx and Morals* (London: Macmillan, 1981), chapter 6.

36. PA, p. 166.

37. My italics.

38. PA, p. 168.

39. PA, pp. 167–71.

9

PROVIDENCE AND THE NARRATIVE OF LIFE

by STEWART SUTHERLAND

Professor of the History and Philosophy of Religion and Principal of King's College, University of London

'. . . work out your own salvation with fear
and trembling for it is God which worketh in
you both to will and do his good pleasure.'
Phil.2, 13–14

I

Theology atrophies if it fails to enter into the arena of the culture in which it is practised. This paper is an attempt to re-consider one element of belief in providence from the cumulative perspective of a number of discussions taking place in contemporary philosophical writing.

However, it is important to say at the outset that I am as yet unconvinced of the theological value of the idea of a 'story', which some would want to press upon us. Equally, despite the interesting book by George Stroup *The Promise of Narrative Theology*[1] it is not yet clear to me that there is something called 'narrative theology' as distinct from the attempts of a number of writers and thinkers to explore the application of the metaphor of 'narrative' to theological issues. I am happy to be included in the latter group, but in so far as I have any contribution to offer, in part it will be to point out how unclear we are about the notion of narrative. Certainly I am not making a contribution to a distinctive style of theological reasoning known as 'narrative theology', for I am not yet sure what such a theological style would be. This should not be seen as a matter for despair, however, for I am quite convinced both that there is much worthwhile intellectual work to be done on the metaphorical application of narrative to theology, and that theologians are making progress here which at least matched similar explorations in the context of philosophy. Of course, it need not be said more than once, but it must be said at least once that the primary location for the idea of narrative is in literature. We foget this at our peril.

Theologically, discussion of belief in Providence focuses upon a number of problems and one main distinction. The distinction is between the general and the special dispensations of Providence. The range of problems is divided on the whole between those which fall under the heading of the 'general' operations of Providence, for example, the sustaining role of God in creation, and those which fall under the heading of the 'special' operations of Providence, e.g. the specific or particular activities of God whether done or 'left undone'. In each case the emphasis of discussion is upon God working through the natural order of the physical and biological world. This applies also to discussions which centre upon the ideas of creation or miracle, where in the one case the focus is upon bringing to be rather than working through the natural order, and where in the other, it is argued by some, including Hume and C.S. Lewis, that the individual acts or events are believed to be against the grain of the natural order. Theological talk of Providence then is often largely a matter of how we can give an account of the relation of God to the natural order of which he is believed to be the creator, and whose history we share.

What is missing from this is the vital but difficult series of questions raised by the text at the head of this paper: '. . . work out your own salvation with fear and trembling, for it is God which worketh in you. . . .'. There are many important issues which arise here concerning the notions of freedom and grace. These are not the primary concern of this paper, although what I do tackle here has a bearing on questions of freedom and grace, and vice-versa. Rather my intention is to explore the Providence of God in relation to the ways in which individuals might seek order and unity in their lives. If, in the words of the text from Philippians, we are seeking to work something out in our living, in what sense if any does the idea of God working in us imply that there is a pattern to be found or fashioned in our living which is the pattern of God working in us? That way of setting the question implies a clearer answer than I can, or would even wish, to give, but it is a useful first shot in the intellectual battle which lies ahead.

This is not the place to begin discussions of the nature of salvation, but the choice of a text which speaks of salvation and of the activity of God in our working out of our *own* salvation is deliberate. Let me rather approach the matter by setting 'salvation' alongside a secular analogue 'fulfilment'. There are many terms which may be located between the two, for example, the idea of authenticity of life whether given the form of existential philosophy or existential theology, but what is essential to note at this stage is that in comparing the ideas of 'salvation' and 'fulfilment' I am not proposing to reduce the one to the other. Rather, I am trying to discover any analogies or comparisons which will help us to devise a way of talking and thinking about, and of course, believing what might be true about Providence and the life of the individual. That question requires rather different treatment from the discussion appropriate to Providence and history, or Providence and the natural order. Of course, the individual always has his or her place in history and equally belongs to the natural order, but as we shall see, part of what we might understand by either salvation or fulfilment is a working out of the difficult question of *how* we are related to either history or the natural order. If we were to be seen *only* as part of history or historical process or *only* as bits of a natural (physical and biological) order, then we should have no use for terms such as salvation or fulfilment. That is perhaps primarily what these terms have in common. They are attempts to locate within history and the natural order, but to do so in such a way as to mark out the fact that there is a problem here of both an existential and intellectual nature. That is to say these terms point to what is fundamental to our humanity, namely that we do ask what our relation is to the cosmos which we inhabit.

Common to both of these terms is a concern to answer the questions: first, who and what ultimately are we?; and second, who and what might we ultimately become?; and third, central to *some* answers to the above, where have we come from?

The attraction of the metaphor of narrative to contemporary philosophers and theologians can now be made somewhat clearer. The search for either salvation or fulfilment involves the search for what gives perspective and underlying unity to human life. Our place in either the perpetuities of history or the immensities of the cosmic natural order is a place in tension between, on the one hand, absorption into or erasure by time and matter, and on the other hand a unique gritty ontological individuality. The question is one of human individuality and identity in the flux of time and space. One way of denying an ultimate ontological fate of absorption or erasure is to begin to talk theologically of salvation, or ethically of fulfilment. Each is an attempt to provide a unifying perspective which marks the life of the individual as of ontological significance. My own preferred form of words is that each attempts to provide a view of each human life *sub specie aeternitatis*, which, if it succeeds, gives to human lives that combination of identity and value which resists ultimate absorption or erasure. The role of the metaphor of narrative is to address us to the question of just what could hold life together in this way: the question of what unity could be found and recounted. It must be admitted that this is an immense weight to place on a metaphor.

[In parenthesis one further admission and one qualification must be made here. The admission is that in focusing upon the individual in this way I am being theologically and philosophically selective.

Culturally I am drawing upon certain dominant aspects of Greek and Christian traditions. This emphasis upon individual salvation or fulfilment is central to European Christianity, but it can be and has been challenged by alternative secular and religious metaphysics. For example, Marxist thought would reject altogether such an individualist ontology, and as Derek Parfit has argued recently in the context of philosophical discussion of personal identity, so would Buddhism (see *Reasons and Person*[2]). There is also a strong element in Eastern Orthodoxy which stresses the idea of the self-in-community rather than the self-as-individual, and even more extreme is Simone Weil's teaching that the loss of the self taught by Christianity is much more than a moral injunction. However, in making the admission that I am being selective and entering the *caveat* that there are other readings of Christianity, I am also committed to a starting point of individualism which I believe to have been dominant in European thought about salvation and fulfilment. Some modification will be made of this in due course, but I do point out immediately that I am not for one moment wanting to substitute a timeless essential identity of persons, for one which, as Marx and many others would insist, takes our historicity seriously.]

II

It is time to begin the exploration of the sort of role which narrative might play in helping us understand what could be meant by salvation or fulfilment. The crucial question which we must first ask of the text quoted is of the relation between the first and second clauses: that is to say between 'work out your own salvation with fear and trembling', and 'for it is God which worketh in you'.

One way of trying to write the narrative implied in the first is to claim to be able to write as if having access to the narrative implied in the second. Thus the story of 'working out' can be transformed into the story of God's acts, of God encountering, speaking to, or revealing himself to the individual in question. Of course writers seldom indulge themselves completely and blasphemously in the attempt to tell the story from God's point of view, but sometimes they do write as if engaged in forms of divine plagiarism. They make the mistake of assuming that they can write about the relation between God and the lives of individuals as if the Prologue to *The Book of Job* were literally true. Or again they assume that we can fill out the story of the second clause, 'it is God which worketh in you . . .' in ways other than telling the story of the first clause 'work out your own salvation in fear and trembling'. In words borrowed from recent Christological writings, I am rejecting the idea that we can write the narrative of the search for salvation or fulfilment 'from above'. We write only 'from below'. This is not a point which I shall argue out here, for I have given my reasons for this in extended form elsewhere,[3] but part of the attraction of the idea of 'narrative' is that it does suggest a way of proceeding of these topics for those for whom theology 'from above' is not on the agenda.

The idea of narrative is one way of raising the fundamental question 'from below' of what a life which seeks to 'work out its own salvation with fear and trembling', looks like. How would we describe it? How alternatively would one try to live such a life? The first point which the idea of narrative brings home to us is that there is a different story for each life. The question of how one describes such a life, or how it may look may seem to be general in form, but in each case the answer is particular. It is *your* story, or *my* story. There may be the offer of salvation which is universal, and there may be a general ideal of fulfilment, but the working out of salvation, or the seeking of fulfilment is always particular.

If this is so, then again what the idea of narrative does here is initially to polarize the universality of a philosophical account of fulfilment, or a theological account of salvation, on the one hand, and the particular working out of either of these in detail on the other hand. It may be true that there is no salvation outside the Church, but it is certainly true that there is no salvation which is not of the individual.

The consequence of this however need not be intellectual despair of ever saying anything at all about salvation or fulfilment, rather it is a re-setting of the questions which may be asked. In such an approach 'from below', neither are we looking simply for a theological account of salvation nor alternatively for a philosophical exposition of the ideal of fulfilment: rather are we directed to ask what sort of texture the narrative of a life has.

We are often tempted to talk here of the 'story' of my life. The difficulty with that is that the term 'story' is ambiguous. It could refer effectively to the chronicle of events in which one participates, or it could refer to something else which I am calling the narrative of one's life. In the first version of his *An Autobiography*, called *The Story and The Fable*,[4] Edwin Muir drew the distinction to which I am pointing in the very title which he chose — *The Story and The Fable*. The distinction in question can be clarified by some quotations from the first chapter of *An Autobiography*. He writes:

> ... there is a necessity in us, however, bland and ineffectual, to discover what we are.[5]

and again,

> Our minds are possessed by three mysteries: where we come from, where we are going, and, since we are not alone, but members of a countless family, how we should live with one another. (*ibid*, p. 56)

The answer to these questions, he believes, cannot be found in the story (or chronicle) of things that we do, and things that happen to us, for such a story is simply a recounting of the natural order of the world, and how one part of it is. It is only, he claims, when we find the fable which can occasionally be discerned, giving form to our experience, only when our biography or autobiography begins to be restricted in that way, that we can hope to see some answers to the question of what we are. The answer however is not the story which is the summary description and chronicle of the web of time, cause and effect to which we belong. His own view is that:

> Human beings are understandable only as immortal spirits; they become natural then, as natural as young horses; they are absolutely unnatural if we try to think of them as a mere part of the natural world. (*ibid*. p. 51)

I do not want to tie what I have to say to Muir's own fable, or autobiography, for my interest here is the sense which he is giving to the idea of a narrative as what can show the connections which, if found and asserted, can show us what we are by offering us variously salvation or fulfilment. Narrative is essentially a way of making connections which while not denying that we are a part of the nexus of temporal cause and effect nonetheless shows us that we are intelligible in ways other than as part of the flotsam and jetsam of the material order.

III

The search for connections, or relations which are not merely, or not reducible to, the contingent connections of the chronicle of our existence ('one damn thing after another!') or the contingent relations pointed to in our idea of causal sequence, might be one way of characterizing the task of philosophy, or theology. The expression of such connections is what we find in areas of literature, art and music. In this paper I am examining the notion of 'narrative' as *one* way of exploring such connections common to philosophy, theology, literature and biography. Two recent but very different works of philosophy illustrate very well the richness of the idea, as well as the difficulty of separating the gold from the dross: Alasdair MacIntyre's, *After Virtue*,[6] and Paul Ricoeur's, *Time and Narrative*, Vol I.[7] I am not convinced that either has fully succeeded in carrying out the rather different tasks in which he believes the idea of narrative has a central role, but their respective examples have much to offer us.

MacIntyre's starting point is his diagnosis of a crisis of our culture:

> We possess indeed the simulacra of morality, we continue to use many of the key expressions. But we have — very largely, if not entirely — lost our comprehension, both theoretical and practical, of morality. (p. 2); There seems to be no rational way of securing moral agreement in our culture. (p. 6)

(This is of course a state of affairs not unknown in theology.) Although I am not convinced of the truth of some of the historical claims which are implicit in his diagnosis, not least the nostalgia for a golden age of moral philosophy, nonetheless I believe that MacIntyre is confronting a most important question. It is in the end the question of the intelligibility, and sense, of moral discourse, and the extent to which these depend upon agreed patterns of coherence and argument.

MacIntyre's point is that we do not have available to us an adequate concept of 'virtue', which of course is essential if we are to be able to 'determine what human qualities are virtues' (p. 172). (The Aristotelian idea, for example, of a *telos* of man performed precisely such a role.) His task is to give an account of such a unitary and unifying concept. He hopes to complete this task by giving a logically ordered account of three ideas — a practice, the idea of 'the narrative order of a single human life', and the idea of 'what constitutes a moral tradition'. MacIntyre argues that the notion of a narrative unity depends upon the concept of such a practice, as does the idea of a moral tradition depend upon the notion of the possibility of a narrative unity in individual human lives, but the dependence is not in either case vice versa. It is, of course, the second of these which is our focus of interest, but again the parallel with theology is plain. Narrative is intended to play a central role in linking together the persisting practices with the idea of the tradition which ultimately provides the structure necessary for the critical evaluation of these practices.

In morality, for example, the practice of keeping promises is both understood and continuing, yet there is the need for a context to provide a means of deciding problem cases (e.g. returning a sharp knife to a neighbour in a demented state caused by the noise of the stereo in No.6, or fulfilling the promise to sell tanks to General Amin, after the nature of his regime has become clear). Equally there are those for whom the practices of religion, prayer, worship etc. continue in particular forms, but in such a manner that they have clearly ceased to be rooted in a liturgical tradition. This, of course, when noticed gives rise to the well-known ecclesiastical vestibule game of liturgical reform. If the latter is played well it will reconnect the practice with a living tradition (if there is still a living tradition), but if it is done badly it will simply re-describe the practice as if it were a *sui generis* activity existing in its own right, after its own kind. Alternatively it may try to re-design the practice by attaching it to something other than the living tradition, or to a different tradition, which is, say, primarily linguistic in character.

MacIntyre's argument in moral philosophy, which I am adapting for theological discussion, is that the bridge from the practice to the tradition is the concept of the narrative unity of a human life. This certainly has application to the theological case, although, as we shall see, the latter provides one means of refining the former.

If, as is occasionally the case, one of my children is trying to understand what I am doing at the moment (as distinct that is from assuming that they already know full and boringly well) then putting pen to paper might be described in a number of ways: 'writing a lecture', 'contributing to theological discussion', 'fulfilling a promise made', 'hoping to impress my colleagues', 'filling in time before lunch', 'avoiding talking to visiting relatives', and so on. Now a few general points can be made about these descriptions. In some cases they compete with each other, in other cases they are disputable, and yet again some are value-laden ('contributing' to theological discussion). Two points are quite central: the intelligibility of what I am doing depends in part at least on my intentions, and these intentions presuppose an ordering of events in my life which is itself part of a longer narrative. The narrative is not simply a chronicle of events, but if there is any unity there, than it will reveal something of the values which I have, the goals which I pursue, and effectively what I consider to be fundamentally important. This does not mean that I always act on an ordered hierarchical set of values, nor does it ignore the fact that my intentions may be mixed. I shall return to these points in due course. Equally the concentration on the narrative of an individual life does not exclude, indeed as the examples show, it depends upon, social context quite considerably – whether in terms of the idea of 'writing on paper' (one has to belong to a very exclusive tribe for that to be relevant) or in terms of 'avoiding one's relatives'.

As we progressively move from MacIntyre's preoccupations to our own, let us re-consider the text at the head of this lecture. Although I am not temperamentally suited to 'confessional' theology, I suppose some philosophers and a few more theologians might be prepared to say that there is a sense in which 'writing a paper' might be seen as 'working out one's own salvation' (albeit that much theological writing shows a marked absence of 'fear and trembling' these days). Now the justification for that connection can only belong to an extended narrative which shows what the connections are in the life of this particular writer, which give substance to the description of writing a paper as, at *one* level, a 'working out of that person's salvation'. It would take a biographer of genius or a theologian and autobiographer of peculiar self-awareness to *tell* such a story convincingly, just as it took the genius of Edwin Muir to move our, and his, gaze from the chronicle to the fable.

MacIntyre provides a useful summary paragraph at a transition point within his argument, and it will serve my purposes equally well:

In what does the unity of an individual life consist? The answer is that its unity is the unity of a narrative embodied in a single life. To ask, 'What is the good for me?' is to ask how best I might live out that unity and bring it to completion. To ask, 'What is the good for man?' is to ask what all answers to the former questions must have in common. But now it is important to emphasise that it is the systematic asking of these two questions and the attempt to answer them in deed as well as in word which provide the moral life with its unity. The unity of a human life is the unity of a narrative quest. Quests sometimes fail, are frustrated, abandoned or dissipated into distractions; and human lives may in all these ways also fail. But the only criteria for success or failure in a human life as a whole are the criteria of success or failure in a narrated or to-be-narrated quest. (p. 203)

In *Time and Narrative*, Ricoeur shows himself to be preoccupied with structurally similar questions about the relation between temporal sequences and the sequences which we regard as history rather than chronicle, but we should be attempting too much to follow this path also in one paper.

IV

In this concluding section of the paper I want to mention two *caveats* about MacIntyre's proposals, and then to use these as the basis for some further reflections on the theological questions with which we started.

The first difficulty which faces us, is that of finding a clear connection between the idea of the narrative unity of an individual life, and the concept of tradition for which MacIntyre is searching. As he eventually makes plain the idea of tradition is rather less full than one might have hoped. In fact, at times it seems to be an account of the social context in which any narrative must be embedded. In a rather gloomy conclusion to the book he suggests some similarities between our own position and the decline of the Roman Empire,

> when men and women of good will turned aside from the task of shoring up the Roman *imperium* and ceased to identify the continuation of civility and moral community with the maintenance of that *imperium*. What they set themselves to achieve instead ... was the construction of new forms of community within which the moral life could be sustained so that both morality and civility might survive the coming ages of barbarism and darkness. (p. 244)

Our own search for what he insists presupposes but is not presupposed by narrative unity has clear parallels:

> What matters ... is the construction of local forms of community within which civility and the intellectual and moral life can be sustained through the new dark ages which are already upon us. (p. 245)

Note first, how modest (and I must agree 'realistic') is his proposal. At best we are attempting to construct what may be the seeds of the tradition which he seeks. Of course, he cannot and perhaps he believes need not be too bold here because he has argued that the concept of the narrative unity of a life is presupposed by, but *does not presuppose* that of the tradition. His argument seems to be that the practices have survived, and perhaps, *en route* to the re-creation of tradition the idea of narrative unity can be given life. It is, however, arguable that unless we find ourselves able to disentangle a fictional (constructed) from a real (discovered) unity then the notion of narrative unity is ambiguous at its most vulnerable point. The problem is that contrary to the view which MacIntyre is taking in moral theory, and the one which I wish to take in theology, the idea of narrative unity seems to require an underpinning from what is more general − in MacIntyre's terms, the idea of narrative unity *does* presuppose the wider idea of tradition. Thus the man for whom the practice of honesty is not in the end deluded wants perhaps more than narrative (fictional) unity in his life. But what more? Equally someone who lives each moment as if it were 'the eleventh hour' (see Kierkegaard's *Purity of Heart*) may want a coherence or unity other than that afforded by the possibly mistaken belief that there is a twelfth hour. But what other coherence would do?

MacIntyre would respond to these sceptical questions by pointing to the fact that there are criteria for failure and success in these matters which may be quarried from those areas of literary theory relating to narrative. In this he has my support, but also my second *caveat* − the very great weight being put on the idea of narrative.

Now MacIntyre is clearly well-read in the relevant areas of literary theory, but there are two features of the idea of criteria for narrative success which must be examined further. MacIntyre is well aware that a degree of incompleteness is an important feature of a successful narrative. Sometimes, as he suggests, this will be because of the inevitable tensions between the extent to which we are free, and the various social, physical and biological constraints which structure our lives. Equally the idea of a distinction between the chronicle and the fable/narrative points to the residue which contingently colours our lives.

However, MacIntyre does seem to be working with the idea of narrative unity as essentially portraying one life within a single, albeit complex perspective. The writings of Dostoevsky display the strengths and limitations of such a conception of narrative. In his classic *Problems of Dostoevsky's Poetics*, Mikhail Bakhtin illustrates well the difficulty I find in MacIntyre's use of the term 'narrative', in commenting upon a view which he believes Dostoevsky to be rejecting:

The unity of consciousness, which replaces the unity of existence, is inevitably transformed into the unity of a single consciousness. (op. cit. Ardis Press, 1973)

The mistaken assumption which I believe MacIntyre's discussion requires is exposed by Bakhtin:

> It should be pointed out that the inevitability of a single unified consciousness by no means necessarily follows from the concept of the one and only truth itself. It is completely possible to imagine and to assume that this one and only truth requires a plurality of consciousnesses. (*ibid*)

Dostoevsky's great contribution to narrative was to write such 'polyphonic' novels, or enquiries after truth. The theological consequences of this are very important and in conclusion it is to those that I now turn.

Our fundamental question is wherein truth resides. The proposed answer is that the answer to specific questions about who we are and where we are going is to be located in the search for what constitutes the narrative of our lives. One secular version of the question concerns fulfilment, and MacIntyre's exploration of the role of the narrative unity of a life in giving sense to that was explored. The religious version of the question concerns salvation: how may we work it out? and in what sense, if any, may we talk of God working in us?

In the metaphor adopted, the concept of Providence is in some sense 'God's story'. But it is not, I suggest, a story about God, but the story which he would/does tell about us. That, however, is the story which, if such there be, is 'from above'. The only story which we can tell of God's providence is 'from below', and it *is*, in this context, the narrative of 'working out our own salvation . . .'

Whether the narrative runs true, or is biography rather than fiction, will, in one sense, depend upon its conformity to 'God's story', for again, if such there be, all biography, autobiography and history, will be either in competition with or to some extent in conformity with 'God's providential story about us'. However, we discern at best *parts* of 'it is God which worketh in you', and, on the proposal of this paper, we do not discern that as a series of discrete events (so-called 'salvation-history' or 'encounter') but to the extent to which the texture of our individual narrative is a 'working out of your own salvation in fear and trembling'. The criteria for effective narrative are very appropriate as guidelines in this.

This is true in so far as the unity we seek in such working out demands clarity of intention and consistency and hierarchy in our intentions. (*Is* writing a paper reasonably or properly *ever* understood as a 'working out. . .'?) It demands further a making explicit of both the need for fundamental values and commitments and also what those values are. It also helps meet the first prerequisite of the ideas of fulfilment or salvation, namely the possibility of disentangling ourselves and our self-understanding from the chronicle of a temporal sequence of causes and effects. This too is the first prerequisite of the intelligibility of the idea of Providence.

NOTES

1. London: SCM, 1984.
2. Oxford: Oxford University Press, 1984.
3. In *God, Jesus and Belief*, Oxford: Blackwell, 1984.
4. London: Hogarth Press, 1940.
5. London: Methuen, 1964, p. 51.
6. London: Duckworth, 1981.
7. Translated by K. McLaughlin and D. Pellauer, University of Chicago Press, 1984.
8. I have discussed this point more fully in *Atheism and the Rejection of God* (Blackwell, 1977).

10

CHRISTIAN NORMS OF MORALITY

by GARTH HALLETT, SJ

Dean of the College of Philosophy and Letters, St Louis University

The choice of a basic norm of objective right and wrong is decisive for all of Christian ethics. Yet it appears that two of the likeliest candidates for acceptance have never been systematically compared and assessed. The present essay remedies this lack, then, having reached a comparative judgment, reflects on this confrontation in the light of issues raised by Gerard Hughes's *Authority in Morals*[1] (hereafter *AM*). What makes one Christian norm more acceptable than another? Where does 'ultimate authority' lie? These concluding considerations confirm the original verdict favouring one of the norms.

TWO NORMS

In *The Theory of Morality*[2] (hereafter *TM*) Alan Donagan examined the Hebrew-Christian tradition and from it elicited the fundamental principle: 'It is impermissible not to respect every human being, oneself or any other, as a rational creature'. (p. 66). He contrasted this norm principally with consequentialism, in particular with the utilitarianism of Mill and Sidgwick, and concluded: 'The duty of beneficence in the Hebrew-Christian tradition is not the indiscriminate and unlimited maximizing of good imposed by utilitarianism. . . . [A]ttempting to choose a moral system by its consequences is not only a mistake in moral theory but also futile'. (p. 209)

In *Christian Moral Reasoning*[3] (hereafter *CMR*) I examined the Christian tradition and from it distilled a broadly teleological criterion of right and wrong, embracing acts as well as consequences and moral as well as nonmoral values and disvalues. Without restriction, value is to be maximized, disvalue minimized. This criterion I contrasted with the appeal sometimes made to natural form (for instance in the condemnation of artificial contraception) and with the ban sometimes imposed on disvalues used as means to values, and I concluded: 'If Christian moral reasoning is to be both consistent and true to its past, it must be based on the balance of values; value-maximization must be its logic and its law'. (p. 224)

This norm (which I shall label *VM*, for 'Value Maximization') appears more plausible than those Donagan considered and rejected, while his norm (which I shall label *PR*, for 'Principle of Respect')[4] looks more plausible than those I weighed and found wanting. So it seems desirable to provide what my book did not, and assess the respective merits of these two rival formulations. First I shall note similarities between them, then dissimilarities, and dwell on those that appear more significant for a verdict between the two principles.

Though importantly different in certain respects, *PR* and *VM* are both presented as general, Christian, substantive norms of objective morality. Of these characteristics the final ones (their being *substantive* norms of *objective morality*) reveal the closest affinity.

Objective. Donagan distinguishes between two kinds of questions: 'those about the rightness or wrongness of actions in themselves; and those about the culpability or inculpability of doers in doing them. Since answers to questions of the second kind presuppose answers to questions about the first, I describe them as 'first-order' and 'second-order' questions respectively.' (*TM* 30; cf. *TM* 3, 55) *PR* figures as the fundamental principle of 'first-order' morality; it concerns 'the rightness or wrongness of actions in themselves'.

Similarly, *CMR* stresses the difference between action-centered queries ('What shall I do?' 'What action should I perform?') and agent-centered assessments of innocence or guilt, (pp. 22–3) and argues the dependence of the latter on the former; (pp. 22, 26, 89–90) then it focuses on the former. 'Such, on the whole, is the perspective here adopted: "concern with antecedent rather than consequent conscience, i.e., with prospective decision-making rather than with retrospective judgment-passing."' (p. 23) Within this chosen focus, *VM* answers the question: 'By what consistent criterion are right and wrong to be assessed?' (p. 2)

Having experienced how commonly such a restriction of attention is mistaken for a substantive reduction or exclusion, and how readily a judgment of conceptual or cognitive priority is mistaken for a judgment of value primacy, I can appreciate Donagan's insistence

> that attention be paid to the contexts within which questions arise about right and wrong, guilt and innocence. When an agent and his moral counsellors are considering the moral permissibility of a proposed action, the first question to arise is, 'Is it (materially, objectively) permissible?' Until they have settled this, no question of formal or subjective permissibility can arise at all. And, when they have settled it, a question of formal or subjective permissibility can arise only if it has been decided that the proposed action is materially permissible. (*TM*, 137)

CMR makes similar points, at greater length (pp. 23–6). Strictly objective appraisal, it maintains, is as legitimate as subjective, and is often preferable. 'To ignore the context, purpose, and intended recipient(s) of the moral assessment and insist upon uniform treatment does not assure that an act's meaning "is most accurately discerned"'. (p. 26)

Morality. In different ways and to differing degrees, both *TM* and *CMR* recognise a distinction between morality and perfection, and this distinction further delimits the scope of their central principles. These assess what is permissible or impermissible (*PR*), right or wrong (*VM*), not what is better or worse.[5] (*TM* 56–7; *CMR* 75–8) This restriction, too, tends to beget criticism. Abstraction is taken for exclusion. Yet neither Donagan's principle nor mine can rightly be accused on this ground of minimalism. 'Permissible' and 'right' are not synonymous with 'better' and 'more perfect,' and clarity is not served by supposing they are. It is true, however, that Donagan restricts the domain of the moral more than some critics and I would.[6]

Substantive. Neither *PR* nor *VM* is a purely formal principle. Each is assigned a decisive role in judging conduct. Neither norm, however, can render concrete verdicts by itself. Each has need of further specifications concerning what is respectful (in the case of *PR*) or what is valuable (in the case of *VM*).

The more general a norm is, the more cases it covers and the more consequential it therefore appears. However, the more general it is, the more abstract a norm also tends to be and the more concrete supplementation it requires in order to render a verdict in specific instances. Since both Donagan's norm and mine are very general, misgivings may arise concerning their practical significance. Thus Jeffrey Stout observes: 'A highly abstract moral principle of the kind Donagan calls fundamental is, for Oakeshott, an abridgment of an abridgment. What use could an abridgment of an abridgment have? None, in abstraction from the tradition it attempts to summarize.'[7] Yet *in* the tradition such a principle may have a crucial role to play.[8] And spotting it there, amid much confusion of detail, may bring clarity and coherence to the tradition.

FIRST DISSIMILARITIES

With respect to generality a first significant difference appears between the two principles, for *VM* is more broadly inclusive than *PR*. *VM* covers the whole of morality, whereas *PR* is doubly circumscribed. It is conceived, first of all, as 'the fundamental principle of morality, with respect to the relations of rational creatures to themselves and to one another'; (*TM* 57) so it omits their relations to God, on the one hand, and to nonrational creatures on the other. (Thus cruelty to animals, for example, is judged contrary to reason, [*TM* 7] but not in virtue of *PR*.)

The principle is restricted, furthermore, to 'that part of common morality according to the Hebrew-Christian tradition which does not depend on any theistic belief.'[9] (*TM*, 29) Of this secular morality, *PR* figures as the first, fundamental principle. From it, 'common morality as a system' (in the doubly restricted sense just indicated)[10] is said to derive. (*TM*, 30)

PR's restrictions tend to elicit various misgivings. It has been questioned, for instance, whether religious belief can be so neatly bracketed.[11] Furthermore, regardless of their validity the restrictions beget unclarity concerning morality as a whole. Suppose duties to God or obligations to animals conflict with duties to humans: which take precedence, when, why? If, for instance, a biological researcher cites advantages to humans and a critic objects to the agony inflicted on test animals, *PR* cannot help adjudicate their disagreement (whereas *VM* can). Donagan does not address such issues, nor is it likely that he could do so without employing some such norm as *VM*. The question also arises: What lies within the bounds of secular morality and what lies without? How do the two realms relate? Is *PR* always decisive? If not, when and how does it need to be completed in deciding concrete problems? Abstracting from the specifically religious or Christian part of morality, Donagan leaves that part in limbo.

Doubtless such unclarity is of more concern to believing readers than to nonbelieving. This is one indication of the audience Donagan had principally in view. Another is the manner of his derivation. The tradition from which he abstracts *PR* is not just the Christian tradition but the Hebrew-Christian tradition, and not just the Hebrew-Christian tradition but also its continuation in modern thought. In *TM* Kant, not Jesus, is the central figure;[12] whereas in *CMR* Kant receives only passing mention and evidence is sought from Scripture, saints, and Christian theologians so as to answer the central query: 'If we wish to be both consistent and true to our Christian heritage, what criterion of right and wrong should we adopt?' (p. 45) Donagan does not ask or answer this more focused question, nor does he proceed on the assumption that Christian tradition is basically sound.[13] His approach is philosophical, not theological. Hence, if the answer to his question turns out to be a better answer to my question than the answer I arrived at, it will be by chance. He provides slight historical evidence for supposing that Christians, if they wish to be true to their past, should embrace *PR* in preference to *VM*. I shall return to this point.

FURTHER DISSIMILARITIES

I have suggested that *PR* and *VM* are comparable in five important respects. Both norms are proposed as 1) objective, 2) moral, 3) substantive, 4) general, and 5) Christian. The first three similarites are close; the last two reveal significant differences. *VM* is both more general and more specifically Christian, at least in its derivation, than *PR* is. These differences are not such as to cast serious doubt on the comparability of the two norms or their status as rivals. More likely to occasion misgivings on this score is the fact that *VM* is offered as a *criterion* of right and wrong, resulting from *criterial* analysis, whereas *PR* is not.

Criterion versus principle

In *CMR* the term 'criterion' is given a Wittgensteinian sense: 'What makes something into a symptom of *y* is that experience teaches that it is always or usually associated with *y*; that so-and-so is the criterion of *y* is a matter, not of experience, but of "definition".'[14] To ask for a criterion in this sense is to ask for a word meaning, not a principle. To ask for the criterion of an ethical term like 'right' and 'wrong' is to ask for the concept's cognitive core as distinct from its emotive, pragmatic, or other noncognitive features. *CMR* describes this core as doubly decisive: 'Criteria are the most fundamental aspect of the most fundamental aspect of ethical discourse. By right and largely in fact they determine the other cognitive features, and the cognitive determine the noncognitive.' Special importance therefore attaches to the question: 'By what criterion, or criteria, should Christians determine right and wrong?'

  CMR recognizes that although 'of all the varied strands in the weave of moral discourse, criteria are the most decisive,' it is not self-evident 'that they should occupy a central position, indeed even a prominent one, in a study of Christian moral reasoning. For criteria might be crucial, but criterial analysis not. Unreflective knowledge might suffice.' (p. 40) In reply the book notes five differences between ethical criteria and others:

1. Ethical criteria differ more frequently.
2. The differences are less readily detected.
3. They are more serious.
4. They are less tractable.
5. We are less competent to deal with them. (40–2)

A reader might grant these premises, yet hesitate to draw the conclusion that ethical criteria require special attention. Ought a thinker like Donagan shift gears and, instead of discussing the fundamental principle of first-order morality, engage in criterial analysis? Does not such a principle have the same practical significance as a criterion of right and wrong, and does it not implicitly define, or help to define, one's moral terms (e.g. 'permissible' and 'impermissible')?

Definite versus indefinite scope

A chief advantage of the criterial approach is that by making explicit what might otherwise remain implicit it draws attention to the linguistic dimension of inquiry and thereby forestalls much confusion and unclarity. This advantage can be demonstrated variously, from setting to setting. Here it might be illustrated as follows. Were Donagan to present respect for rational creatures as a defining criterion of the 'permissible,' it would be clear that all permissible actions must pass the same test: all must satisfy *PR*. However, abstracting as he does both from defining criteria and from religious beliefs, he leaves open various possibilities: a) *PR* might apply to all actions and might decide all of them (though religious beliefs might sometimes have to determine what is truly respectful); b) *PR* might apply to all actions but might not be decisive for all, since religious considerations (e.g. the love of God) might sometimes take precedence; c) *PR* might apply to the majority of actions but not to all, and might be decisive for all it covered; d) it might apply to the majority of actions but might not be decisive for all it covered, just for most; e) and so forth. The unclarity that thus enshrouds Christian ethics in *TM* infects its central principle as well. The reader is not told the precept's scope.

Rich versus meagre historical support

A criterial approach is not the only way to confront issues like these, but it does assure that they are confronted. It has the further benefit of deepening and enriching the process of historical consultation. Sifting Christian tradition, *CMR* examines much more than the explicit moral principles Christians cite in the course of their moral reasoning. Explicit principles, like explicit definitions, are revealing but are relatively rare. To see what people mean by their words — whether 'currency' and 'protein' or 'right' and 'wrong' — you must observe when, where, and why they employ the words. Thus among the evidence *CMR* weighs for and against the criterion of value-maximisation, explicit general norms

like *PR* or *VM* rarely surface. Indeed no such norms appear in the mass
of moral reasoning surveyed in the first of the book's three historical
chapters.

Yet in each instance the mode of appraisal was similar:

(A) Jesus looked to the good of the handicapped man, recognized no
comparable value in delay, and so argued the rightness of healing him
on the Sabbath. (B) Similar weighing of advantages prompted Paul to
recommend celibacy over marriage and to proscribe eating meat
when a brother would be harmed. (C) Ignatius generalized the
approach in his method of tabulations pro and con. (D) Thomas
applied it to self-defence, comparing more- and less-violent modes of
self-preservation and pronouncing against the former. (E) He
recognized that similar balancing might sometimes tell against the
general norm of restitution and saw this as typical. (F) Believers in
precepts, like Ramsey and Mitchell, adduce the advantages of rules
over no rules or of this rule over that. (G) They have sometimes
pressed their reasons more strongly, not only in favor of specific rules
but also against all exceptions. Value is best served by their
exclusion. (H) Rahner countered similar rigidity in the practice of
obedience by citing possible countervalues and insisting that they be
taken seriously in assessing right action. (I) Similarly, Mackey noted
the usual advantages and occasional disadvantages of conformity to
church teaching and advised that these contrasting values guide
decision. (J) With respect to political structures, Niebuhr advanced
negative arguments, Maritain positive ones, in behalf of democracy.
The right regime is the one that best promotes human welfare. (K) At
a loftier level Teilhard's apologia evinced the same thrust. It would be
wrong to pluck the cosmic fruit before it is mature. Value should be
maximized. (pp. 71–2)

Had Donagan attended to such evidence as this he could hardly have
passed over *VM* as he did. When in his brief review of sample norms he
comes to Aquinas's 'first principle in practical reason' that 'good is to
be done and pursued, and evil shunned,' he does not mention the
maximisation of good over evil as a possible interpretation. Instead, he
takes the principle's moral import to be: 'Act so that the fundamental
human goods, whether in your own person or in that of another, are
promoted as may be possible, and under no circumstances violated.'
This norm he finds less adequate than Kant's. 'For while most acts of
respecting human nature as an end in itself are also acts of respecting

certain fundamental human goods as to be promoted and never violated, not all are. For example, respecting as an end in itself one human being who attacks the life of another, who is innocent, does not appear to exclude using deadly violence on him, if only so is the life or fundamental well-being of his innocent victim to be safeguarded.' (p. 64) With this objection VM agrees. However, so did Thomas (e.g. *Summa Theologiae* II–II, q. 64, a. 7). As Margaret Farley observes: 'Aquinas' first-order precepts regarding the protection and pursuit of human goods no more absolutize these goods than does Donagan's system. There is not one of the three basic inclinations which Aquinas lists in *Summa Theologiae* I–II, 94, 3, which he is not willing at some point or other to subordinate to what may be a higher good (whether the good of the total individual being, or the common good, or the good of ultimate "happiness").'[15] The like may be said of Christian tradition as a whole. Hence, whether as exegesis of Thomas or as a reading of Christian tradition, VM looks more plausible than Donagan's twentieth-century rendering derived from Grisez.[16]

Broad and clear versus narrow or misleading

Farley's remarks suggest further points of comparison between PR and VM. As Thomas's applications of his principle often suggest VM, so do Donagan's applications of PR. Repeatedly, the respectful thing to do is the one that maximises value; and where it is not, one may question, not the norm of respect, but Donagan's judgment of what is respectful. So a principal question to consider in evaluating not only the Christian credentials but also the moral merits of PR and VM is this: How genuinely do they differ? If suitably interpreted, would they perhaps yield identical verdicts?

Donagan's treatment of lying helps to focus the issue. 'For benevolent purposes,' he concedes, 'it is sometimes permissible to dupe children, madmen, and those whose minds have been impaired by age or illness. Yet even with regard to them, the weight of Jewish and Christian opinion is on the side of veracity, except where it is beyond doubt that a truthful statement or evasion will cause unjustifiable harm.' (p. 89) Why unjustifiable? In virtue of what principle? Perhaps in virtue of respect for every human being, rational or irrational, in the sense of a desire for his or her welfare, but not, it would seem, by reason of respect such as PR enjoins and such as Donagan urges against lying to responsible adults: 'The duty of veracity appears to be independent of the institution of contract and to rest simply on the fact that the respect due to another as a rational creature forbids misinforming him, not only for evil ends, but even for good ones. In duping another by lying to him, you deprive him of the opportunity of exercising his judgment on the best evidence available to him.' (p. 89)

Here Donagan's key value comes to view: autonomy.[17] Those who do not possess it cannot be deprived of it; those who do possess it should never be denied its exercise. However, a dominant value is not the same thing as a universal principle. So the foregoing analysis, with its contrasting cases, serves to sharpen the following dilemma: either respect for others as rational beings is one value among many that determine right and wrong (in which case it fits within the larger perspective of *VM* but cannot adequately ground *PR*'s broad claims), or 'respect' is made to embrace all values (in which case the labelling is unenlightening and misleading).

Some critics take Donagan's term 'respect' at face-value and therefore complain of narrowness. Farley notes that 'Donagan's theory . . . favors autonomy over well-being and the self as individual agent over the self in mutuality with others.'[18] Stout agrees that what we need 'is a view of ourselves that is rich enough to sustain both a healthy respect for autonomy and a genuine regard for the positive dimensions of well-being.'[19] 'It is love-like attitudes,' Wertheimer urges, 'that seek and take satisfaction in the well-being of their objects; respect does not take satisfaction at all, and does not aim at the good of its objects. Respect for truth may motivate honesty and candor, but not, as love of truth does, the quest for wisdom, certainty or scientific knowledge.'[20] Critiques like these are telling, however they are viewed. For the previous dilemma can be restated thus: either *PR* is indeed too narrow and the complaints are just, or the critics have been misled by a deceptively narrow formulation of a broader, more comprehensive viewpoint.

Why not call a spade a spade? When one tells untruths to the young, the senile, or the insane so as to shield them from harm or assure their welfare, one does as Aquinas says: one seeks to do good and avoid evil. When one tells the truth to a responsible adult, despite the consequences, so as to allow the person to exercise his or her own judgment, one seeks a different good: autonomy. There is no need to bundle all values under a single heading. Such terminological imperialism only generates confusion.

To illustrate the inadequacy of Donagan's formulation, consider Sartre's well-known case: shall the student stay with his mother who needs him, or try to join the Free French? According to Sartre, Kant's principle is no help. 'The Kantian ethics says, "Never treat any person as a means, but as an end." Very well, if I stay with my mother, I'll treat her as an end and not as a means; but by virtue of this very fact, I'm running the risk of treating the people around me who are fighting, as means; and, conversely, if I go to join those who are fighting, I'll be treating them as an end, and, by doing that, I run the risk of treating my mother as a means.'[21]

Kant could reply that to show preference to one person, or group, over another when values conflict is not to treat the one party as an end and the other as a means. And Donagan might reply similarly were Sartre's objection couched in terms of respect for rational creatures. (See his comment quoted above about taking an aggressor's life.) But this answer would not show the relevance either of Kant's principle or of Donagan's variant. Mere respect for persons does not indicate which person or persons to prefer. If the young man is moved by the millions who suffer from Nazidom and leaves to join the Free French, or is impressed by the sureness of the benefit to his mother and opts to stay with her, his decision is not based on greater respect for one party or the other but on the greater or surer good to be achieved. The balancing of values is prior to, not dependent upon, the judgment of respect. So once again, here as in countless other cases, why not call a spade a spade? Why hesitate to acknowledge the rule of value-maximization?

REASONS FOR *PR*'S NARROWNESS

It appears that one of Donagan's reasons is Kantian[22] and agnostic. He is ready to specify the supreme value that should govern all conduct within the realm of 'common morality,' but thereafter he disclaims any competence to judge what is best for others.

Aristotle's description of [happiness] has not been bettered: activity in accordance with human excellence (*arete*), in a complete life (*Eth. Nic.* 1098a 16–20). That happiness in this sense presupposes the enjoyment of primary human goods, such as health, a certain amount of wealth, and a respected place in a free society, has been brought out by Rawls. There is no doubt at all that normal human beings naturally seek happiness. But they do not all in fact seek it; and when they do not, it may be presumed that they have reasons for not doing so which they consider of overriding importance. That is why Kant consistently held happiness to be the natural end of man but not an unconditional rational end. Action in pursuit of happiness is always intelligible in rational terms, but it is not imposed by reason. (p. 225)

Donagan may be impressed by the reasons people have had for not pursuing happiness or the enjoyment of primary goods (and not by their reasons for denying respect to others), but Christian thought has not joined him in concluding that one person's value-judgments are as good as another's. In this it has arguably been more consistent than Donagan. In any case, a principle based on such scepticism about all values except one hardly mirrors Hebrew-Christian thought through the centuries.

Donagan's remarks on beneficence suggest a second reason, in tension with the first, for *PR*'s narrow focus on respect: 'If a man respects other men as rational creatures, not only will he not injure them, he will necessarily also take satisfaction in their achieving the well-being they seek, and will further their efforts as far as he prudently can. In short, he will observe the general precept: *It is impermissible not to promote the well-being of others by actions in themselves permissible, inasmuch as one can do so without disproportionate inconvenience.*' (p. 85) Given this entailment, Donagan might say there is no need to mention other values; respect brings all values with it. However, which values? The 'well-being *they seek*,' as in the first sentence, or 'the well-being of others' *tout-court* (without subjective restriction), as in the second sentence? The first phrasing preserves autonomy. The second permits value judgments of one's own, admits other values than autonomy, hence implicitly calls for balancing of values when values conflict, as they regularly do.[23] Understood in this second manner, *PR* differs from *VM* only in its wording, and its wording seems doubly deficient. For one thing, 'love,' 'care,' or 'concern' more aptly indicates a beneficent attitude than does the word 'respect'. For another, an effective norm of right conduct must do more than name an attitude. Donagan is rightly critical of those who 'proclaim *agape* (as theologians like to call it) as the sole valid guide for action: and, as the sole and sufficient rule of conduct, "Love, and do what you will!"' (p. 62–3) 'Respect, and do what you will!' succeeds no better. The works of respect, like those of love, require clearer specification, as for instance in *VM*.

Donagan's critique of C.D. Broad's and W.D. Ross's 'newer intuitionism' suggests a third likely reason for his unwillingness to broaden *PR* and give clear recognition to other ends besides autonomy. According to this view, writes Donagan:

> A moral agent must ... be familiar with all the more significant characteristics that count for or against doing the actions that have them. ... Supposing that he is, and that he succeeds in reviewing all the morally significant characteristics of the various courses of action open to him, he may then proceed to the second stage: that of weighing the various considerations against one another, in order to judge what course of action is indicated by the greatest balance of favorable considerations over unfavorable ones. (p. 22)

Against this position (and implicitly against *VM*), Donagan initially objects that 'since the new intuitionist theory confers no definite weight on any consideration, every agent may assign to each of them whatever weight seems good to him.' (p. 23) In a sense this is obviously true, but also irrelevant. People may and do reach varied verdicts on any matter, whether theological, historical, scientific, or valuational. However, Donagan continues:

> Philosophically, the chief objection must be that it is fraudulent to describe what the new intuitionists take to be the process of moral deliberation as one of 'weighing' or 'balancing' considerations. For that metaphor to be appropriate, there must be a procedure for ascertaining the weight of each consideration, either comparatively or absolutely, a procedure analogous to that of putting objects on a balance or scale. It is an appropriate description, even a happy one, for deliberation in terms of a moral system in which different considerations are ordered serially; for in such deliberation, which consideration has priority over the others is determined by reflecting on their respective places in the series — a process unquestionably analogous to weighing different objects in order to find the heaviest. But by repudiating anything that might order the various considerations it acknowledges, and accepting as 'weighing' or 'balancing' any process whatever in which a man, hesitating before alternatives supported by different considerations, without conscious insincerity overcomes his hesitation, the new intuitionism deprives that description of any definite sense. (pp. 23–4)

In utilitarianism, the single factor 'happiness' might perhaps order values as greater or less (according as they promised more or less happiness). In his own system, respect might be thought to perform a similar function. However, once multiple, independent values are admitted, as by Broad and Ross (and *CMR*), no verdict is possible. Considered by themselves, disparate values are not comparable.

When unpacked, this critique looks no more impressive than variants one encounters in Finnis, Grisez, and others.[24] With or without scales to check one's impressions, it is meaningful to speak of weighing objects in the hands and judging whether one is heavier than the other or both are roughly equal in weight. With or without thermal measures, it is meaningful to speak of feeling objects and judging whether one is warmer or colder than the other or both are roughly the same temperature. And none of Donagan's remarks reveals any reason to suppose that a similar procedure with regard to values is less meaningful or sound. (See *CMR* 167–68.) His apparent claim that serial ordering must precede individual comparisons of weight, heat, value, or what have you, rather than result from such comparisons, does not even make evident sense.

Donagan himself performs and enjoins much balancing of values with no other norm to guide him than *PR*. Yet as we have seen, the rule of respect cannot serve to order value considerations, and in fact does not. In *TM*, values determine respect more than respect determines values. Thus Donagan's practice conflicts with his theory. In instance after instance he applies *PR* by means of value-balancing. Indeed, he grounds *PR* itself on comparative value considerations. 'They are: first, that rational creatures are negatively free because they exhibit a kind of causality by virtue of which their actions are not determined to any end by their physical or biological nature; and second, that because of that causality, they are creatures *of a higher kind* than any others in nature. These characteristics, according to Kant, provide rational creatures with an end which their own reason must acknowledge: their own rational nature.' (p. 237; emphasis added)[25] Donagan accepts these considerations as 'rationally compelling,' though not 'intuitively self-evident,' and proceeds to base his system on a piece of patent value-balancing.

Though similar balancing in his treatment of particular precepts is veiled by his talk of respect for rational creatures, it sometimes protrudes unmistakably through the verbal camouflage. Comparisons of disparate values (justice, life, convenience, cost, community, self-respect, enjoyment, etc.) are made repeatedly, and repeatedly determine what is 'respectful' and therefore permissible. A few samples from among many:[26]

> Respecting as an end in itself one human being who attacks the life of another, who is innocent, does not appear to exclude using deadly violence on him, if only so is the life or fundamental well-being of his innocent victim to be safeguarded. (p. 64)

Inasmuch as the relief and enjoyment afforded by a drug compensate
for any ill effects it may have, then it is permissible to use it. . . . For
anybody to place any kind of drug-induced enjoyment before the full
use of his capacities as a rational creature, is a plain case of failure to
respect himself as the kind of being he is. The objection is not to the
enjoyment in itself but to the inordinate value set upon it. (p. 80)

Nobody is morally obliged to promote the well-being of others at
disproportionate inconvenience to himself. One does not fail to
respect another as a rational creature by declining to procure a good
for him, if that good can be procured only by relinquishing an equal
or greater good for oneself. (p. 86)

Solitude and civil anarchy are both human evils. Hence a man owes it
both to himself as a rational creature and to others, to obey even the
defective laws of his civil society, while doing what he can to rectify
defects and to prevent abuses. Only in extreme cases can direct
disobedience, or general civil disobedience and rebellion, be justified.
(p. 100)

War is so horrible an evil that only a very clear and great cause can
justify it. (p. 111)

Fervently desirous of preventing the abolition of Palestinian Jewry,
he did draw the line where reprieve would be bought at the price of
moral cohesion and self-respect. . . . There are minimum conditions
for a life worthy of a human being, and . . . nobody may purchase
anything — not even the lives of a whole community — by sacrificing
those conditions. (p. 183)

To avoid pain, or trouble, or even exertion is a perfectly good reason
in itself for doing something; but not when there is adequate reason
for putting up with it. (p. 242)

I cite these passages as *ad hominem* evidence that value comparisons of
the forbidden variety — judging more or less, without calibration or the
mediation of any common measure other than value itself — are
possible, legitimate, and decisive. The same and similar passages
suggest the justice of Wertheimer's critique. 'Donagan's tradition,' he
observes, 'has never provided a facsimile of a philosophically adequate

description of what this thing, respect, is that it directs us to have. Instead we are given assorted claims about an odd lot of behavioral expressions of respect. . . .'[27] The underlying rationale that makes sense of the preceding 'odd lot' is *VM*, not *PR*.

In confirmation of this verdict, consider a case of apparent value-balancing which Donagan examines with special care, indeed with desperate ingenuity. The famous potholer caught in the rocks may, he concedes, be blown away so that those behind him will not drown. But the reason is not, he argues, that otherwise 'many lives will be lost and far greater misery will obtain' (as Kai Nielsen contends). Rather, the reason is that the potholers in question may have agreed, tacitly and legitimately, that if, 'through nobody's fault, they should be confronted with a choice between either allowing certain of their number to be killed, or doing something that would, against everybody's will, cause the deaths of fewer of their number, the latter should be chosen.' (p. 178) In killing such a spelunker, his companions would be carrying out his own wishes, not sacrificing him for a greater good. Even in his death, autonomy would triumph. But suppose there was no such tacit agreement? Well, 'perhaps it would have force even if it were virtual: that is, even if all members of the group, were they to think about it, would agree that everybody in the group would think that so to conduct themselves was the only rational course.' (p. 179) Suppose, though, that there was no such tacit or virtual agreement: what then? And would they be right in thinking that 'so to conduct themselves was the only rational course'? Would even the tacit agreement be permissible, as claimed? If so, why? Might they as legitimately agree to blast out anyone whose predicament threatened to delay their supper? I think it is clear that in Donagan's reasoning the balance of values is decisive and the judgment of what is respectful and permissible is derivative.

The passages quoted, and Wertheimer's summary verdict, suggests that a fourth reason for the narrowness of *PR* is no sounder than the preceding three. As a ground for preferring Kant's interpretation of the primary principle to that of Aquinas, Donagan cites its simplicity. (p. 65) The structure of any system of morality based on *PR* is logically very simple, he explains, and,

> The structure of the fundamental principle is itself simple. It contains only one concept peculiar to moral thought, that of (moral) permissibility. And its sense is that no action which falls under the

concept of not respecting some human being as a rational creature can fall under the concept of being permissible. The second concept it contains, that of (not) respecting some human being as a rational creature, is not peculiar to moral thinking. It has a place in descriptions of human conduct in anthropology and psychology, and of course in everyday descriptive discourse. (p. 66)

Aquinas's principle, by contrast, speaks of good and evil rather than of respect, and therefore adds further concepts 'peculiar to moral thought.' So does *VM*.

Wertheimer's assessment suggests how illusory is this contrast. Bundle all manner of values under the single heading 'respect' and the most varied disvalues under the single heading 'disrespect,' and one may create the impression of simplicity together with richness. But the simplicity will be purely verbal. And why stress simplicity, if the good we rightly strive for is a many-splendoured thing? 'Simplex sigillum veri,' it has been said; yet long experience suggests that the contrary has more often been the case: 'Simplex sigillum falsi.'

A series of illustrations in *CMR* (the limitation of intrinsic good to human good, to states of consciousness, to moral good, to virtue, to man's final end, to the world to come, to the beatific vision, to God alone) documents the danger of undue simplification. (pp. 129–33) 'As the mind's thirst for unity leads to repeated reductions in the speculative order (materialism, idealism, determinism, and so on), so the heart's kindred yearning reduces value after value to a servant of the one.' (p. 132) Donagan's yearning would seem to be more of the mind than of the heart, but his Kantian reduction leads to a similar outcome. As each of the cited reductions reveals inner incoherence (*CMR*, 133–37), so does his. The varied values he eliminates from *PR* play their inevitable roles. The comparisons he declares meaningless he nonetheless performs repeatedly. His practice, it seems, is sounder than his theory, and indicates the need to rethink and reformulate the theory.

METHODOLOGICAL CONSIDERATIONS

The preceding confrontation elicits reflection on the respective roles of reason and faith, philosophy and religion. At first glance the claims of faith and religion seem strengthened. *CMR*'s full, focused consultation of Christian tradition has revealed a more acceptable norm than did *TM*'s skimpier survey and heavy reliance on Kant. *VM* not only looks more consonant with Christian tradition than *PR*, but is commended by its broader coverage, its greater clarity, its superior adequacy as a guide to more varied cases. However, *reason* conducted the consultation of tradition; *philosophical scrutiny* noted the coverage, the clarity, the greater adequacy. So where does 'ultimate authority' lie? With Christian tradition (Scripture, Fathers, councils, saints, moralists, preachers, popes) or with reason?

This issue, addressed by Hughes, is also raised by his practice. In contrast with *CMR*, and even with *TM*, he arrives at a verdict basically similar to *CMR*'s without having any recourse to specifically Christian data. Although his work is subtitled 'An Essay in Christian Ethics,' the task he sets for himself is simply, 'to produce a theory of ethics which at least gives promise of being able to deal with contemporary problems in a way which might satisfy the radical critic, and which is sufficiently precise to meet any reasonable demand for clarity and guidance.' (*AM* 29) This end he seeks to attain by defining right action in terms of human welfare, and human welfare in terms of human needs. The procedure is purely philosophical.

Certain reactions to my book alert me to a problem implicit in this contrast between *AM* and *CMR*. How explain Hughes's failure to consult Scripture or tradition? How justify my insistence on doing so? In brief response, several reasons may be noted that perhaps explain, but do not justify, a purely philosophical approach. Although all are suggested by passages in *AM*, I am more interested in the reasons themselves than in their attribution. Hughes's procedure may have some other explanation.

First, to enunciate defining criteria is, in a sense, to indicate where 'ultimate authority' lies. As *CMR* observes, 'the whole process of ethical deliberation, whatever the form it takes (consultation of authorities, calculation of values, discernment of spirits, etc.), is governed by the underlying criteria. They determine what evidence is germane, what arguments are appropriate, and what reasoning is conclusive or persuasive. Even when other considerations are pertinent, perhaps decisive, they are so only be virtue of the constitutive criteria of right and wrong. Alter the criteria, and they too would alter.' (p. 39) However, criteria must not be confused with procedures, as they often are; (cf. *CMR*, 171–2) otherwise criterial primacy may be confused with procedural primacy. *CMR* states a single Christian *criterion* of right and wrong (in the defining, Wittgensteinian sense indicated earlier); it acknowledges a variety of legitimate Christian *procedures* for determining right and wrong, without stating a preference for any one of them. In particular, it does not assign 'ultimate authority' to value-balancing and deny it to consultation of Christian authorities.

In *AM*, Hughes's position is variously stated. In one place he writes: 'The ultimate authority in ethics is to be found in the facts about ourselves and our world on which morality rests, as these are organized in an acceptable ethical theory'. (p. 95) Here there is no mention of method or procedure, and the 'facts about ourselves and our world' might constitute a criterion of morality in a manner indicated by the 'acceptable theory.' However, elsewhere a procedural sense is evident: 'The ultimate authority in ethics is the authority of the facts in so far as these can be discovered and interpreted by the normal methods, scientific and informal, of human inquiry.' (p. 91) It is conceivable that this difference was not noted and that criterial primacy was confused with procedural. However, it seems likely that the stated procedure is a procedure for applying the criterion of right and wrong, not for establishing it. So I shall pass to other possible motives for bypassing tradition.

It is not immediately evident what the claim of 'ultimate authority' might mean if given a procedural sense. But something of its purport is suggested by the restrictions Hughes places on 'legitimate appeal to authority' and by the fact that he formulates no comparable set for legitimate reliance on one's own unaided efforts. Since the conditions he states are proposed for 'human inquiry generally,' they apply to *CMR*'s inquiry, which consults authority, and to *AM*'s, which does not. So they may explain this difference between them. The full listing goes as follows:

(1) The question must be one which we have not settled satisfactorily ourselves.
(2) There must be some external grounds for believing that the authority appealed to is likely to be correct on the point in question.
(3) The grounds for believing in the authority must be sufficiently strong that they outweigh any tendency we may have to disagree with its conclusions on internal grounds.
(4) It is undesirable to rely on authority in circumstances where it is practicable to settle the point in question without making any appeal to authority. (p. 92)

These four conditions, whose validity I shall not assess, are all relevant to our case. *CMR*'s recourse to Christian tradition might conceivably be faulted on any one of these four counts or on several. I do not believe, however, that such criticism would be valid. For instance:

(1) If it be suggested that we have settled the criterial question 'satisfactorily' ourselves, through philosophical reflections like those in *AM*, the use of this success-word should not mislead us; it means merely that we are confident, or have firm grounds for believing, that our solution is correct. However, since we are fallible, it makes good sense to consult the verdict of authority, especially on so complex, debated, and debatable a topic as a general criterion of right and wrong.

(2) If it be urged, in such a case, that it seems 'to be in accord with human dignity, and to show a proper respect for human intelligence, that we should refuse to allow ourselves to appeal to authorities in matters where we could perfectly well reach a satisfactory under-standing of the question for ourselves,' (*AM* 94) once again I would distinguish between reaching a satisfactory understanding and knowing for sure that we have. If the point of inquiry is to find the truth, there can be no indignity in consulting whatever evidence is available.

(3) If, however, 'appealing to' and 'relying on' (in conditions 1, 2, and 4) mean something more than merely 'consulting' or 'having recourse to,' then *AM*'s restrictions on legitimate appeal to authority may be less pertinent than they appear for the procedural issue that concerns us. It is not only legitimate but fitting and right, I would say, for a Christian ethician, when addressing a question as difficult as that of a general criterion of morality, to seek light from Christian tradition and, when proposing his solution for acceptance by fellow Christians, to cite what evidence he finds. For as Hughes remarks, 'The Christian believes that he has general theological grounds for his confidence in the inspiration of Scripture, and the continuing guidance of Christ's Spirit in the Church.' (*AM* 95)

These same grounds warrant going farther, I suggest, and adopting what J. Philip Wogaman has termed a 'methodological presumption' in favour of Christian tradition.[28] If talk of Christian 'authorities' is to retain meaning, then Christians must be ready to say, in parallel with Hughes's third condition: 'When reason and authority appear to conflict, the grounds for accepting one's own conclusions must be sufficiently strong that they outweigh any tendency we may have to disagree with them on grounds of authority.' With respect to *VM* I perceived no such countervailing grounds, and indeed no conflict between reason and Christian tradition.

From the preceding double comparison, first with Donagan then with Hughes, it appears that for Christians *VM* is doubly commended. Not only is Value Maximization a clearer, more coherent, more adequate guide than, for instance, Donagan's Principle of Respect; it is also, to my knowledge, the only such norm supported by a fairly thorough sifting of Christian historical evidence.

NOTES

1. Gerard J. Hughes, *Authority in Morals: An Essay in Christian Ethics* (London: Sheed & Ward, 1983. Washington: Georgetown University Press, 1984).

2. Alan Donagan, *The Theory of Morality* (Chicago: University of Chicago Press, 1977).

3. Garth L. Hallett, *Christian Moral Reasoning: An Analytic Guide* (Notre Dame: University of Notre Dame Press, 1983).

4. The five abbreviations I shall use are therefore the following:
AM *Authority in Morals*
TM *The Theory of Morality*
CMR *Christian Moral Reasoning*
VM Value Maximization
PR Principle of Respect

5. For Donagan's reasons for choosing 'permissible' and 'impermissible,' see *TM*, 54. I preferred 'right' and 'wrong' as being somewhat ampler, though still moral.

6. See pages 304−5 of Newton Garver's review of *TM*, in *Ethics* 90 (1979−80).

7. 'The Philosophical Interest of the Hebrew-Christian Moral Tradition,' *Thomist* 47 (1983), 185.

8. Cf. *TM*, 71: 'Among those who share in the life of a culture in which the Hebrew-Christian moral tradition is accepted, the concept [of respecting every human being as a rational creature] is in large measure understood in itself; and it is connected with numerous applications. . . .'

9. Donagan tends to equate the part of morality that does not depend on theistic beliefs with the part ascertainable by human reason. See e.g. *TM*, 6. In this he is not true to the tradition he aims to represent.

10. Donagan's repeated references, without distinction or restriction, to 'common morality' (as here and on p. 31), to 'the fundamental principle of morality' (eg. pp. 57, 58), to 'the first principle of morality' (eg. p. 59), and the like, though understandable as convenient shorthand, tends to obscure the limitations of his system and its guiding principle.

11. See Jerald H. Richards, 'Alan Donagan, Hebrew-Christian Morality, and Capital Punishment,' *Journal of Religious Ethics* 8 (1980), 321−4.

12. 'For Donagan,' writes Stout, '"the Hebrew-Christian moral tradition" is little more than a list of canonical texts drawn up with Kant in mind.' See 'Philosophical Interest', 189.

13. It is just deserving of consultation. See *TM*, 28−9.

14. *CMR*, 36, quoting Norman Malcolm, *Knowledge and Certainty: Essays and Lectures* (Englewood Cliffs: Prentice-Hall, 1963), 113.

15. Margaret A. Farley, Review of *TM* in *Religious Studies Review* 7 (1981): 236.

16. Cf. *CMR*, 114−5. From Saint Thomas's works as a whole an equally strong case can be made for a purely formal sense of his norm, equivalent to 'Do what you ought to do, don't do what you shouldn't.' The formula is therefore profoundly ambiguous. Hence the need to look deeper than mere formulae.

17. 'Respecting a being as a rational creature is respecting him as autonomous − as having the right, subject to the moral law, to decide for himself what his own good is, and how to pursue it.' (*TM*, 77)

18. Review 235.
19. 'Philosophical Interest', 177.
20. Roger Wertheimer, 'Critical Review,' *Nous* 17 (1983): 305.
21. Jean-Paul Sartre, *Existentialism*, translated by B. Frechtman (New York: Philosophical Library, 1947), 30–1.
22. 'Kant was no less plagued by the notion that . . . human desires and purposes are hopelessly "subjective" and relative, and hence not at all of a sort that can provide a basis for duties and obligations that are objectively binding upon all human beings. . . ' Henry Veatch, 'Variations, Good and Bad, on the Theme of Right and Reason in Ethics,' *Monist* 66 (1983), 54–5.
23. Donagan envisages possible conflict between respect and beneficence (pp. 154–7) not just between autonomy and beneficence, but does not explain how this is possible if beneficence is a requirement and test of respect, as dozens of passages in *TM* suggest (see a number quoted later in the text).
24. See Garth Hallett, 'The "Incommensurability" of Values,' forthcoming in *The Heythrop Journal*.
25. Cf. *TM*, 232: 'Having this power to judge his producible ends, which as such, is a higher kind of power than brute animals possess . . . , human beings, as rational, are of a higher kind than any others they have yet encountered in nature. Nor can there be any creature higher in kind, although there may be some higher in degree.' In *TM* this judgment of 'higher' translates into 'only': subhuman values drop from view.
26. See also eg. pp. 78–79, 82, 104, 152, 169, 173, 186–7.
27. 'Critical Review' 304. 'Upon close examination,' writes Stout ('Philosophical Interest', 182), 'we find that Donagan's fundamental principle bears virtually no weight'. Rawls, too, has stressed the indeterminacy of mere 'respect for persons' and the impossibility of deriving specific precepts from so ill-defined a basis. See John Rawls, *A Theory of Justice* (Cambridge, Mass.: Harvard University Press, 1971), 585–6.
28. *A Christian Method of Moral Judgment* (London: SCM Press, 1976), 40, 166–9.

FREDERICK C. COPLESTON
A Bibliography

This bibliography does not claim to be complete. It lists only the first publication of a work and ignores later editions – *Aquinas*, for example, afterwards appeared as *Thomas Aquinas* – and the many translations of *A History of Philosophy*. It does not include shorter book reviews, though some major ones have been listed.

1934   "Bergson and Intuition", *Modern Schoolman*, XI, 61–5.

"De Unicitate Formae Substantialis", *Divus Thomas*, XXXVII, 582–93.

"Pacifism and the New Testament", *The Church Quarterly Review* CXXV, 70–89.

1935   "Pirandello's Propaganda", *The Month*, CLXV, 156–61.

"Russia's Awakening", *The Month*, CLXVI, 429–36.

1936   "Escape from Self-Isolation", *The Month*, CLXVII, 154–9.

1937   "The Continuity of Philosophy", *Blackfriars*, XVIII, 592–8.

"The Quest for Beauty", *Modern Schoolman*, XIV, 64–6.

1941   "Nietzsche and National Socialism", *The Dublin Review*, CCVIII, 225–43.

"Henri Bergson", *The Month*, CLXXVII, 47–57.

"A Prophet of Perpetual Peace", *The Month*, CLXXVII, 344–54.

"Nietzsche *versus* Hitler", *The Month*, CLXXVII, 444–54.

1942   "Friedrich Nietzsche", *Philosophy*, XVII, 231–44.

Friedrich Nietzsche: Philosopher of Culture. London: Burns and Oates.

"'Know Thyself' – But How?" *The Hibbert Journal*, XLI, 12–17.

1944   "The Centenary of Friedrich Nietzsche", *Studies*, XXXIII, 465–74.

St Thomas and Nietzsche. Oxford: Blackfriars.

1946   *Arthur Schopenhauer: Philosopher of Pessimism*. London: Burns and Oates.

"The Challenge of Friedrich Nietzsche", *The Month*, CLXXXII, 467–70.

A History of Philosophy, I: Greece and Rome. London: Burns and Oates.

"Pantheism in Spinoza and the German Idealists", *Philosophy*, XXI, 42–56.

1947   "Existentialism and Religion", *The Dublin Review*, CCXX, 50–63.

"Leibniz and Spinoza", *The Month*, CLXXXIII, 369–71.

"Man without God", *The Month*, CLXXXIV, 18–27.

"The Philosophy of the Absurd", *The Month*, CLXXXIII, 157–64.

"A Visit to Germany", *The Month*, CLXXXIV, 269–77.

"What is Existentialism?" *The Month*, CLXXXV, 13–21.

1948   "The Existence of God: A Debate between Bertrand Russell and Father F.C. Copleston, S.J.", first broadcast on the BBC's Third Programme (for publication, see under 1957).

"Existentialism", *Philosophy*, XXIII, 19–37.

Existentialism and Modern Man. Oxford: Blackfriars.

"Filosofia na Inglaterra", *Revista Portuguesa de Filosofia*, V, 420–2.

"The Flight from Metaphysics", *The Month*, CLXXXV, 150–65.

"Sartre on the Index", *The Tablet*, 1948, 292–3.

"A Visit to Berlin" *Studies*, XXXVII, 409–20.

1949   "Concerning Existentialism", *The Month*, CLXXXVII, 46–54.

"The Nature of Philosophy", *The Month*, CLXXXVII, 363–72.

"The Present Situation in Philosophy", *The Month*, CLXXXVIII, 379–90.

1950   *A History of Philosophy, II: Mediaeval Philosophy, Augustine to Scotus*. London: Burns and Oates.

"The Human Person in Contemporary Philosophy", *Philosophy*, XXV, 3–19.

"Some Reflections on Logical Positivism", *The Dublin Review*, CCXXIV, 71–86.

"A Note on Verification", *Mind*, New Series LIX, 522–9.

1951   "A Christian Philosopher: George Berkeley Republished", *The Tablet*, 27–8.

"The Church and the Mind, I: The Catholic Church and Truth", *The Tablet*, 114.

"The Church and the Mind, II: The Catholic Church and Science", *The Tablet*, 322.

"Mounier, Marxism and Man", *The Month*, CXCII, 199–208.

"Philosophy and Language", *The Month*, CXCI, 270–8.

1952   "The Church and the Mind, III: The Catholic Church and Politics", *The Tablet*, 114.

"The Church and the Mind, IV: The Catholic Church and Philosophy", *The Tablet*, 136.

"The Church and the Mind, V: The Catholic Church and the Non-Christian Religions", *The Tablet*, 156.

"David Hume and St John of the Cross", *The Month*, CXCIV, 69–81.

Medieval Philosophy. London: Methuen.

"The Mind of Leibniz: A New Edition of the 'Theodicy'", *The Tablet*, 28–9.

1953   "Contemporary British Philosophy", *Gregorianum*, XXXIV, 271–87.
       "The Function of Metaphysics", *Philosophy*, XXVIII, 3–15.
       A History of Philosophy, III: Ockham to Suarez. London: Burns and
       Oates.

1955   *Aquinas*. Harmondsworth: Penguin Books.
       "Bergson on Morality", *Proceedings of the British Academy*, XLI, 247–
       66.

1956   *Contemporary Philosophy: Studies of Logical Positivism and Existent-
       ialism*. London: Burns and Oates.

1957   "The Existence of God: A Debate Between Bertrand Russell and Father
       F.C. Copleston, S.J." [in] *Why I am Not a Christian and Other Essays* by
       Bertrand Russell. London: Allen and Unwin (see 1948 above).

1958   *A History of Philosophy, IV: Descartes to Leibniz*. London: Burns and
       Oates.
       L'Universita nell' Inghilterra Moderna. Palermo: Quaderni di Studio.

1959   *A History of Philosophy, V: Hobbes to Hume*. London: Burns and
       Oates.

1960   *A History of Philosophy, VI: Wolff to Kant*. London: Burns and Oates.
       *De Motu Trascendentiae: Quaedam Linea Reflectionis de Problemate
       Absoluti*. Rome: Gregorian University Press.
       "Man and Metaphysics", *The Heythrop Journal*, I, 3–17, 105–17, 199–
       213, 300–13.

1961   "Man and Metaphysics", *The Heythrop Journal*, II, 142–56.

1962   "Berkeley and Catholicism", in *A Catholic Dictionary of Theology*.
       London: Thomas Nelson, 260.
       "The Crazy Gang: The Madness of Metaphysics", *The Month*, CCXIII,
       206–14.
       "In the Clothing of Sheep: Philosophy and Religion", *The Month*,
       CCXIV, 219–28.
       "Uncertain Guides: The Philosopher in Politics", *The Month*, CCXIII,
       325–33.

1963   *A History of Philosophy, VII: Fichte to Nietzsche*. London: Burns and
       Oates.
       "Medieval Visions: The Nature of Philosophy. A New Account of
       Medieval Thought", *The Month*, CCXV, 151–5.
       "No Honest Woman: The Nature of Philosophy", *The Month*, CCXV,
       347–55.

1964   "An Atheist's Values", *The Heythrop Journal*, V, 402–9.
       "Hegel", in Maurice Cranston (ed.) *Western Political Philosophers*.
       London: The Bodley Head, 91–8.
       "Religion with and without God", *The Month*, CCXXI, 73–7.

1965 "In Appreciation. From an Historian of Philosophy", *Continuum*, II, 311–13.

"Probe at Woolwich", *The Month*, CCXXII, 360–7.

"Wittgenstein frente a Husserl", *Revista Portuguesa de Filosofia*, XXI, 134–49.

1966 "Dialogue with Humanism", *The Month*, CCXXII, 114–23.

A History of Philosophy, VIII: Bentham to Russell. London: Burns and Oates.

"Randall's Career of Philosophy", *The Journal of Philosophy*, LXIII, 724–34.

1967 "The Future of Belief", *The Month*, CCXXIV, 126–31.

1968 "Foreground and Background in Nietzsche", *The Review of Metaphysics*, XXI, 506–23.

"Man, Transcendence and the Absence of God", *Thought*, LXIII, 24–38.

"Words and Marx", *The Heythrop Journal*, IX, 5–16.

1970 "An Evolving Faith: Leslie Dewart's New Book", *The Clergy Review*, LV, 298–304.

"The Special Features of Contemporary Atheism", *The Month*, CCXXIX, 72–9.

1971 "Hegel and the Rationalization of Mysticism", in W.E. Steinkraus (ed.) *New Studies in Hegel's Philosophy*. New York: Holt, Rinehart and Winston, 187–220.

1972 *A History of Medieval Philosophy*. London: Methuen.

1973 "Contemporary Atheism", *Ateismo y Diaologo*, VIII, 25–31.

"The History of Philosophy: Relativism and Recurrence", *The Heythrop Journal*, XIV, 123–35.

Philosophy and Religion in Judaism and Christianity. London: Westfield College.

1974 "The Logical Empiricism of Nicholas Autrecourt", *Proceedings of the Aristotelian Society*, 249–62.

Religion and Philosophy. Dublin: Gill and Macmillan.

1975 *A History of Philosophy, IX: Maine de Biran to Sartre*. London: Search Press.

1976 *Philosophers and Philosophies*. London: Search Press.

1977 "Ethics and Metaphysics. East and West", *Proceedings of the American Catholic Philosophical Association*, LI, 75–86.

"Father Martin D'Arcy", *The Month*, CCXXXVIII, 22–4.

1979 *On the History of Philosophy and other Essays*. London: Search Press.

1980 *Philosophies and Cultures.* Oxford: Oxford University Press.

1982 "Are there Recurrent Problems in Philosophy?" in Linus J. Thro (ed.), *History of Philosophy in the Making.* Washington (DC): University Press of America, 197–211.

      Religion and the One: Philosophies East and West. London: Search Press.

1983 "Philosophy and Ideology" in Anthony Parel (ed.), *Ideology, Philosophy and Politics.* Waterloo (Ontario): Wilfrid Laurier University Press, 17–36.

      "Christianity and Marxism", *The Month,* CCXLV, 230–2.

1984 "The Liberation of Philosophy", *The Times Literary Supplement,* 15 March, 298.

1986 *Philosophy in Russia: From Herzen to Lenin and Berdyaev.* Tunbridge Wells: Search Press.